LIVING THE VOWS

LIVING THE VOWS

The Emotional Conflicts of Celibate Religious

Robert J. McAllister,
M.D., Ph.D.

1817

Harper & Row, Publishers, San Francisco
Cambridge, Hagerstown, New York, Philadelphia
London, Mexico City, São Paulo, Singapore, Sydney

FIRST EDITION

Library of Congress Cataloging-in-Publication Data

McAllister, Robert J.
  Living the vows.

  1. Monastic and religious life—Psychology.
I. Title.
BX2440.M33   1986   255'.001'9   85-45359
ISBN 0-06-065425-6   19.95

86 87 88 89 90 RRD 10 9 8 7 6 5 4 3 2 1

To all those whom I have discovered and rediscovered in my own life during the preparation of this book.

To all those whom I have helped to discover themselves.

Contents

Acknowledgments

My sincere thanks to Patricia O'Brien Freeman for many helpful suggestions and for untiring diligence in editing and preparing the manuscript. My gratitude to A. W. R. Sipe for his personal encouragement in support of this work and for his professional service as author's agent.

I am especially indebted to my wife, Jane, for insightful comments, invaluable discussions, and inexhaustible confidence, and to my daughter, Laura, for her support and encouragement. To them both I offer my apologies for time taken from them to pursue this venture, time that they generously gave in their abundant love.

Preface

Some Christians vow religious obedience, chastity, and poverty, not to place themselves beyond the human condition, but to manifest and to facilitate their service of God. Professed religious endeavor to imitate Christ and to follow his call to discipleship. This spiritual ideal of discipleship has attracted disciples throughout the Christian centuries, and it continues to do so today.

Nonetheless, Christians who profess religious vows are not beyond the human condition. They are endowed with the same riches and conflicts of human emotions as is the rest of humankind. Some religious view their emotions with a good measure of suspicion, and try to repress them as much as possible. This thinking reflects the influence of Manichaean philosophy, which places the responsibility for human depravity on the human spirit, emotions, and body. The Christian tradition as a whole, however, does value the physical and emotional human being as a gift of God: affected by sin, to be sure, but good in itself (good enough to be assumed by the Son of God).

Most Christians generally live their life in uneasy peace and intermittent conflict with their human emotions, but professed religious strive to rise above the conflict through asceticism and discipline. Many assume that the very profession of religious vows places them beyond the emotional problems that afflict their brothers and sisters in faith.

Religious certainly know that the emotions and passions are a part of their human nature, and acknowledge this by creating rules to moderate them. Other Christians expect the religious to be little moved by such emotions as anger or greed, and assume that the ideal way to live the religious life is to sail just above the rough waves of the emotions. Religious themselves, of course, know differently.

The education that religious receive, however, serves to help them in these emotional struggles. In school, religious of every age learn wisdom that proclaims an insight into human nature. They are influenced by the thought of Aristotle, Plato, Saint Augustine, and Saint Thomas, and form an understanding of themselves along these philosophical lines. New disciplines, such as psychology and anthropology, combine with the older ideas, and together have led religious to a greater understanding of the human being in this world.

As can be expected, no one method of understanding and assisting the human spirit has prevailed, but those who study human psychology do agree that the conflicts of the human spirit can be approached by various methods of therapy. The methods surely differ in their philosophical bases and in their success rate, but the point is that many methods of therapy are effective.

Christians entering the life of a religious community bring with them a unique configuration of emotional treasures and conflicts. They bring their family past with them; they bring their ways of coping with their emotional problems. Then, they find themselves in a situation where the emotions must be disciplined. The new crises they meet in religious life test their mettle, and, on occasion, throw them off balance. Thus, the need for therapy.

Dr. McAllister's intriguing book not only argues for the place of psychological counseling in religious life but also presents in details its many forms. He writes from a professional knowledge of human psychology and psychiatry, but, as important, he draws on many years of counseling experience with religious men and women. He paints verbal pictures of religious we have met, resented, and pitied.

Dr. McAllister's love and respect for religious life remains undiminished throughout the book. He does not write to expose the foibles of these human beings who profess a certain type of Christian discipleship. Rather, he hopes to exhort them to seek counseling when necessary, and to encourage them to live a peaceful human existence in conformity with their authentic desires.

Religious will profit from this book, since it reviews many aspects of their dedicated life. Community leaders especially will find many valuable comments on their tasks: the need for confidentiality, the need to respect the private and inner lives of the people they serve, the need to distinguish the role of professional counselor and the function of an authoritative leader in a religious community.

Dr. McAllister adroitly describes the nature and the limits of intimacy in religious life. Many religious today express the need for some kind of intimacy in their lives, but they frequently go astray in their understanding and expression of this need. They will benefit from Dr. McAllister's sympathetic understanding of the need for affection and his tracing of the limits of intimacy in religious life.

Religious hope to form a fruitful and life-giving community, both for themselves and for the people they serve. Dr. McAllister acknowledges the value of community, and he also offers a good critique of community. The religious community cannot provide every form of intimacy, affection, and closeness. His comments will provoke thought, especially for those who expect too much of the religious fellowship.

In short, this book is valuable for all religious. All need to attend to the workings of the human spirit; all need the reminder that not all problems can be solved with a determination of will or a "spiritual" remedy; all must know that religious are afflicted by the regular run of psychological illnesses evident in the rest of the human community; all need to attend to the goal of their striving: the creation of a healthy human life of service and love.

Abbot Jerome Theisen, O.S.B.
Saint John's Abbey
Collegeville, Minnesota

A Note to the Reader

Living the Vows accurately portrays the emotional problems celibate religious face, but all names, locations, and other identifying characteristics mentioned in the book have been changed, and case presentations represent composites rather than the story of any specific individual.

1. Introduction

This book is intended as a series of essays on religious life written by one who is an outsider, an "extern," in community language. It is not based on research or statistical validation of data; it has developed from the struggles of many individual religious. Out of their emotional conflicts and from their psychic pain, a distillate has formed that seems to have some general, if not universal, application.

This book is written by one who has worked in a professional capacity with religious women and men for over thirty years. Most of this work has consisted of individual psychotherapy with religious; religious in formation and in vows, religious in the process of entering and in the process of leaving, religious redefining or re-establishing the fullness of their chosen state. These men and women typically struggled with emotional conflicts about their communities, about their state in life. Usually they came for psychiatric care because of their inner turmoil, less frequently because of the turmoil they created within their community. Most came willingly. Some came involuntarily. All came because they searched for something more than what they seemed to have, because they believed they could be better persons than they experienced themselves to be.

I acknowledge with gratitude the insights into religious life that they have given me. They have allowed me to move inside the sanctuaries of their hearts and see the sacred things deeply rooted there. They have also exposed themselves at times as tarnished vessels that held those hallowed truths. For all the matters that have been sorted through together in therapy, I hope that the painstaking and sometimes painful process has never dulled their sensitivity to others, diminished their self-esteem, or lessened their faith. During a treatment session, a perceptive priest once asked me in a rather embarrassed tone if working with religious had ever been a source of scandal. A negative answer came readily. There is mystery in every person, and the gradual and graceful unfolding of that mystery in treatment, no matter where it leads, brings a sense of awe and deep respect. I trust that those who read this book will look for truth, not tragedy, will search for the reverent, not the reprehensible, and will reserve judgment about others as a way of discovering more about themselves.

The lengthy struggles, the intense sufferings, and the gradual conflict resolution of those who worked so hard in therapy have inspired this book. Their conflicts seemed not to be unusual but only more sharp, more intense, and more disturbing than those of their fellow religious. References to individual patients are not based on the histories of specific persons but are composites and derive from many sources. They are used as vehicles to describe the emotional conflicts of many celibates, rather than the emotional struggle of a particular celibate. All names are, of course, fictitious. If someone believes that he or she has discovered himself or herself or a friend in these chapters, it only seems so. These chapters arise from therapeutic work with over five hundred religious spanning a period of thirty years. Comparable stories, similar scenarios, the same problems, and parallel sets of symptoms recurred with startling frequency as those religious men and women went through the adventure of treatment. It was the existence of such reappearing patterns and repeated experiences that supported the objective of writing a book to explore and expound these common themes.

Readers may question some of the case histories as extraordinary and some of the conclusions as surprising. Formation directors and spiritual directors, especially, may doubt the frequency, if not the authenticity, of these conflicts. A primary contention of this work, however, is that the emotional conflicts depicted here are not exceptional but, indeed, fairly representative of conflicts faced by a large percentage of religious personnel. These inner conflicts and their behavioral expressions overshadow the lives of many religious who choose to conceal these dark afflictions from confessors and directors and, most of all, from religious superiors.[1] Those therapists who work intensively with religious will find the stories of their patients duplicated throughout these pages. Psychiatrists hear the confessions that cannot be told anywhere else. Superiors cannot be told because they might be obliged to act upon the information. For the same reason, formation directors cannot be told. Spiritual directors cannot be told because they are seen as friends, as mentors, as supportive allies, and also as persons who may take a firm position in relation to the directee's choices. Confessors need not be told because details are not required and reconciliation promises reprieve. But psychiatrists probe and pull and pry. They search for causes of emotional disarray and behavioral disharmony. They piece together the history of the individual's emotional development as they carefully sort through the particulars of family interaction, social development, educational process, and psychosexual maturation. They ferret out the causes of anxiety, depression, anger, fear, and eroticism. As they examine the causes of these emotional reactions, they also clarify their

---

[1] One who writes about religious life today encounters some difficulty with terminology. Some communities no longer use the word *superior*. They have adopted words that connote a more egalitarian association and a less autocratic atmosphere. No matter what term is used to designate these authoritative figures, religious communities continue to have these figures. To call them coordinators or administrators or facilitators does not automatically lessen their authority. For expediency, the term *superior* has been retained here; it is used to identify those persons in religious life who have positions of authority over other religious members in relation to their vowed state. The term includes, therefore, members of the hierarchy, pastors who have assistants, major superiors of religious orders, local superiors of religious communities, and superiors of small living groups, regardless of the titles any of them may use.

effects on the individual's past decisions, present reactions, and future directions.

Throughout this searching exploration of the individual's psychological condition there is firm assurance that exposure will not bring about abandonment or rejection by the therapist. Neither will the treatment contract permit the therapist to prompt the responses or to guide the decisions of the individual religious. Others who participate more directly in the life of the religious may permit their own views to interfere with their recommendations. Because of other responsibilities, the goals of the director, for example, may have to take precedence over the good of the directee.

Religious in emotional conflict have difficulty finding an unbiased listener, much less an open-minded counselor, within the religious setting. Persons in authority represent the law, the rule, the requirements of the vowed state. No matter how understanding they are, their response to the religious in conflict requires a request for conformity. "These are the duties you have assumed. You must try to meet these obligations." Spiritual directors and confessors direct attention to moral values and count upon the individual to push toward higher goals. Their position calls for discernment, prayer, and faith. "These are the struggles in your path to perfection. You must pray for guidance and God's help to make your commitment a more vital witness." Friends in religious life have preconceptions and sometimes conflicts of their own that make them unable to be without bias. They tend to give the ready answers that they hold for themselves or wish for their friends. "These are difficulties that a lot of people in religious life encounter. You must try to put them out of your mind and out of your life and get on with the work at hand." Under these circumstances psychiatrists and other counseling professionals become the confidants of those religious whose inner disharmony causes personal distress or professional dysfunction. They provide a more deliberative approach. "Let us explore together the things that trouble you. Let us look beneath the surface problems to understand their causes, their significance, their seriousness. Through this process you will better comprehend this distress and its meaning in your life. With the resultant insight you will then be in a better position to benefit from spiritual help, to cope with certain adversities, and perhaps to make some changes that appear to you to be warranted as a result of your discoveries."

Psychotherapy is not the only source for the thoughts that are here. Discussions with other psychotherapists, review of various source materials, and observations of religious outside of the office setting have contributed to the case material as well as to my theoretical concepts. In addition, I have worked with various religious groups for many years as a lecturer, a visitator, a short-term and a long-term consultant, and a facilitator. These experiences have provided opportunities to study community life from another perspective and to compare that data with information acquired in the office setting. I am indebted to those many religious communities that have allowed me to enter so deeply into their daily lives and to know them within their more private world.

During the last three or four decades, society has become increasingly aware of the affective element in human decision making and in human behavior. Religious communities have attempted to follow this cultural trend. Although they have become aware of the emotional component, for the most part they have not successfully integrated it into their formation training or their community life. Many psychological issues confront modern celibate religious: The psychological aspect of vocational choice remains a confused issue. The concepts of emotional growth and emotional maturity lack clarity, although large expenditures of time and money support these objectives. The interjection of feelings into community interaction brings awkward periods of silence, immediate group rejection, or the unpleasant aftermath of factious discord. Conflicts relating to intimacy and the religious vows provide considerable uncertainty and some demoralization. Some advisers to individual religious and to religious communities only add to the confusion because of their own inadequate understanding of the psychological implications of these factors for the celibate.

It is problems of time management and energy appropriation that create many of the emotional symptoms of assiduous religious. Substance abuse among religious does not disappear because it remains undiscussed. In addition, religious sometimes suffer because their spirituality does not sufficiently answer their experiences of loss. Unhealthy family relationships also can cause lasting emotional impairment, but religious often expect idealistic resolution of family controversy. Religious authorities face peculiar problems that occasion emotional strain and possible psychological deterioration.

All these topics have an emotional impact that varies from subtle to stark, from limited to diffuse, and from irritating to disabling. This book explores the affective aspects of these issues as they involve the lives of contemporary religious women and men. These emotional struggles cause some religious to develop frank psychiatric symptoms, others to exhibit serious disquietude, and others to question the significance of what they do and the merit in how they live. If these emotional matters are examined openly and understood clearly, the psychological deterioration of some religious may be prevented or lessened, the restlessness of others may be relieved or reduced, and the dedication and satisfaction of many may be enhanced and purified.

The author hopes that readers of this book will not find in it any reason to doubt the value or the validity of the religious life for themselves or for others. It would be regrettable if material in this book were used as argument against the concept of the celibate religious life. That concept, that ideal, is not diminished by the material presented here: to survey the roughness of the road should not deter those who judiciously choose to make the journey. The author prays that as a result of this delineation of emotional conflicts many will make their choice more prudently and, for those who choose the road of celibacy, at least some will journey more smoothly and more securely on that difficult but glorious pilgrimage.

This book examines a number of issues with the intent to provide clarification and understanding to those who are caught in the emotional conflicts that these problems cause. In addition, the book is intended to stimulate further study by those who are concerned with the future of religious life. A key question in the subject of celibacy is the psychological basis for such a vocation.

2. The Psychological Aspects of Vocation

To have a vocation to the religious life is considered equivalent to having a call from God. Much has been written about the theology of vocation; the concept is not difficult to comprehend and discuss. However, for the individual who asks the question, do I have a vocation? the conceptual answer and the theological discussion do not suffice.

Is vocation to religious life some special call communicated in an unusual manner, or is it, rather, an intellectual choice that one makes after mature consideration? If it is the former, then it eludes psychological evaluation, for it escapes the natural process of decision making. Many who work with vocations seem to support this idea of vocation. They expect to find the call to religious life secreted away in shadowy events that unfold to reveal this great gift to the individual aspirant. In hushed tones they speak of "God's call," and the quietness suggests that speaking loudly or frequently about it might cause it to disappear. It must be referred to only with awe and a sense of reverence.

On the other hand, if vocation involves an intellectual choice based on a seasoned process of deliberation and decision, then it requires maturity and responsibility to be valid. It cannot, then, be approached with such awe and reverence that it overwhelms the individual and makes careful reflection impossible. From a psychological point of view, vocation should be more than a five-year-old's wish to "bring Jesus to the babies in the missions," a ten-year-old's intense desire to win parental approval by becoming a religious, or an eighteen-year-old's brief emotional elation during a period of prayer. Are not individuals more likely to know God's will for them by searching the delicate structures within themselves than by straining to find some sign scrawled across the external events of their lives?

In considering a tentative decision to serve God in religious life, an individual should examine early experiences and patterns of relationship within the family. A realistic assessment of personal abilities and deficiencies is important. One's need for solitude and for intimacy, one's tolerance for loneliness and for group living demand attention. To give serious and prayerful thought to these and similar issues establishes the psychological basis of vocation. This is a responsible approach to the question of vocation. It is not mystical, but prayerful. It is not mysterious, but practical. By contrast, there is the story of the young priest who had served as an altar boy in a rural parish. When the bishop of the diocese visited that parish, the deportment of the lad impressed him, and he said to the boy, "Have you ever thought of being a priest?" Deeply touched by this great man's interest in him, he considered that remark as constituting his call. Ordained two years, he still insisted that the bishop was responsible for his becoming a priest. A more mature process would have been to begin to consider the priesthood as a result of the bishop's remark and then to go through a period of deliberation, with little or no attention to the offhand remark of a visiting dignitary who knew absolutely nothing about him except that he behaved well in that particular setting on that particular occasion. Had he done this, he could then have said that he himself was responsible for his becoming a priest, with God's help, of course. Facing that decision more responsibly, he might also have concluded that the idea of the priesthood did not suit him well.

Individuals in religious life sometimes arrive there without ever having made a mature choice about it. A fifty-year-old sister said that she had decided at age ten to become a religious. At that time her mother was close to dying in childbirth.

She knelt and promised God that if her mother survived, she would enter the convent. During psychiatric treatment she wondered why uncertainty about her vocation threatened her peace of mind. A priest who had exhibited sexually scandalous behavior for several years following his ordination and who had been eventually exiled from his diocese by his bishop remarked in relation to his vocation, "From all time I was supposed to be a priest—I knew about my vocation from the earliest age of reason." During psychotherapy at age thirty-six, he decided that he had never had a vocation. Decisions regarding a religious vocation that are made at an early age must be viewed as immature decisions. One might assume that immature decisions regarding a vocation would be adequately challenged in religious formation. Though they are challenged, they are often not adequately challenged. In pre–Vatican II years, the challenge occurred in the austerity of the training. Formation years were rigorous. The unspoken (but sometimes clearly stated) position seemed to be: if a person can accept this structure, then she or he is acceptable to God. Occasionally, out of misguided fervor, the novice director or the novice judged that the more harshness a person accepted the more acceptable that person became. To suggest that someone challenge a vocation might be misconstrued as an attempt to discourage the vocation. This idea stands in sharp contrast to the practice of sheltering vocations by quickly reassuring the religious aspirant who exhibits doubts about his or her vocation.

A boy of seven who thought of being a priest decided, in his childlike manner, that he wanted a clear sign of God's call. When he went to bed at night, he regularly left a sheet of clean, white paper beside his bed, and he fantasized that God would write in golden ink his call. But God did not respond. Then the boy made up a new test. If God did not want him to be a priest, then God should write no with his golden pen. One might smile at the boy's innocence and faith. But one can no longer smile when he reappears thirty years later as a chronically unhappy priest. His course into the priesthood began in that immature fantasy and was fed by his troubled childhood.

As a boy he felt rejected by both his parents. His father was emotionally cold and psychologically absent from the home. His mother was controlling, unaffectionate, and insensitive. Both parents were strict and unforgiving. The boy was insecure and emotionally needy. He wanted someone to want him, and thus he maneuvered God into the position. Then he had to pay the price for God's call: he had to be worthy of it. He regarded authority as severe, demanding, and unfeeling. In his teen years he resented that God had called him, because he felt that he did not want to be a priest. However, he learned from his parents that feelings are not important, and he learned from religion teachers that feelings often lead people to sin. He hoped that some calamity would befall him so that he would be unable to be a priest. Naturally he could not pray for such a turn of events, because God would hear him. Nothing happened. He became a priest, an unhappy one. Could he have been adequately challenged in seminary life to make his career choice a more mature one? The key to such a challenge would have been in the hands of someone who came to understand the origins and background of his vocation. It could not be challenged successfully on theological grounds, because he knew God had called him. It could not be challenged by the austerity of formation, because that only increased his worthiness. It could not be challenged by personal contact with seminary professors, because he had been "ordained" at seven.

The challenge to vocations that frequently occurs in present-day formation is the challenge of dialogue, of spiritual direction or discernment, and of group dynamics. These methods do not always place the burden clearly on the shoulders of the candidate. Most formation directors have a special interest in preserving the vocation. The same predisposition appears frequently among retreat directors, religious superiors, and others who work with those in formation. A young woman in formation years struggled in an appropriate fashion with the question of religious life as a suitable choice for herself. She encountered this problem as a part of her psychotherapy. During a break in her schedule, she visited a prominent retreat director who had encouraged her to enter religious life. The young religious told the director about her struggles. He replied, "Continue steadfast in your vocation, my dear. Jesus will be enough for you." Theologically that is good advice for anyone, unless it binds the individual not to alter any tentative decisions. Psychologically it lacked depth and perceptivity. It was truly pious platitude.

Those who work in formation acquire some natural bias. It is not bad to have this bias; it is simply bad not to recognize it. Parents naturally have some bias in what they want their children to do in life. Because of that bias, they consciously and unconsciously encourage and support some choices and some behaviors, and they discourage other directions. Spiritual directors, formation directors, and religious superiors also have biases. The decreasing number of vocations contributes to that bias in many instances. One could expect them to offer greater support for a choice to be a religious than for a choice not to enter—or to leave—religious life. When people invest themselves wholeheartedly in a particular project, they typically lose objectivity in relation to that goal. In law or business, advice from one who acts as an authorized agent for a project to one who has a right to an impartial opinion represents conflict of interest. Psychiatrists and other counselors who are well trained attempt to preserve a neutral position in regard to the choices their patients make; years of supervised experience help them attain this posture and alert them to the difficulties in maintaining an open-minded attitude. Most religious who deal with vocation questions do not have the benefit of such training and experience.

Everyone looks for certainty, especially in matters related to religion. This area in which people seek the most certainty is precisely that which leaves the realm of physical reality and solid experience and takes them into a world where mystery and vision conflict with reason and order. Young religious today approach the question of vocation without much better preparation than the neophyte of years past had. This call from God remains a mystery. Mystery causes doubt, and doubt seeks resolution through assurance. When one is insecure and uncertain, without a clear path to certainty, one looks to others to provide the answer, to communicate the reassurance that solid ground is underfoot. The director who says, "It seems to me you have a vocation," or even more directly, "You have a vocation," can in no way plead neutrality. For persons in formation, especially if they have doubts about their vocation, such statements serve as a powerful influence. Uncertainty is uncomfortable. Doubt creates anxiety. The discomfort and the anxiety can be alleviated if someone else confirms the chosen course as correct. But discomfort and anxiety also promote growth, stimulate evaluation, and incite change. The neutral position of the director is, "I do not know if you have a call from God to be a religious. It is your task to make that decision as wisely as possible."

For the superior or director of the religious in permanent vows, the vocation question assumes greater complexity. In addition to its theological and psychological aspects, the question now includes ecclesiastical difficulties and community implications. Religious caught in the anguish and turmoil of reassessing a previously made commitment need sufficient time for and suitable aid in the decision-making process. On the other hand, the religious authority sometimes must urge the individual to resolve the indecision, so that it does not become a perpetual ambiguity for the individual and for the community. Some years ago, a psychiatrist cared for a sister who had been in community for about fifteen years. Sister Anna had characteristically established a passive-aggressive relationship with each of her immediate superiors by displaying both excessive dependency and hostility toward them. This pattern had angered her superiors and had seriously disrupted her life in community. She progressed well in therapy and became more aware of her angry feelings and better able to express them. Her ability to gauge these newly discovered facets of her personality was not well calibrated or controlled, however. One day she impetuously called her superior a "big, fat dummy." The next morning she received a wig and necessary secular clothing and was dismissed from the convent through the back door. This was hardly sufficient time for her to decide that she did not have a vocation. Others made the decision for her.

Individuals in formation sometimes fluctuate between wondering if they should leave and wondering if they will be dismissed. In professed religious the dilemma shifts slightly. They are frequently afraid to ponder the question of leaving, but a fear that they could be dismissed often haunts them. This fear is not totally unfounded: On one occasion the dismissal of a professed religious followed a psychiatric examination conducted with the sister's written consent (after she had been given a clear explanation of the purpose of the examination). The evaluation confirmed that because the individual exhibited severely and chronically disruptive behavior in community and experienced little personal satisfaction or even composure in religious life, dismissal did not appear to inflict an injustice. In another case, a diocesan priest was dismissed when his maladaptive sexual behavior was brought to the attention of his bishop. Although the priest had sought psychiatric care and no threat of public scandal or litigation existed, the bishop suspended the priest's faculties and ordered him to leave the diocese that same day. The severe and obdurate behavior of the bishop intensified the priest's despondency and complicated his return to a healthy ministry.

Occasionally a religious gets caught in an impasse resulting from a doubtful individual commitment and an ambiguous community response. The individual behaves in an aloof and indifferent manner, unwilling to interact as a community member but unable to terminate community membership. The community, unable to persuade the reluctant member to participate more fully and unwilling to demand a resolution of the ambiguity, becomes disengaged. The individual moves to the periphery of community life and community involvement, where friction lessens because of minimal contact. Emotional distance becomes the mutually acceptable goal, and geographic distance sometimes assists the process of estrangement. On occasion, such arrangements may be justified, but they usually benefit the community more than the individual. Religious who live and work separated from community without any significant contact for long periods of time may be compensating for their inability to relate to community members. They may also lose close contact with God in their position of isolation because the development of their spiritual life no longer receives nurturance from their community. This represents a particular hardship and a hazard for the missionary and for the religious in a specialized field whose work necessitates considerable time and distance away from community. Financial realities of modern religious life often require a person's taking a job wherever available. In these latter situations, regular communication and periodic visits maintain an affectionate bond between the absent member and the community. These supportive ties hold the separated individual spiritually and emotionally close to the group.

It is not unusual, however, to find a sister, priest, or brother geographically separated from community, not out of necessity, not out of positive benefit to all concerned, but out of compromise or convenience. These arrangements sometimes serve as a kind of unofficial leave of absence. Because there is no demand for clear decision, direct confrontation, or definitive resolution of conflict, both the community and the individual slip easily into an accepted standoff. The individual religious lives in self-imposed exile as an alternative to facing the problems back home. The superior, indeed sometimes the community, lives in uneasy peace as an alternative to dealing with the displaced member. The participants rarely acknowledge their rejection of each other. No one asks the question, Where does this path lead? perhaps because the answer is so clear and so discomforting. For the separated celibate it leads nowhere—and nowhere for the religious in this situation is total alienation from community, increasing loneliness as the years go by, bitterness that grows to galling proportions, and a sense of abandonment by others and by God. This unhappy "solution" for problem religious occurs with increasing frequency, but, because of the pain it causes, its frequency does not justify it.

Father Al feels alienated working as a physician hundreds of miles from his religious community. The check he sends periodically to his superior sums up his relationship with his community. He lives an unhealthy and empty personal life, unable to affiliate with other religious in the area or even to associate with others in the church. He rarely attends liturgical functions. He has carried his alienation from his community into his social life and into his spiritual life. On the other hand, he cannot bring himself to declare another choice and to acknowledge by a new decision that he made a serious misjudgment in choosing the celibate state. In private conversation he acknowledges a mistake, but he will not act on it. Year after year he goes on in an increasingly isolated existence, lacking nourishment for his spiritual needs and support for his emotional needs. His situation steadily deteriorates.

It takes courage and equanimity on the part of a religious superior to corral that wandering sheep and say, "We want you here with us, in this fold, if you can find life here. But if you cannot, then perhaps you should seek another pasture that we pray will be richer and greener for you. Most of all, you cannot be part of this flock if you have no part of us, because if we are separated, you may starve or fall among wolves, and we may forget you or not respond to you when you are in need."

A vocation can be psychologically tested by the ordinary and prosaic question, What do you want to do? Perhaps its simplicity makes this question appear sterile. Many religious in formation and in vows find it difficult to answer. They respond by reference to God's will in an attempt to avoid the issue. The examiner should not accept such an answer and might set the following scene: "Suppose Jesus walked through the door, came and sat down with us, and said to you, 'My friend, I have given you the gift of life, and I really mean it to be yours. I want you to be happy with it, and I want you to choose what you would like to do with it. I will bless your life whatever choice you make. What do you want to do?' " Even in this setting, religious experience difficulty in gratifying what they consider self-will.

Theologians, religious authorities, and spiritual directors state that a vocation consists of a call from God, a call that the person may decide to accept or reject. Some say that the sign of a vocation depends upon the official approbation of the proper religious authority. Although not in disagreement with these theological and ecclesiastical positions, the psychology of vocation requires a different point of view. Psychodynamically, the decision within the individual gives rise to the vocation, and it is not the vocation that produces the decision. The person's decision represents the psychological foundation of the vocation. The burden of that decision rests squarely upon the aspirant to religious life. The inspiration of God and the selection by the religious authority do not release the individual from that solemn moment when vocation involves personal, deliberate, free choice.

Although religious may be unable to state directly what they would like to do, they sometimes state it indirectly. A psychiatrist was asked to evaluate a young seminarian who had a problem of nocturnal enuresis. This young man was studying his third year of theology. His years in seminary had been relatively smooth. No problems had emerged except that of nocturnal enuresis. He had tried in every way possible to control the problem: He stopped drinking liquids in mid-afternoon. He set his alarm for the middle of the night. He tried going to bed late. He tried getting up early. Nothing helped.

During the interview he protested frequently, "I cannot possibly be a priest if I wet the bed." He discussed the embarrassment it would cause, the difficulties it would create in a rectory or in traveling, and the final, harsh reality that one could not be a priest if one wet the bed. In a tentative manner, the psychiatrist asked, "Have you ever considered not being a priest?" He replied that he had not thought about that possibility, but perhaps he should look into it. He refused the subdeaconate two months later and left the seminary within another month. He never wet the bed after he left the seminary. He could not say he did not want to be a priest; he could only wet the bed and then say, "One cannot be a priest if one wets the bed." When he no longer had to be a priest, he no longer had to wet the bed.

The webwork that surrounds vocation and commitment is demonstrated in the following case history. Alice had entered her community at age sixteen. Twenty years later as she considered her vocation, she said, "I entered because I couldn't take it at home anymore. I saw religious life as people who loved one another." She was the third of four children. Her father was an alcoholic. Her mother was a rejecting woman who never praised her but never let her forget a mistake. Two months before she entered religious life, her mother told her she would never stay. During postulancy her mistress encouraged her to discuss her family life. She responded with silence. In novitiate she questioned whether or not she belonged in religious life. The mistress of novices told her she had a vocation to that community. Twice when she renewed temporary vows, she expressed doubt about her vocation. Her provincial reassured her on both occasions. When she made her final vows six years after entering, she felt that she should not be taking her final vows at that time. Twenty years later, she commented, "I'm not sure I knew what I was doing."

Within the year after novitiate she developed severe stomach pains, with accompanying nausea, vomiting, and general malaise. Six months after final profession, she began psychiatric care. She took an overdose of pills on two occasions and threatened suicide on many others. She saw three different psychiatrists over a period of six years and took various psychotropic medicines. Finally she accepted hospitalization in a private institution for one year and then received additional outpatient treatment for ten months. During all that time the question of her religious vocation was never raised as an issue in therapy. She began treatment with a new psychiatrist who insisted that the subject of her religious vocation be considered. Alice endured a painful exploration of her beginnings in religious life, her experiences in religious life, and her attitudes about religious life. The years prior to her entry into religion and the interrelationships of her family members served as background for these inquiries and provided clarification of their meaning.

She prayed and felt that no one heard her. She recognized that it was difficult "to share a little in community because I want to share everything." She acknowledged intense anger toward others in community and feared she would "be condemned to hell for these feelings." She volunteered the comment, "I think I try to make myself have the stomach problems either consciously or unconsciously so that I can get out of things." As she began to consider seriously the question of her religious vocation, a priest visited her community and spoke about a lack of prayerfulness as the cause of people leaving religious life. Fortunately, Alice recognized the absurdity of his position, and she continued the disturbing task of evaluating her vocation. She stayed with her therapy and completed the work. She said, "It is hard to acknowledge that I made a mistake. The convent is not home for me. It never has been. It never can be." She might have said that life in community as she had perceived it resembled her home life too much, because it made her feel alienated, unappreciated, and constantly evaluated. She had not been able to tolerate her own home, so she escaped to the convent. She brought her background with her and found experiences in community that repeated the emotional events of her past. She decided that life outside of religion would offer a wider range of corrective opportunities and healthy choices than she had found in community. She expressed some appropriate anger toward previous therapists, especially those in her inpatient program, for not investigating the vocation issue.

As she packed to leave, she found her original acceptance letter and the formula of her final vows. She destroyed them. "It was not what I wanted to do." She described a feeling of "releasing within myself." The stomach pains that had been treated unsuccessfully for twenty years with various medications suddenly stopped. She left the community free of stomach medicine, free of stomach aches, free of psychotropic medicines, and free of the burden that she had never really committed herself to carry.

Some might disagree with the idea of challenging a vocation. A psychiatrist had in treatment a young man about to be ordained to the priesthood. In a letter to the psychiatrist the formation director of the community wrote, "We have persons within the community who provide guidance in whether or not a person has a valid vocation." Based on this attitude of the director, the psychiatrist avoided the topic of his patient's vocation. The evening of his ordination day, the young priest picked up a teenage boy and spent the night with him in a motel. The psychiatrist knew about this pattern of behavior, which had occurred for a number of years prior to ordination. It continued following ordination for a number of years until he again sought psychiatric care. His new psychiatrist was unwilling to separate his vocation from his pathological behavior. The juxtaposition of the two areas in treatment helped him gain control of the behavior. Unfortunately, the first psychiatrist had received the director's letter as a warning not to become involved in the question of religious vocation. In another case, the provincial of a large religious community refused to allow the sisters of her community to see a certain psychiatrist. She decided this because the psychiatrist had encouraged one of the sisters in treatment to examine her vocation from the standpoint of her emotional health, and as a result she had left religious life.

Psychiatrists who work with the deep and long-standing emotional conflicts of religious and who in that work examine the origins and course of vocational choices usually believe that vocations cannot be challenged to excess. This is particularly true if the challenge is straightforward and positive: "This is a serious choice. You should make it responsibly and freely." The force of family and strong unconscious impressions from childhood support the call. Early sentiments about church and religion, feelings of insecurity associated with the search for God, the desire for goodness and salvation, the pursuit of noble goals, the longing for uniqueness—all of these nurture the vocation objective. Unless there is serious questioning, serious consequences can ensue for some young people, who reach to catch the brass ring and fall into years of discouragement, disillusionment, and finally despair. Those who stretch so far to make the momentous pledge of religious vows require generous hearts motivated by righteous idealism. Unless the psychology of vocations unmistakably emphasizes a sense of true freedom, hesitation or vacillation is seen as moral weakness, and a choice away from the religious life appears to be a choice away from God.

Fortunately, most parish communities now realize, through direct contact, that former religious continue to be generous people dedicated to worthy pursuits. This increased acceptance of those who leave the religious life contributes to a freer choice for those who remain in vows and makes the decision for those who leave a more salutary alternative.

The call to religious life obviously involves the mystery of grace, but so do all the important decisions of life. The spiritual background of the vocation decision does not preclude the necessity of judicious examination on the part of the candidate or the relevance of careful evaluation by those who indirectly

participate in the decision as superiors, directors, or therapists. If the religious vocation is not accepted as a psychological process and as a personal decision, then it is exempt from
any valid scrutiny and also from any immediate responsibility.
Everyone has at times made an honest but erroneous decision
based on emotional immaturity, insufficient information,
unwarranted assumptions, or the wanton enthusiasm and
inept advice of others. If such limitations are recognized in
other areas, they also need to be acknowledged in relation to
an individual's decision to enter religious life.

The importance of thorough inquiry into the psychological
aspects of an individual's vocation cannot be overemphasized.
Such investigation will prevent some aspirants from making
an improper choice to enter religious life, and it will assist
others who are in religious life to discover the unsoundness of
their choice.

In order to make a sound decision a person needs a certain
amount of factual information. When considering marriage, it
is important to know the personal characteristics and limitations of the fiancé. When considering the possibility of entering a religious community, it is important to be aware of the
characteristics and limitations of religious communities.

3. Characteristics of Community

"Community" has become a catchword in contemporary society, and especially in ecclesiastical settings. Religious and laity talk of "building community," "finding community," and "having community." The idea has the familiar ring of "family," as parish leaders speak of "our parish community" and "our Christian family." Considerable confusion surrounds the concept of community. The theological basis for a Christian community seems lost at times in the emphasis on the psychological advantages of community relationships. Community becomes an efficient cause of various benefits rather than a result of special relationships. Community becomes synonymous with emotional closeness. Community entails not only a sharing of goods or labor or goals, but also a sharing of oneself, emotionally, intimately.

The early Christian community shared their worldly goods so that none would be needy among them. They shared their time in common prayer; they shared their concern for the material and spiritual needs of one another. The need for parish groups, for Christian organizations, for religious communities, and for larger ecclesiastical bodies concerned about the temporal and spiritual welfare of members remains unchanged. The different community groupings within the church rightfully design remedies that respond to these material and spiritual exigencies. The bonds that hold people in community groups should result in certain benefits for those who are members; however, some questions arise: What results can legitimately be expected from the bonds that bring a particular group together? Do some communities promise more to their members than they can give? Do they promise what they cannot produce?

Certain communities exist as a result of the personal relationships among the members. They discover that bonds of affection, communality of interests, and mutual directions and goals press them to form a community. Some religious orders began in precisely this fashion. A few individuals shaped bridges of mutual affection connecting each one with the others. They made these bridges stronger by increased familiarity arising from intimate discussions. Finally, these reinforced bridges supported the traffic of common objectives, similar motivations, and shared life.

Individuals build family units in much the same manner. Mutual affection develops between two people. Intimate conversations strengthen this rudimentary relationship. They explore common interests and goals. They decide that the strength of their love for each other furnishes a basis for marriage. From this background a union develops that provides for the material and the spiritual needs of the couple and their offspring. In the provision of these secondary benefits the original emotional bonding of the parents must be kept intact.

In some families the pursuit of material goods becomes more important than the preservation of an intimate union. The affectionate interactions of family members and their love for one another fade into the background, and the accumulation of money and things takes precedence. One young cleric who had difficulty with his emotional sterility commented, "I was always aware of my father's love when he gave me an extra ten or twenty dollars if I was going out for the evening. It was his way of showing he loved me." A priest, Father Bernard, had severe problems relating to his confreres in community. In therapy he described his family background. When he was a child, his parents both worked, his father usually holding two jobs. His parents always bought everything Bernard and his three siblings might need, and the children never had to ask for anything. Bernard recalled that when he was seventeen his parents came into his room and gave him the keys to a new car they had just purchased for him. He enjoyed the new car, but he felt cheated because his parents had not joined with him in the satisfaction of discussing, planning for, anticipating, shopping for, and finally choosing the car. Bernard played varsity basketball for three years in high school. His mother attended one game, and his father never attended any, because he worked such long hours. They never seemed interested in any of his activities, and they never spent time with him. The marital relationship apparently suffered because of their busy schedules. The parents spent little time with each other and never went out together socially. They argued violently over money, which the mother controlled. In their quarreling each parent sought the support of the four children. Bernard viewed his father as a weak, disheartened, and uninterested person who inspired little masculine identification in either of his two sons. He perceived his mother as a domineering and demanding person whom he tried to avoid. He judged both of his parents as preoccupied with money and material things and derelict in their marital commitment as well as in their parental obligations. Material goals took precedence over mutual affection, and money became a substitute for love in their home.

Other families lose touch with the importance of their human love for one another in their search for spiritual values. They may abandon close family ties in the process. Families sometimes become engrossed in church work, perhaps deeply involved in a particular cause, such as Right to Life, Marriage Encounter, or peace and justice issues. They may be devout, prayerful, and dedicated. Occasionally it happens that these same families have a spouse or a child at home who suffers seriously from lack of demonstrated love. In one such family the mother was intensely devoted to spiritual values and the spiritual needs of others. She attended retreats, workshops, and lectures. She spent hours helping religious personnel in their service to others. The priests and sisters in several of the city parishes admired her for her good works; among the laity she had a reputation as a very spiritual person. However, her unhappy husband regarded their marriage as a farce and a failure. Their seven children felt neglected and unloved.

An eighteen-year-old daughter in another spiritually dedicated family made a suicide attempt. In the course of treatment, she revealed that she had been the victim of rape at age sixteen. She had never told her parents, because they "did not have time for me." They were deeply engrossed in the Right to Life movement. At various times they took foster children into their home at the request of the Catholic Charities office. They participated in religious education programs from grade school through high school. They gave emotionally at church, over and over and over again. They apparently had nothing left to give emotionally at home. Their daughter received little indication of affection from either parent. They had formed a family community and had responsibilities to that community, but they turned away from those responsibilities to devote themselves to church involvements.

When people join together in a community out of mutual love, they often establish lofty goals. The most important thing they can accomplish is the preservation of the love that brought them together, that gave them life as a group, as a family. This kind of love is not self-perpetuating. It must be faithfully tended. It must be carefully guarded. It must be held so dear that the attainment of external community goals, whether material or spiritual, only enhances those internal bonds and does not lessen them.

The healthy family group represents the prototype of this kind of community. Some religious orders can look back at their origins and say, "Yes, this is how our community began." This kind of community takes shape naturally when several persons find a force of affection and a depth of understanding that draw them together in such a way that differences do not cause division and difficulties disappear in a deepening appreciation of each other. Everyone longs for the kind of community that holds out the promise of unconditional love, the largesse that loving parents give their children. Frequently psychotherapeutic work focuses on the problem of helping an individual accept the reality of poor family relationships. Everyone carries the dream of someday belonging to a perfect family. "My parents will someday understand me." "My father and mother will no longer be difficult to live with." "My teenager will return, will be whole again, will be happy." There is the constant desire to deny reality and, in that denial, to re-create the family—loving, healthy, complete, and living happily ever after. The mental picture of "family" has a tremendous attraction for everyone. Each individual has a powerful yearning for family. The thought of family carries a sense of nostalgia, whether or not one has ever really known a good family environment. The longing is neither diminished by bad experiences of family nor ever completely satisfied by good experiences. Perhaps it is a longing for something that is really not there, a remembrance of something that never quite was. Perhaps what people seek, what they have always sought, is not family, but truly unconditional love—and family is only the echo of eternity that keeps ringing in their ears.

Perhaps this explains why community has become such an attractive concept. With the growing disintegration of family unity under contemporary social and economic pressures, the idea of community emerges as a solution to loneliness and alienation. Community claims to be the first kin of family, the promise of perpetuating the warmth of previous family ties or the hope of discovering the affection that family never gave. Most communities, whether they are parish communities, neighborhood communities, or religious communities, cannot furnish to others what they have not found for themselves. These communities are not formed out of mutual affection and understanding, or through emotional bonding. Instead, definite decisions and practical objectives bring them together. They are established because common goals, similar beliefs, geographic propinquity, temporal need, or official fiat unite

them. Any or all of these reasons may be active in the formation of a particular community. These communities develop
from the top down. They come into existence to accomplish
something; the achievement of this goal is their *raison d'être*.

The "family" kind of community, by contrast, occurs as a
spontaneous outgrowth of loving relationships. It exists because those relationships exist. If the mutual caring no longer
exists, the family-community dies. It may then change to a
goal-oriented community and provide food and shelter and
even spiritual encouragement for its members, but it has lost
that one vital ingredient, emotional love.

This lengthy discussion of community sets the stage for an
exploration of religious community. Clarification of the psychological limitations of religious communities seems essential. It
may be controversial to state that modern religious communities cannot establish family-communities. They come together
to respond to the temporal and spiritual needs of their members and to join in common efforts for the benefit of the church
and the welfare of society. The diocesan clergy form a religious
community in this sense as well as in many others. Religious
communities, like the other communities that emerge from
need, do not include promises of emotional love or mutual
affection in their bonds of formation. To offer aspirants such
promises represents either deceit or poor judgment. To suggest to members of religious communities that bonds of emotional love and mutual affection are an integral part of
community relationships creates confusion and disappointment. As previously mentioned, some communities came into
existence through the affectionate interrelationships that the
community founders had for one another. Although those
emotional bonds represented an essential character of the em-
bryonic community, they typically did not survive the growth
and expansion that took place and that brought a variety of
persons and personalities into the original group. These communities developed in a manner similar to closely attached
families, which gradually lose their strong interrelatedness with
the continuous inclusion of outsiders through marriage.

Formation directors sometimes enroll their directees in "sharing groups." The directors express the expectation either openly or implicitly that those in formation should perceive this group as a kind of family unit, a loving group of friends whom one can trust and with whom one can engage in limitless self-disclosure. It would be nice if it were so. A person does not come to trust others based on studying together, living together, praying together, or having a common superior or director. In fact, those who work in marriage tribunals recognize that couples may live together for years and never establish a relationship of mutual trust. One individual does not come to trust another individual based on third-party assurances. After all, confidence tricksters work in pairs, one assuring the innocent party that the other is absolutely reliable. An individual establishes trust in another based on personal experience of that other person's trustworthiness. That is how it should be. The process takes time, and if there are eight or ten people in a community, it takes time to discover whether or not a person can trust each one of them.

Self-disclosure, sharing one's private thoughts or revealing one's innermost feelings, should come only after the individual builds a firm sense of trust and a strong awareness of a secure relationship. To gather a group of religious novices in a room and ask them to engage in self-revelation because "we are all here out of spiritual motivation and therefore we can trust each other completely" shows not just naïveté but also indiscretion. One might as appropriately ask them to disrobe completely "since we are all religious and self-exposure creates confidence." Even family members need to preserve a deep respect for privacy, both physical privacy and—just as importantly—emotional privacy.

A Catholic high school student made some perceptive comments about a high school retreat that concentrated on sharing private thoughts and family secrets in an atmosphere of lighted candles and hand-holding closeness. The student remarked, "It was just like a one-night stand, false intimacy with no basis in a real relationship. While we were in the situation, we talked about everyone's caring for everyone else, but the minute we walked away we didn't really care about each other. I didn't want the burden of knowing about the personal, private problems of people I'm not close to. They had no right to tell me those things. It was phony, because we were trying to pretend we had some feelings that we didn't really have."

Some religious communities attempt to operate on the erroneous idea that "if we reveal ourselves to one another totally, we will understand one another and love one another. We will find community. We will have family." Even lovers do not reveal all their thoughts and feelings to each other. They need to select what they say to each other as well as how they behave with each other. It is important to be open with those who are emotionally close; but neither closeness nor openness permits indiscriminate communication. This is true because almost all emotional relationships, particularly the intimate ones, include ambivalent feelings. The more strongly persons bond to one another the more they need to be sheltered from the lapses of love, the inconstancy of caring, that occur in intimate relationships because of ambivalence. Openness with others should not be misinterpreted as open season on others. A need to communicate is not a license to destroy.

The novice, the newly professed, and the veteran religious nurture great expectations for permanent intimacy in community living. They search for this phantom of community love, this vision of unconditional acceptance, and they engage in lively but inconclusive discussion about where it can be found. Is it in a house of prayer? Is it in a small community of four or five people? Is it in a large group of forty or fifty? Is it in a religious order? Is it in the diocesan clergy? Is it in a university setting? Is it in a parish with the people of God? Some religious claim they briefly found it, but it quickly faded away. Others say they have never experienced it in community, but the writings and lectures of popular leaders encourage them to continue the search. Rarely does anyone question whether it may be a myth, an imaginary panacea for personal unhappiness and community unrest.

Occasionally a small group of religious decide that they can find this elusive, loving community if they receive permission to live together. Religious superiors recently have tended to promote experimentation, so the superior agrees to the request, perhaps secretly hoping that this group will unravel the mystery of intimacy and return to share their discovery. This small, inexperienced community makes a shiny new rule: "We will be open with one another. There will be no hidden conflicts within the group. We will support each other and build a loving community." Before long, one of the members spends several hours talking with a person outside this small community. This continues with some frequency. One of the other community members questions why this person chooses to spend so much time with an outsider. Eventually a confrontation occurs, because the code of this model community requires openness, no hidden conflicts. "Why are you spending so much time with your noncommunity friend? What do the two of you talk about? How can you be a part of this community and spend so much time with someone else?" This attitude implies that a person's emotional investment must remain within the group. Love, affection, close interaction, intimate conversation must be kept within the small community. The group must be kept inviolable. The errant member characteristically must elect to recant the transgression against the community or to defend the other relationship and become ostracized from the small group. Although this example sounds exaggerated or a little dramatic, it is not uncommon.

Bret, a seminarian attending a coeducational college, spent considerable time in the company of a young female student. Bret decided to enter psychotherapy with the hope of clarifying some sexually traumatic incidents in his childhood and of resolving some conflicts regarding a celibate life. Several of his confreres disapproved of his contacts with the female student and took the matter to the superior of their small community. The superior confronted Bret, questioning his allegiance to the seminary community. "You are violating a bond that exists within this group. You are being unfaithful to your fellow seminarians, your community. You should find your needs for affection satisfied within this house." Of course, the superior did not know that Bret had terminated a brief homosexual relationship with one of the young men in the house just a few months previously. The majority of the small community, perhaps following the superior's implicit lead, became quite hostile to Bret. He refused to give ground, because his relationship with the young woman was quite innocent and without duplicity. The response of his community made life unpleasant, and as a result he made a precipitous choice to leave the seminary. (His therapist considered the choice a judicious one in spite of its abruptness, however.)

Sometimes a few people form a small living group based on their belief that they have a firm affection for and understanding of one another. After living together for a few months, they may request the assistance of a facilitator. The facilitator serves primarily to help them come to terms with the realities of their various personalities and backgrounds and to accept the less-than-perfect world they found rather than the perfect family they fantasized they would create. One living group of eight female religious used a facilitator profitably and formed a community that functioned harmoniously. They had apparently achieved mutual understanding of, if not emotional attachment to, one another. Their little group lived together calmly for about eighteen months. Then another sister asked to live with them. Her age, her similar attitudes and interests, and her friendship with the group members indicated that she would be a compatible addition to the group. They interviewed their sister in religion and refused to accept her as a group member. They gave as the reason that the equilibrium and harmony of the group might be disrupted if they added another member. In other words, although they thought they had found a loving community, they refused to test the fragility of their newly discovered family. What a tight web some bonds become! Their web choked the life out of their group: within one year they dissolved as a living group, with some residual bitterness toward one another.

Families can also become self-absorbed and exclude others. They can become too self-centered and show no concern for the needs of others. They can become too possessive and oppose any outside attachments or interests. Healthy families reach out to others and respond to their needs without losing the affectionate bonds that hold the family itself together. They recognize the expansive nature of love and accept the inclusion of others in enlarging circles of concern without destroying the inner circle of family love. The structure of contemporary religious communities does not provide a basis of intimacy and emotional love that permits them to imitate the process of expansive love manifested by healthy families. The extension of their concern to others must be based on spiritual motivation that originates in prayer, meditation, and thoughtful reflection, rather than in the flames of compassion for others that mutual love kindles in an affectionate family.

Religious women and men might attain greater peace if they acknowledged the psychological limitations of living in religious communities and did not try to escape the cross by pretending it is the day of resurrection. Religious who live together, whether it is in a diocesan rectory or an isolated convent, on a college campus or in a house of prayer, do not live with one another because they have discovered a mutually overwhelming affection. They live together because they must, rarely because they choose to. Even in these times when religious frequently participate in the decision about where they will live, in reality they rarely choose all of their living companions. They more likely avoid those with whom they know they cannot live compatibly. Out of necessity, they often accept a living situation where complete congeniality is lacking.

Previously, religious lived together because they had a common ministry. Now there is a great diversity of ministries within the same living group. In addition, opinions about many issues vary greatly, in contrast with earlier times, when religious superiors strongly influenced community attitudes. Religious living in the same house may hold different convictions about peace and justice issues, the role of women in the church, the authority of the pope, celibacy, the validity of the religious life, and the permanence of religious commitment. Religious achieved harmony more easily when arguments centered on what team would win the World Series or whether it rained during the May Queen crowning the previous year. In those earlier days, community members discussed only certain topics, and these did not include many controversial issues. Harmony based on controlled discussion came at too high a price, but open discussion among persons holding a variety of opinions costs something too.

The bonds of emotional love sometimes collapse in a family, but the members remain tied to one another by material needs and residual loyalties. In families like these, adults visit older parents, not because of affection, but because of a sense of duty. Siblings continue contact with each other, not because of emotional attachment, but because of a sense of obligation or tradition. The continuation of relationships out of duty, obligation, or tradition serves a useful and suitable purpose in many families. If those same family members must pretend that strong bonds of affection hold them together in a steadfast relationship of emotional love, considerable psychological conflict appears. Such hypocrisy distorts reality and strains those who practice it. If their natural responses tell them that their relationship is based on responsibility, not on love, they should not have to declare to all who will listen, "We love each other dearly, and this great affection we have for each other makes us rejoice in those times when we can be together." In families that have lost the ties of affection but maintain the association of obligation, reunions on holidays and other occasions bring marked emotional stress, especially if everyone must maintain the pretense that love has brought them together. It is a reunion of bodies, not of spirits. The strain of the mandatory meeting boosts the consumption of alcohol, disturbs digestion, fans smoldering resentments, and reminds a more honest few to try to avoid this tradition the next time if at all possible. If the family members recognize that they meet out of responsibility rather than affection, then such stress is greatly reduced.

Religious who study or work at some distance from their community may experience emotional tension when they return home for a vacation. Psychiatrists sometimes encourage religious in treatment to avoid returning to their community until they have resolved some of their own misconceptions and exaggerated expectations regarding community membership.

In therapeutic settings religious often express their disillusionment with the limitations of community relationships. One priest, living in a house with three other priests, mentioned that he never let anyone know when he was going out and never greeted anyone upon his return. "They would only ask out of curiosity where I was going or where I had been. They do not really care about me." One is reminded of the book about adolescents titled *Where Are You Going? Out. What Are You Doing? Nothing.* Another priest told how he fabricated stories about himself to impress others in his community. "They pay little attention unless you are extraordinary." A sister related how the members of her small living group demanded that she discuss her psychiatric treatment with them because "we should not have any secrets from one another." She incurred their anger by her refusal. Another sister described how she had put up a wall within herself because she had no interest in the people with whom she lived. Another sister commented bitterly, "What's the use of fighting for my rights in community? I don't have any rights. But I'm tired of being easy to live with in community." A seminarian said, "Everyone is nice and pleasant where I live, but if I fell down, no one would be there to pick me up. They are indifferent." A sister spoke of feeling "almost total aloneness in the convent."

The idea of Christian community is a valid intellectual concept. The Christian community of a religious group or a parish unit provides a sound basis for mutual support and represents a relationship that has many practical advantages. However, an intellectual notion cannot control or contain the realities of emotion. In a religious community or a parish unit, participation in intimate discussions of personal experiences and open declarations of mutual trust and loving interdependence do not produce affective bonds. Emotional responses do not follow intellectual directions. Emotions drag their feet in the clay of primitive being. They have their own existence independent of a person's cultural trappings or spiritual raiment. Emotional reactions to others, likes, dislikes, trust, distrust represent complex affective responses that do not coincide with social niceties or reverent refinements. Behavior in community should be governed by social propriety and the spirit of Christian love, rather than by emotional response. Even though others may arouse emotional antipathies, charity and amity demand courteous exchange. If religious communities require tactful exchanges and respectful relationships with one another, everyone can achieve that goal independent of personal emotional reactions to others. If, on the other hand, a religious community attempts to make psychological love and emotional closeness its goal, everyone is exposed to the traffic of personal affection, exclusive relationships, private dislikes, jealousy, erotic attachments, rejection, and all the contradictions of shallow emotional love.

Searching for affectionate bonds forms a significant goal for an individual. However, a person must seek such ties in the unfolding experience of developing relationships and realize that intimacy depends on profound communication, mutual trust, assurance of fidelity, and, finally, lasting affection. If the religious community sets forth psychological closeness as a goal, community members eventually wonder why they do not receive the fullness of community life; they become critical either of themselves as emotionally deficient or of the community as collectively apathetic. In reality, it is the notion of community that has been falsely extended to include a sense of intimacy, which it cannot produce, and to promise an atmosphere of affection, which it cannot provide.

Religious communities have definite limitations in providing for the emotional needs of community members. Religious cannot expect a community atmosphere of unconditional love, because the spiritual and material bonds that hold a group of adults together in modern religious communities do not support that degree of emotional caring. Religious communities cannot provide the kind of psychological relationships that healthy families develop, because communities lack the benefit of common origin, the depth of personal attachment, and the closeness of a shared life. Therefore, religious communities should not mistakenly assume that they can proffer to candidates or to professed members a life that compares with family life or creates relationships similar to family relationships. Community life is not an alternative type of family life but rather a different model of life and of relationships. One of the most significant limitations of community life will be examined in the following chapter on intimacy.

4. Intimacy in Religious Life

During the past several decades considerable research data have accumulated dealing with the concepts of imprinting, bonding, and attachment. An important discovery in all this work postulates that the human offspring very early in life develops the ability to bond to another human being and that later attachment patterns in adult relationships depend upon these early experiences. With striking clarity the research data indicate that small children who are reared in circumstances of emotional isolation grow up to become adults devoid of the ability to bond to other adults in a meaningful manner. On the other hand, positive attachment patterns in infancy carry over into the interpersonal relationships of adulthood. This abundance of scientific data establishes that, as a result of early life experiences, some adults enjoy an attachment to others, whereas other adults cannot participate in close emotional bonding.

The need for emotional closeness varies considerably in different individuals. Schopenhauer's fable about the two porcupines at the North Pole presents the picture: In the freezing climate the two porcupines discover that they can ward off the cold by bringing their warm bodies close together. They also discover that they experience pain when they move too close to each other because the sharpness and length of their quills set a limit on their friendliness. Everyone has his or her own "porcupine index": that degree of closeness to another that brings maximum warmth and minimum irritation. This porcupine index could also be called an emotional quotient, or EQ, similar, in a sense, to the intelligence quotient, or IQ. The EQ presumably has a distribution that follows the normal curve. Only a small percentage of people find pain in every situation of closeness. At the other end of the curve, only a small percentage of people tolerate great depths of closeness without encountering some irritation. The rest of the people scatter along a continuum between these extremes, with most of them located nearer the middle. The majority of people desire closeness and respond well to it, but they also maintain a comfortable emotional distance from those to whom they are attached.

Many lecturers and writers describe the value and importance of intimacy in the life of the religious. Usually the proponents of this position recommend that the individual religious secure an intimate relationship with one or more others and through that intimacy discover the real value of self. By implication and sometimes by direct assertion, these advocates of intimacy encourage religious to believe that without such an experience a person cannot be fully alive or genuinely open to others. Under the pressure of this propaganda, religious may feel inadequate about themselves and ineffective in their work because they have not experienced the prescribed intimacy.

This search for intimacy takes on the character of the quest for the Holy Grail. The goal sounds so specific, so concrete, so vital, so sacred. It is a great prize that one must grasp steadfastly when the opportunity comes, so that one might be saved. Anything less than the true cup of closest intimacy cannot be considered worthwhile. Love for one's parents, a firm bond with a sibling, enduring friendship with other religious or with laypersons, an abiding affection for a distant classmate from years ago—none of these appear to qualify as genuine intimacy. The quality, the depth, the permanence of these relationships do not meet the criteria of true intimacy. There is the implication that adult intimacy involves a kind of ultimate relationship that has not previously been experienced. But how does a person know when she or he has achieved the ultimate in intimacy if some avenue of closeness remains to be explored? If one starts on a pathway but is unable to recognize its end, one may take a step too far and fall into difficulty. If intimacy makes a person more real, more open, more alive, then would not greater and greater intimacy continue to enhance all these personal qualities?

Sister Connie approached a psychiatrist to discuss some conflicts she was having with the department chairperson at the college where she taught. During several introductory interviews Connie repeatedly mentioned one of her department associates. She had spent a great deal of time with this gentleman over the previous two years. They met in his office or hers at least once a day. They often ate lunch together at a restaurant off campus. They sometimes walked in the park in the afternoon after classes ended. He and his wife invited Connie to their home for dinner approximately once a month. On two or three occasions when his wife left town to visit her parents, he invited Connie to a restaurant for dinner. Connie said they talked about all sorts of things when they were together. They talked about work, about faculty appointments, about students, about budget. They also talked about their past, about their families, about their adult years. He talked about his children, about his marriage, about his wife. She talked about her religious life, about her conflicts with community members, about her provincial. They discussed their ideas, their goals, their dreams, their feelings. Occasionally she gave him a painting of hers for his office. Occassionally he gave her a poem he wrote.

After relating all this to her psychiatrist, Connie asked if he thought that her relationship with her colleague contained any hazards for her. She prefaced her question by emphasizing how important this relationship had been to her during the past two years. Her friend made her community conflicts and her difficulties with the department chairperson less disturbing. Their discussions motivated her to improve her teaching and to be more compassionate toward her students. She felt that in knowing him she came to understand herself better. He gave meaning to much of her everyday life. Connie, of course, denied any romantic attachment in their friendship. Obviously she sought confirmation from the psychiatrist for the value of their relationship. The psychiatrist suggested that Connie consider their affiliation from the man's wife's point of view. Connie found it difficult to think about that. She became angry and refused to make any further appointments. The intimate relationship she had established with her associate troubled her at some level. Quite possibly her purpose in seeking psychiatric help was to allay her misgivings and elicit support for her behavior. When the psychiatrist encouraged her doubts, she turned away from something she did not want to see.

The religious who believes that an individual needs an intimate relationship in order to achieve maturity and function in a healthy manner may readily use another person to achieve that goal. The idea that one will be a better religious after one has experienced an adult love relationship rarely takes into account the consequences of this event for the other person. Searching for intimacy to discover oneself contradicts the essential character of the relationship. The desire for intimacy should motivate a person to give of self in search of another, not to take from another in search of self.

A young priest discussed with a psychiatrist his friendly relationship with a female co-worker. The psychiatrist asked a number of questions in order to understand the depth and force of their relationship. He asked if they went out to dinner together. The priest said they did not, but later in the interview mentioned that he took his friend to supper occasionally. He chose to believe that eating supper was less formal, less significant, and less intimate than going out to dinner with her. In treatment he gained perspective on his self-deception and decided that either supper or dinner brought their relationship to a level that he considered inappropriate for him and unfair to her. As these case histories indicate, one must examine the results greater intimacy has for those involved.

The most valid argument for the importance of the

experience of intimacy relates to the period of infancy. To develop normally an infant needs the experience of bonding to a nurturing person. Without that experience, a permanent defect in relating closely to others results. If the individual religious knew intimacy as an infant, then he or she does not need to discover intimacy as an adult in order to be a healthy, whole person. If the individual religious did not encounter that attachment as an infant, attempts to find it in adult life rarely produce good results. Healthy adults seek intimacy for personal satisfaction, not to become whole. Adults who never attached in their infancy avoid intimacy, because it brings pain, not pleasure.

The purveyors of "get your intimacy now" philosophy base their invitation on the assumption that intimacy contributes to personal growth, to an understanding of others, to an acceptance of oneself. They present intimacy as a necessary, and certainly pleasurable, means to achieve a worthwhile end. Without doubt, the intimacy of attachment behavior in infancy contributes to healthy emotional development. Does adult intimacy necessarily produce further growth, or can it become an end in itself that provides pleasure but not betterment? Can an intimate relationship cause damage to those who are involved? Two young people at a rock concert, wrapped in the same blanket, smoking the same marijuana cigarette and drinking from the same bottle, disclosing the details of their past lives and exposing their immediate feelings as they are swept along through the inner fog by the sound of acid rock, can profess an intimate relationship. Their intimacy does not produce growth. It does not clarify their view of themselves or expand their appreciation of their environment. Like others who become intimate, they too desire this feeling of intimacy to continue forever. The ephemeral character of their relationship precludes permanence. Their moment of intimacy leads nowhere, except perhaps to another rock concert.

An intimate relationship that carries a person to higher goals, to better behavior, and to nobler thoughts obviously nourishes personality growth. Beyond enjoyment, intimacy holds no real value for those who are intimate unless it fosters values in their lives. There is an essential difference between intimacy that turns inward and feeds on itself and intimacy that enhances personal insight and encourages understanding of others. Those who search for intimacy should recognize that not all intimate relationships promote emotional health and psychological growth. Furthermore, and contrary to popular opinion, psychological health and personal growth are not contingent upon an ongoing intimate relationship.

Some equate the *desire* for intimacy with a *need* for intimacy. They suggest to religious that their desire for intimacy requires fulfillment to make their lives wholesome and complete. Many persons never find that which they seek in this world, whether it is wealth, fame, and power or intimacy, peace, and happiness. Many single adults, divorced persons, widows and widowers continue to have a desire for intimacy, but they manage to live healthy and fruitful lives without an intimate relationship. Indeed, many married people never find intimacy in their married state. Although rewarding relationships may fill their lives and provide a degree of social interaction, for many people the desire for intimacy remains unsatisfied. A realistic view of life cannot establish intimacy as an essential ingredient for healthy adult living.

Work with married couples often exposes marked differences in their needs for intimacy. One spouse may desire a great deal of intimate interaction, whereas the other may be quite uncomfortable in the closeness of married life and find various ways of avoiding an intimate relationship. Incessant activity provides a barrier to closeness. Outside interests can take up the time that intimacy requires. Children can be used as a buffer to keep the spouse at an emotional distance.

A woman, married for thirty-two years, came for psychiatric help because her husband avoided spending time with her, refused to engage in meaningful discussions with her, and insisted on taking his vacations without her. The psychiatrist originally speculated that this man no longer loved his wife and probably sought an intimate relationship with someone else. The husband agreed to a series of interviews. These interviews revealed that, in fact, he still loved his wife as he always had, but he experienced no desire to spend time with her. In the beginning of their marriage he worked hard to support his wife and their four young children. She kept busy with the children and found companionship in their presence. After they left, she turned to her husband for intimacy and could not understand his inability to respond to her emotional needs. Treatment helped her accept her husband's emotional unresponsiveness and his need to avoid closeness. Emotional deprivation in his childhood made him unable in his adulthood to establish a close relationship with anyone.

Similarly, every religious does not desire the same degree of intimacy, nor can each one tolerate the same degree of intimacy. Carl, a fifty-year-old priest, sought psychiatric help because of a conflict in his life caused by a superior's refusal to give him an assignment he wanted. Carl described his life as exciting and flamboyant. Indeed it was. He knew many influential and wealthy people and used his contacts with them to his advantage. His outstanding work for his community brought him national prominence. His verbal fluency and suave manner opened doors for him and pocketbooks for his cause. The extent and the success of his work required him to have a personal secretary. After a short time together, their relationship became a physically intimate one and remained so for ten years prior to the time he came for therapy. His life story unfolded in the psychiatric setting.

A painstaking review of his relationships with others showed an absence of genuine intimacy. His father, a harsh and aloof man, rarely talked to any of his four sons. His mother, a devout and gregarious woman, declared her love for her children to everyone who would listen but never demonstrated that love to them. Carl, the youngest of the four boys, could not remember his parents ever reading a story to him, ever kissing him good night or even coming into physical contact with him, ever tucking him into bed at night, or ever responding to any of his childhood needs. They expected good performance at school, obedience to their authority and that of others, and exemplary behavior to uphold the family reputation.

Carl never dated as a youth. When he finished high school, he entered the seminary. There he excelled. His keen intellect, wit, and charm made him popular in the seminary and later in his community. He never trusted anyone, and he never formed a close relationship with anyone. After ordination he advanced rapidly and soon held a position of considerable responsibility in his province. His contacts with family members served as a nuisance in his active life, and he quickly discarded family ties.

As a child Carl did not experience any authentic affection from others. As an adult he did not evidence any genuine caring for others. He only gave to gain more in return, and he never really gave his love. Perhaps he had none to give. He used his friends as stepping stones and displayed no loyalty to anyone. His relationship with his secretary kept her tied to him. Her organizational abilities and her professional competence served him well and promoted his career. He used her as he used others. Finally, he used her to get even with his superior for refusing to give him the assignment he requested. In a civil ceremony, he married his secretary, not out of love for her, but out of anger toward his religious superior.

Ostensibly Carl sought psychiatric care to straighten out his life and to return to the commitment of his vows. In reality he wanted to use psychiatry for his own gain, as he used everything else. After six months Carl found marriage too demanding, too confining, too drab. He wished to make peace with his community in order to regain his prestige and return to his extravagant lifestyle. His problem was not what to do about himself but rather what to do about the bride he wanted to discard. He commented, "I need lots of people to love me. It's the hero in me." Many people had loved him. On the other hand, he had never been truly intimate with anyone. He never could be.

Families often maintain intimate ties, but that happens because affectionate bonds extend from every member to each of the others. Family members possess a common heritage, and strong, stable bonds hold them together. Because of their shared background, they often have similar needs for intimacy. Members of religious groups, however, differ greatly both in their emotional development and in their genetic makeup. Consequently they exhibit remarkable diversity in their desire for intimacy. They do not come together with the familiar history, the common memories, and the shared experiences that enable some families to build and maintain ties of permanent closeness. Religious communities can provide an atmosphere of harmony, a setting for friendship, a climate of congeniality. But the desire for intimacy seeks a partner, a soul mate, a person who understands how one thinks and feels and who sometimes understands without the use of words.

Persons in religious formation often struggle with their desire for intimacy and wonder how this desire can be fulfilled. To tell them that relationships within the community provide the answer to their wish for closeness misleads them. One does not find intimacy through group contact. An intimate group may form because individual intimacies within the group expand to include all the members. This is far more likely to occur in a small support group, such as a Caritas group, than in a large community or in a small living group. Even in small support groups, the opportunity to form deep affectionate bonds with all the other participants rarely occurs. To a person interested in religious life but searching for a high degree of intimacy, one must honestly say, "Religious life does not provide a setting for intimacy. If one can develop an intimate relationship with God through one's prayer life, one discovers love. Religious do not always attain that goal. Some find the spiritual relationship too intangible to satisfy their need for human closeness. Marriage is the state of life that makes intimacy its touchstone. In religious life one must be willing to forgo the deepest human intimacy. One may find and cherish close friends, one may maintain and enrich family ties, one may love and be loved, but deep intimacy is not a characteristic of religious commitment."

A young man in seminary formation recognized this struggle within himself while under psychiatric care. Clarence sought help because he felt "depressed, lonely, isolated." He slept poorly, always felt tired, and had difficulty concentrating on his studies. He described self-hatred as a familiar feeling. On one occasion as he discussed this feeling, he commented, "I might have to kill myself because I am so alone." Clarence described his father as undemonstrative, a lonely man, living "behind a big emotional wall." His mother tried to control Clarence and consistently made him feel inferior. His parents had fought throughout his childhood and adolescence. His father withdrew emotionally from everyone for weeks at a time. His mother behaved in an extremely volatile manner and, in her rages, "would roar away" in one of the family cars. As a child, Clarence had feared abandonment. He distinctly remembered at age five feeling it was his responsibility to keep his parents together. He always tried to please his parents, but that presented a dilemma. They constantly disagreed, so if he did something to please one of them, it usually displeased the other. Finally, he chose sides and worked hard to make his mother happy.

Clarence excelled as a student and participated in several extracurricular activities. Before entering religious life, he completed college. His parents never acknowledged any of his achievements. He dated several different women during his high school and college days. Typically these relationships ended badly. He would begin to feel unloved, to do more and more to please the woman, to become angry when his efforts failed, and finally to feel abandoned. He entered religious life because the sense of fellowship appealed to him. He expected to find friendship, a sense of belonging, intimacy. During a therapy session one day, he commented wistfully, "I am angry at my community because they have failed me. I thought they would offer me emotional warmth. I thought they would help me to be more open, to be more real, and they have not done so." This young man clearly yearned for a close relationship with someone. Earlier his inclination led him to search for that bond with a woman. He failed repeatedly because his developmental scars interfered. He thought that he might find the answer to his yearning in the camaraderie of a religious community. As treatment progressed, he became increasingly aware that community life did not satisfy his desire for intimacy and that, in fact, the structure and limitations of community excluded the possibility of such satisfaction. He also became aware that this desire represented a powerful and significant aspect of his personality. He rekindled his hope that a heterosexual relationship could develop into a permanent state of intimacy. Clarence left religious life and entered into a marriage that appeared to bring him the intimacy he sought.

Of course, marriage is not the only situation in life that permits and promotes intimacy. Deep and lasting friendships sometimes reach a similar kind of closeness. However, outside of marriage, intimacy encounters a number of limitations and restraints. Close friends may be separated by great distances and for long periods, divided by the limitations of separate life schedules and lifestyles, and kept apart by the priorities of other commitments. The unique intimacy of marriage cannot be captured in any relationship that does not have similar opportunities for sharing time and physical space, for participating in a broad range of experiences, and, finally, for creating a world of mutuality. In that kind of intimacy, the perception of a new world takes place, for intimacy adds a certain depth to the sensibilities of each spouse. The solitary individual sees the world from a single position. In the vast intimacy of a devoted marriage, a remarkable approximation of thoughts and feelings occurs; nonetheless a separateness remains. For persons who are so close yet distinct, this kind of unity provides a kind of stereoscopic view, so that all of life has a little more depth, a little more color, and a little more clarity than if it were seen through the eyes of one person alone. A wise priest once suggested that religious might achieve this stereoscopic view of life by relating to God's view of the world. That represents an ideal for everyone. Unfortunately, most people diverge so far from God's view of things that a comparison of views only reveals their distorted vision and demonstrates their disharmony.

Spouses who are close help keep each other authentic. The husband finds himself reflected back in his exchanges with his wife. In the intimacy of their union he knows that she knows more about him than he sometimes knows about himself. If he is wise, he will learn from her knowledge, but his lack of learning will not disturb their intimacy. For her knowledge does not partake of outside judgment, but becomes, rather, another part of him. In a similar manner, a wife finds herself mirrored in her husband's knowledge of her. Perhaps this exchange in deepest intimacy foreshadows for the couple their final unanimity with God.

The celibate life deprives the individual of this alter ego, this guardian of authenticity. The absence of this intimate counterpart forms the existential loneliness of the celibate. An attempt at attachment that falls short either in duration or in depth neither brings lasting satisfaction nor diminishes the need. However, in their unwillingness to accept their aloneness, religious may come upon an intimacy that is less than genuine, a love that is less than lasting. Sometimes they mistake sexual attraction and erotic stimulation for intimacy and attempt to achieve emotional closeness through physical contact. Some advocates of intimacy for religious encourage this naive approach to a very complex relationship. Their promotion of physical intimacy appears to come from their own inability to appreciate the meaning of genuine intimacy or from their own unwillingnesss to acknowledge the psychological and moral consequences of physical intimacy.

In regard to intimacy, religious frequently err in their refusal to acknowledge that emotional closeness often disposes people to desire physical closeness, and physical closeness inclines toward sexual contact. One cannot claim that this is universally true, but neither can a reasonable person deny the direction that intimacy tends to take. Like unsophisticated adolescents, religious sometimes argue that their openness about their feelings of affection provides a safeguard against sexual involvement. After a couple reaches the point of discussing their romantic feelings toward each other, they move imperceptibly toward displaying their erotic interest in each other. Open discussion and the honest expression of feelings play a valuable role in the resolution of certain personal and social conflicts. However, in the areas of affection and erotic desire, silence and restraint help prevent conflict for those not free to express their affection physically.

Although physical closeness often comes to mind when people consider the topic of intimacy, the concept includes a great deal more. The bonding behavior of infants necessarily involves physical contact with a parental figure. This first experience of physical intimacy produces the basis for emotional attachment to others that extends beyond the limits of physical nearness and immediate presence. From these early intimacies of life, the person develops a sense of individual worth and separateness. Mature adults maintain varying needs for continuing attachment, emotional intimacy, and physical closeness. Married life provides the natural setting for attaining a high level of emotional and physical intimacy. Celibate religious life, on the other hand, does not promote an atmosphere of emotional intimacy and does not permit an environment of physical intimacy. Those who choose the life of a celibate religious must recognize the constraints on intimate relationships that become their portion in that vowed state. The vows of marriage include words of affectionate bonding, of personal intimacy, and of permanent attachment, but the vows of celibate religious allude to private sacrifices, public dedication, and spiritual rewards. Awareness of the demands of religious life and of their own emotional needs is essential for celibate religious and for those considering the celibate religious life.

5. Conflicts in Observing Obedience

The idea of obedience is rather alien in contemporary society. The phrase "obedience to the state" is more likely to conjure up notions of totalitarian oppression than to signify conformity to the laws in a democracy. Obedience suggests subservience and domination. The propriety, indeed the necessity, of children obeying their parents is no longer the subject of sermons—or the psychological approach that puts a book on the best-seller list. Authors and lecturers discuss the obligations of parents to be concerned about and listen to the thoughts and feelings of their children. Understanding their children becomes the goal of good parents. Popular speakers and writers rarely mention the concepts of obedience and discipline.

In this era of human rights, powerful social forces influence the thinking of everyone. Although the champions of individual rights do not attack the concept of obedience, they create a psychological atmosphere that markedly minimizes the role of authority. The rights of individuals curtail the dominion of the state. The rights of children and adolescents restrict the authority of parents. The rights of students limit the regulations of the schools. The rights of citizens curb the jurisdiction of the police.

In the area of religion, individual conscience has advanced theologically to center stage. Personal conscience as the proximate norm of morality has moved from the footnotes in old theological texts to the title pages. The concept of individual conscience recognizes the unique developmental history and the particular psychological state of each person. Unconscious motivations and mitigating emotional factors influence the direction of the individual's moral decisions. Recognition of these psychodynamic forces and emphasis on their power in human behavior have also created a bulwark against the demands of external authority. Confessors, spiritual directors, and counselors tend to support the individual's interpretation of and response to his or her world. The position of external authority succumbs to the primacy of the individual conscience. Occasionally, religious even oppose their superiors as a matter of conscience.

Not only does obedience to civil and ecclesiastical authority allow for interpretation and exception, but the situation of the individual vis-à-vis the strict moral law also seems to permit some singular conclusions. Some Catholic laity have shopped for "the right confessor" for many years. This became a common practice in regard to birth control. It expanded to other moral concerns, such as sterilization and homosexuality. Religious, too, tend to look for support and approval from spiritual directors and confessors who agree with their position.

Concern for individual rights and respect for individual conscience provide a significant background for consideration of the vow of obedience. Appeal to authority in present-day society rarely evokes a sense of compliance in anyone. The contemporary theological, psychological, and social climate severly limits the authority of the religious superior. In times past community members viewed religious authority as sanctioned by God. Obedience followed without questioning. If a decision of the superior seemed unreasonable or even ridiculous, the individual religious found inner security in knowing that God's will had been expressed, and resigning oneself to the decision represented the right course. The vow of obedience required acceptance of the superior's authority. Spiritually, the vow represented the sacrifice of one's own will to God's will, as expressed through God's delegate, the religious superior. Psychologically, the vow represented an unqualified submission to the uncontested authority of another human being.

For some, this was not an easy sacrifice. Many dedicated but spirited men and women found each surrender a psychological irritant, although at the same time a spiritual unction. They possessed their own sound ideas, their own inner forces, their own high visions. In their endorsement of obedience, they accepted the ideas of superiors without relinquishing their own intellectual creativity; they followed the direction of the designated authority without abandoning their personal ideals; they worked in assignments they did not choose without losing their enthusiasm for the life they had chosen.

Religious authority no longer symbolizes autocratic power. Religious authority has lost its solemnity. An attitude of co-operative endeavor replaces the emphasis on obedience. Mature religious find new meaning in the vow of obedience and new virtue in its practice. The principles of participatory management may not belong to their vocabulary, but the concepts have become part of their relationship with authority. These religious join with their superiors to further the works of the community. They recognize that someone must be in charge and that the person in charge must sometimes make decisions with which everyone does not agree. Although they participate in the decision-making process, they accept the fact that such participation is still constrained by obedience.

In the past for some religious, the vow of obedience simplified life. They enjoyed a dependent role and found comfort in allowing others to make decisions for them. For some, that was the attraction of religious life. Psychologically, they responded to religious authority as others in society respond to the cults that offer eternal salvation and the clans that offer permanent security. All the individual must do is follow the dictates of the leader, without question, without reservation, without evaluation. This kind and degree of submission still appeals to the personality of some individuals. It relieves them of responsibility for decision-making. It offers them assurances of being on the right side of things. Fear of failure, concern about mistakes, and anxiety about the future all seem to be eliminated through this abandonment of oneself to the care and control of another.

Sister Dorothy grew up in a rigid home atmosphere. Her father dominated the household and gave special privileges to his sons. The females in the family accepted submissive roles. The family tradition required the women to be subservient, get married, have babies, and take care of the house and children. They were expected not to engage in intellectual discussions and not to be concerned with financial matters. Her mother's piety always impressed Dorothy and seemed to her to help her mother cope with the restrictions of her female role. The sisters in her grade school encouraged Dorothy to consider religious life, and she viewed them as women who had escaped male domination.

Dorothy entered the convent during her senior year in high school. She readily accepted the discipline of her formation years. Those in authority found her serious and submissive. Spiritual guides found her prayerful and devout. Others appreciated her cheerful disposition, enthusiasm, and pleasant smile. Everything went smoothly during those years. On schedule, she made temporary vows and then permanent vows.

Dorothy accepted each assignment she received in the same way that she had accepted postulancy, novitiate, and juniorate. She taught a class of fifty third-graders before she had the training or the credentials commensurate with the job. She taught art if requested, mathematics if needed, shop if no one else was available. For one year, she taught music to several grades, although she had neither the training, the talent, nor the inclination to do so. She regularly attended summer school in a desperate attempt to equip herself for the tasks she was already performing. Each time she achieved some professional competence and some psychological comfort in teaching at a particular grade level in a particular setting, she would be assigned to a different grade or transferred to a different school.

She always appeared to accept these changes graciously and generously. Her pleasant disposition and submissive attitude undoubtedly encouraged superiors to choose her as a person whom they could easily reassign.

As the years went by, state requirements regarding credentials became more stringent, parents became more demanding, and students became more difficult. And Dorothy's inadequacies became more obvious. She had never acquired a professional dignity that elicited respect from others; she had maintained a subservient attitude toward others and a disparaging attitude toward herself. She had never been able to direct her own studies toward any distinct goal, because she had never requested that her superiors clarify their goals for her. Unfortunately, Dorothy's childhood experiences and her vow of obedience, as she interpreted it, hindered a healthy personality maturation. She had never obtained a distinct image of her own individuality or a sense of her own independence. Her developing identity fused with that of her pious and submissive mother and then transferred to the prayerfulness and obedience of religious life. Her psychological immaturity was, in fact, a greater obstacle to her career than were her professional limitations.

Dorothy's inadequacy as a teacher became increasingly apparent and forced her superiors to remove her from the classroom. Dorothy could not understand how she had failed. She had been obedient, prayerful, and diligent. She thought that was all that was necessary. She became despondent, and at that point, she began a lengthy course of psychotherapy. Although her personality remained somewhat childlike, she became more aware of her own strengths and weaknesses, more cognizant of the limitations of authority figures, and more resolute in assuming responsibility for her own actions and the direction of her own life. She became moderately successful in another career that provided an opportunity for initiative with the safeguard of regular supervision.

Some religious who previously satisfied their extreme dependency by forcing superiors constantly to tell them what to do now turn directly to God, since God's delegate has seemingly abandoned them. They have learned something about the process of spiritual discernment but not enough to use it in an appropriate manner and only in situations in which it is called for. They avoid decision making by trying to invoke the process of discernment at every turn. They can hardly decide what to eat for breakfast without first discerning God's will. They ignore judgment and volition, God-given tools for daily decision making. Instead of sharpening these tools, keeping them in good repair, and using them regularly, they set them aside and go directly to the Toolmaker for further assistance. They look for spiritual signs to indicate their daily path, divine directions to guide their way. They previously avoided responsibility by waiting for superiors to give them orders. Because superiors made the decisions, superiors carried the burden of any failures that occurred. They now place responsibility on God for their decisions and leave God with the burden of poor results. The poorly prepared priest who begins his homily by attributing his remarks to the Holy Spirit tries to escape responsibility for a bad sermon. In justice, he should charge his inept preaching to his own busyness, or possibly to his own laziness, but certainly not to the guidance of the Holy Spirit. The theological principle that every creature depends on God for everything should not deter a person from using those gifts of intelligence and volition that make humans stand above all other creatures. These precious gifts are the tools of the trade for humanity. The individual can use them creatively, joyfully, and expansively or can shun them and turn back to the Maker, the Giver, and say, "I'm afraid to trust those tools. They are inadequate for the task you have given me."

Sister Danielle's provincial superior asked her to consider taking the position of administrator in one of the community's schools. Danielle gave the matter a great deal of thought. She reflected on her own timidity, her lack of assertiveness, her perfectionistic traits, and her impatience with others. She knew that she often felt tense and, during these periods of heightened anxiety, experienced marked insomnia and had difficulty maintaining her external composure and accomplishing even simple tasks. For these reasons, Danielle decided she should not accept the position of administrator. She prayed about her decision, thought about it some more, and then informed her provincial.

Five years later, obsessive ruminations caused Danielle to seek psychiatric care. In therapy she discussed her early life. Her parents were rigid, perfectionistic people. They disapproved of their daughter's exuberance and spontaneity. To avoid their displeasure, Danielle subdued her natural enthusiasm for life and became solemn and submissive. She always felt guilty because her mother had to work so hard caring for the five children. She helped her mother in every way she could, but she resented the obligation to do so. She often thought of running away from home.

When Danielle first decided not to serve as an administrator, she believed it was the right decision. As time went on, she began to doubt her decision. The provincial had made the request. Was that not an indication of God's will? Perhaps she had not prayed enough before deciding. Maybe she was just being willful. Why had she not sought advice from her confessor? She had surely been disobedient. God must certainly be displeased with her. Perhaps she was experiencing these emotional difficulties because she had been so selfish and headstrong. During treatment Danielle struggled obsessively with that decision as well as many others she had made. She enclosed herself in a relentless web of doubt.

Danielle considered contacting her provincial and requesting an assignment as an administrator. This drive to undo her earlier decision seemed ill advised. The psychiatrist tried to reassure her about the soundness of the previous decision without telling her directly that a position of administration would probably be severely detrimental to her emotional stability and disastrous for those who worked with her. Danielle was not easily reassured. She discussed the matter with her spiritual director, who, unfortunately, advised her that it was probably God's will that she accept the administrative assignment, since her superior had asked her to do so.

An erroneous oversimplification would suggest that it is older religious who accept the subservient interpretation of obedience and younger religious who define obedience in terms of collegiality. However, the distinction between those religious who actively enter into decision making and those who passively stand by to be led by others does not rest with age alone. Many older religious always contributed to decisions made by their superiors, especially if those decisions involved their work or interests. Characteristically, they achieved those goals with less temerity and clamor than their younger counterparts currently exhibit.

By contrast, some younger people in religious life display little desire or ability for self-direction. By temperament or by training, some people are content to play passive roles. Although they follow some leaders with enthusiasm and others with reluctance, their basic stance is submissive. Their vow of obedience creates little conflict for them. However, the vow of obedience as others understand it and live it may cause them considerable consternation. They may secretly envy the more assertive style of associates, and they may be envious of the liberties that others discover in the modern version of obedience.

A definition of maturity must maintain a breadth that encompasses a range of behaviors. An active pursuit of independent thought and self-directed behavior can occur in a mature manner or in an immature manner. The religious who expresses personal preferences and discusses these forthrightly with the superior, keeping in perspective the needs of the community, behaves maturely. A less mature religious may seek self-determination without regard for other members of the community and defend the position vociferously and contentiously in discussion with the superior.

Most communities these days have one or two members who assume a position of defiant independence that strains the patience of each new superior. These errant members demand much and contribute little. They insist on special assignments or will accept none. They request attendance at workshops, classes, and retreats that exceed their personal budget and sometimes strain community finances. They separate themselves from community exercises, community meetings, and community relationships. They sometimes bolster their position by maintaining that their spiritual director, therapist, or physician advises these behaviors for their personal development, spiritual needs, or psychological health. Although their behavior purportedly seeks self-determination, it is, in reality, selfishly determined and markedly immature.

A lack of assertiveness and a pattern of passivity can occur in a healthy or unhealthy fashion also. Concepts of competitiveness that permeate contemporary society cast a heavy shadow over those who are nonaggressive. Present-day culture encourages a disparaging attitude toward those who can but who will not stand up for their own rights or the rights of others. The righteous aggressiveness of those who fight against aggression in the world usually carries an air of disdain for those who maintain a passive attitude. Is aggression in one coat less disordered than aggression in another? Do not both have their victims? The range of emotional health must include those who take a passive position in life as well as those who take up every challenge and enter every controversy. Healthy religious can choose to avoid confrontation and follow in a submissive fashion those who are elected or appointed to be in charge of them. But this style of obedience is not popular in communities where confrontation is the order of the day and submission is acceptable only after all defensive avenues are exhausted. Neither the inherent goodness nor the internal stability of an individual can be equated with the number of causes espoused or the force of the uproar for rights. On the other hand, religious who acquiesce to the demands of everyone and prostrate themselves as a kind of community doormat must be considered emotionally immature.

Other variations in the meaning and context of obedience

cause individual conflict and community turmoil. For some, the vow of obedience has lost its luster beside the blaze of individual rights, and superiors have lost their credibility alongside the supremacy of individual needs. Many religious push to find the limits imposed by obedience, rather than searching for the emotionally healthy parameters and the spiritual benefits of obedience. For them, obedience represents only restrictions and coercion. Other religious, who view obedience in a positive manner, discover psychological bounty and new spiritual vistas in their commitment.

The re-evaluation of the vow of obedience has released years of pent-up anger in some religious. They behave like adults who were the victims of child abuse, carrying a reservoir of concealed anger that overflows from time to time with little or no provocation and engulfs others in its violence. For these religious, their submission to authority during their earlier years in religious life represented only an external acceptance. They have stored up and mentally catalogued every detail of harshness or unfairness. The constraints of a rigid interpretation of obedience helped them repress an accumulation of anger. Community structures of the past restrained their wrath and bolstered their defenses against its expression. Now they are free from the restrictive interpretation of obedience, and they rebel vehemently and sometimes viciously against authority figures. They excuse their behavior with the popular idea that it is healthy to express anger—and they express it unceasingly and insatiably.

Healthy people recognize their own emotional reactions to life events. They also know that the outward expression of internal emotional responses demands behavioral restraints and temporal limits to be considered healthy. The manifestation of grief by the widower becomes pathological when it exceeds a reasonable period of time. The display of anxiety by the soldier's wife becomes unhealthy when she runs up and down the street calling for her husband. Demonstrations of fear by nuclear-age adolescents are reasonable, but not if these adolescents become unable to venture from their homes. Anger, too, can be expressed in healthy ways and in unhealthy ways. The repression of anger may be emotionally damaging to the angry person; however, the expression of anger may also be destructive both to the angry person and to the person who is the object of the anger. Expressions of anger that harm others or that continue in an endless chain of bitterness diminish the goodness of the one who is angry and assail the worth of the one who is attacked. Demeaning remarks, constant criticism, false accusations, unfair observations, and harsh allegations can weaken the confidence and destroy the courage of another. Those who encourage an individual to express anger should also encourage him or her to evaluate the method and the consequences of its expression.

Most religious superiors have had experience with individual religious who are defiantly disobedient. Any attempt to discuss differences with them intensifies their fury. Their verbal criticism slips quickly from policy matters to personal attack on the superior. Generally no benefit comes from the encounter. The anger is not resolved, for it is more deep-seated than the policy or decision in question. Nor does it revolve around the personality or style of this superior. The next policy, no matter how broad, the next decision, no matter how fair, the next superior, regardless of style or personality, will arouse the same flailing anger. For the superior, the encounter may be unnerving because it is so irrational, discouraging because it is so relentless, and damaging because it is so merciless. The provincial superior of one religious community sought psychiatric care after completing her term in office. As provincial, she had been repeatedly subjected to exchanges of this kind. A mild-mannered, sensitive woman, she interpreted these diatribes as attacks against her rather than as assaults against authority. She became deeply depressed and required a lengthy period of treatment to regain her quietude and self-esteem.

The vow of obedience is not the real issue for these angry

religious; often there is present a personality problem that originated in a faulty developmental process. Research indicates that religious life attracts an unusually high percentage of persons with personality disorders.* One of the most frequently encountered personality disorders in religious life is the passive-aggressive personality. People with this disorder may react in a pathologically passive manner in one situation and in a morbidly aggressive manner in another situation. Religious communities no longer encourage or reward passivity as they did in the past. This change of attitude stimulates passive-aggressive personalities to shift to the aggressive mode in their interaction with authority figures.

The religious who consistently responds with exaggerated anger may have experienced some gross injustice in the past, either prior to life as a religious or during it. Sister Donna, age seventy-two, was sent by her provincial for psychiatric evaluation. In the previous few years she had been defiant toward authority and argumentative with other community members. She had become suspicious of the intentions of those in authority and secretive about her own behavior. One might initially assume that senile changes could be responsible for this irritability, suspiciousness, secretiveness, and defiance. However, her alertness, vitality, interest in her environment, intact memory, and unguarded attitude toward the psychiatrist eliminated the possibility of senile deterioration. It became evident that Donna was doing what older people often do. She was reviewing and attempting to integrate the experiences of her life as she entered her Golden Jubilee year. Looking back at her religious commitment brought her peace, and analyzing her observance of the vows brought her satisfaction. However, in considering her relationship with her community, she could find neither peace nor satisfaction.

---

* See M. W. Kelley, "The Incidence of Hospitalized Mental Illness Among Religious Sisters in the U.S.," *American Journal of Psychiatry* 115 (1958): 72; R. J. McAllister and A. J. Vander Veldt, "Psychiatric Illness in Hospitalized Catholic Religious," *American Journal of Psychiatry* 121 (1965): 881.

During therapy Donna discussed some incidents of previous years that remained smoldering fires of resentment and bitterness. At one time in her career, she taught at a high school for girls in the Midwest. Something happened at the school that resulted in the sudden dismissal of four students. The president of the school, a member of Donna's community, summoned Donna to her office and informed her that she had made a request to the Mother Superior to have Donna transferred immediately to another area. The president spoke in veiled terms about the reputation of the school and the possibility of a lawsuit. Donna did not know why the four students had been dismissed, nor did she know why the president had requested her transfer. She assumed that there must be some connection between the two events, but she had no way of knowing what the connection was. Within four days Donna left, with no good-byes allowed. The Mother Superior ordered her never to discuss the matter. Obediently Donna had never discussed it, but neither had she understood it—nor forgotten it.

Donna spoke about other incidents in her community life that she had endured silently but resentfully. When she had abdominal surgery, her superior asked her to return to the classroom three days after she came home from the hospital, even though the doctor had recommended two weeks of rest before she returned to work. On another occasion, she had received permission from her immediate superior to attend a summer workshop. Before summer came, a new superior took over and arbitrarily rescinded the permission.

Donna believed that obedience required silent submission, but her inner sense of fairness rebelled against these injustices. Although other involved community members had long ago forgotten these incidents, Donna thought about them frequently as her jubilee year approached. Each time she remembered them, she recalled the hurt, and her anger increased. In therapy, she re-experienced the trauma, relived her anguish, and exposed the extent and force of her anger. She acknowledged that her community now had no way of righting the wrong, no way of making peace with her, nor even the capacity to understand her distress. She realized that the attainment of peace, the resolution of conflict, and the forgiveness of others sometimes require a solitary solution, a private accomplishment, a personal surrender. She made peace with her community within her heart. Her irritability and suspiciousness went away because the reasons for them were no longer there.

Another dilemma of many religious with regard to obedience was addressed by a priest in therapy. Father Duane had exhibited some behavioral difficulties that caused concern on the part of his superiors, including his provincial superior. His superiors transferred him to another assignment so that he could receive psychiatric care. Toward the end of Duane's treatment, his therapist encouraged him to ask his superiors about his next assignment. In the kind of dialogue that commonly occurs between religious superiors and community members these days, his provincial advised him to search for an acceptable position. Upon finding such a position, he was then to consult with the provincial for approval prior to applying. Father Duane commented, "It looks as if I can take any job that suits me as long as it suits the provincial."

A similar dilemma was faced by Sister Debra. The provincial directress of ministries told Debra to find a job commensurate with her education and experience. Debra, a dietician, found a suitable job in a hospital. The directress of ministries, although not a dietician, decided unilaterally that Debra could not do the job and refused to let her apply for it. Debra was in psychiatric care to deal with some phobic traits. She requested a meeting with the directress, her provincial, and her psychiatrist. In the meeting the directress appeared threatened and became increasingly determined to exhibit her authority rather than to explain the reasons for her decision. The provincial quickly aligned herself with her designee, the directress. Debra, in an assertive moment, asked what would happen if she applied for the job contrary to their recommendation. Without hesitation, the provincial replied that she and her council would then consider the possibility of involuntary exclaustration (dismissal from the community but not a release from vows). Debra spent six months working in the kitchen at the provincialate before the directress allowed her to apply for and accept a job in dietetics. Though the vow of obedience does involve sacrifice, those in authority sometimes make unjust demands. The resultant anger can continue for years.

Research indicates that another kind of personality disorder frequently appears in religious communities—the sociopathic personality. Individuals with this personality disorder are usually intelligent, verbally adroit, and determined to attain self-serving goals. They expend considerable effort to prove that they are the exception to regulations and policies. The firm guidelines of previous community structures usually held their sociopathic traits in check. These individuals ingeniously maneuvered their way through the maze of rules, but rarely with complete success. Dialogue, confrontation, sharing, and collegiality are their specialties. They master all these interrelational skills; however, they view them only as tools for influencing others, not as techniques for understanding others. They persuade superiors to allow them to do what they want to do, whether it is to take a vacation in Hawaii (because they need the rest due to excessive strain), to buy an expensive camera (because they need a hobby to express themselves), to travel to a distant retreat (because that retreat director is the only person who can spiritually enrich them), or to have the best room in the house (because their condition of questionable health warrants it). They do what they want to do, but with permission. They do not disobey, but they circumvent the spirit of obedience.

In practice, obedience represents an association between the personality and history of the individual religious and the personality and history of the superior. The vow of obedience demands a variety of sacrifices from different religious as each one brings a unique history of submission and rebellion, passivity and aggression, dependency and self-assertion. Excellent leadership makes the vow of obedience easy and provides a psychological basis to reinforce the pattern of obedience. Poor leadership makes the vow of obedience difficult and requires a spiritual basis to overcome the burden of obedience.

Changes in social and political attitudes regarding authority and individual rights have influenced the thinking of religious personnel and have brought about changes in their understanding and practice of religious obedience. Today, major decisions in religious communities are commonly made through a process of open discussion, shared information, and mutual agreement among community members. Religious communities increasingly provide opportunities for individual religious to explain their preferences, express their disagreement, and discuss their negative reactions. As greater numbers of religious superiors encourage community expression, the burden of salutary dialogue rests more heavily on community members. Although the channels of communication have been opened, there remain serious responsibilities to communicate in a mature manner, to respect those who communicate less ably, and to remember that the final goal of communication is mutual understanding.

There have been changes not only in the understanding and practice of obedience, but also in the area of chastity. Conflicts regarding the vow of obedience characteristically involve the relationship between the individual religious and the superior. Conflicts regarding the vow of chastity more commonly involve relationships with peer religious or with laypersons.

6. Conflicts Regarding Chastity

To consider the subject of chastity without a clarification of theological thinking and teaching in this area may be somewhat imprudent. To examine this subject without reviewing the particular social climate of the times is somewhat risky. People certainly recognize that changes in theological thought and shifts in social mores influence not only the individual's observance of chastity but also the individual's interpretation of chastity. On the other hand, one can argue that modifications in the theological position have evolved to a great extent from a deeper understanding of the psychodynamics of human behavior. In addition, changes in sexual mores occur primarily as a result of the dynamic conflicts involved in the individual and group management of sexuality. Therefore, in considering the matter of chastity from a psychological point of view, one may assume that the psychodynamic intricacies of sexuality often anticipate and sometimes direct theological formulations as well as social directions.

From a psychosexual viewpoint, one might describe celibacy as an attitude of thought and a choice of behavior that, for the purpose of achieving some higher gain, directs the individual away from genital gratification. The vow of celibacy neither eliminates nor forbids sexual feelings. Sexual feelings are a physiological and affective response to erotic stimuli. The celibate often confuses sexual feelings with sexual wrongdoing. Sexual arousal represents a normal response to a sexually stimulating experience. Sexual arousal is a psychosomatic reaction containing components of physical response and of mental awareness and desire. If a person encounters a sexual stimulus, a response occurs that has the same components that other emotional responses have.

When a person meets a frightening situation, the physiological component of the emotional response includes an increased heart rate, cessation of digestion, and increased blood flow to peripheral muscles. The person also experiences the psychological component of the emotional response: a feeling of physical fear and a desire to get away from the person or circumstance causing the feeling. All of this reaction makes up the psychophysiologic response of fear, an essentially automatic response over which one has no control and thus no responsibility. Judgment, decision making, and thus morality have not yet entered the scene.

When a person comes upon a sexually stimulating situation, the physiologic component of the emotional response includes an increased blood supply to the genital organs, causing tumescence and a sensation of fullness and pleasurable tension. The individual also experiences the psychological component of the emotional response, a feeling of physical attraction and a desire to get close to the person causing the feeling. Just as in the fear response, in the sexual response, the two components occur automatically and involuntarily. To this point, choice is not involved. Therefore, neither is morality.

Obviously the matter becomes complicated when sexual feelings induce fear. Contradictory emotional responses then take place. The feeling of attraction and a desire for closeness stand opposite the feeling of danger and a desire for distance. Conflict ensues and causes sexual anxiety.

Religious sometimes behave like those anxious adolescents who interpret their own curiosity about sex and interest in sex as a violation of their innocence. Sexual development sometimes embarrasses and confuses adolescents, because they do not understand the changes that are taking place. As their sexual organs mature, so do their sexual awareness and sexual responsiveness. In the process of their psychological maturing they experience a need to be in control of themselves, of their decisions, of their behaviors. They struggle to wrest control from their parents and to take charge of themselves. Not surprisingly, then, it disturbs them to go through changes in their body and in their thoughts that seem totally beyond their control. The adolescent boy, made self-conscious by an erection as he observes an attractive girl or even thinks about one, may become angry at his own sexuality because he interprets his reactions as a loss of self-control. The adolescent girl whose breast development embarrasses her or whose menstrual flow restricts her comfortable participation in various activities may be frustrated by her sexuality because it decreases her control of her behavior. To many adults the term *self-control* suggests control of one's sexual impulses.

A sixteen-year-old girl who frequently refused to go to school came for psychiatric care. After several interviews, she trusted her therapist sufficiently to explain her reason for not attending school. Although she denied an interest in sexual matters, vulgar sexual terms sometimes occupied her thoughts. When this happened she could not get these words out of her mind, and she feared that one might slip out unexpectedly in her speech or in her writing. During these episodes she became afraid to complete written assignments because she might write one of those words. She feared answering in class because she might say one. Her lack of control over the presence of sexual words in her mind frightened her and made her determined to control her sexuality. Her restriction of her developing sexuality manifested itself in an absence of menstruation and a denial of any sexual curiosity or interest.

Therapists frequently see religious whose attraction to the religious life appears to have originated in their rejection of adolescent sexuality. Their psychosexual history is interwoven in their vocation history. A priest, age fifty-eight, began masturbating at age fourteen. He abhorred the behavior and became scrupulous about it. He decided to become a priest because "the vow of celibacy would put an end to the problem." In religious life, his obsessive-compulsive neurosis flourished. He became a chronic worrier, a perfectionist, with a number of obsessive thought patterns and compulsive behaviors. Compulsive masturbation recurred after the fervor of novitiate days subsided. Another priest was told by his mother during his adolescence that masturbation causes cancer. He thought the priesthood would help him eliminate the behavior, but periodic lapses continued and caused him intense concern for his physical well-being.

In therapy women religious sometimes associate their interest in religious life with a lack of interest in their sexuality as an adolescent. One sister told how she assumed a stooped posture as an adolescent to conceal her breast development. She decided to hide her feminine contours in religious garb. Needless to say, she later gave up the traditional habit with considerable reluctance. Another sister recalled her fright when, as a teenager, she became aware of her attraction to boys. Her mother had diligently warned her about men but had also fixed in her daughter's mind the idea that women were responsible for the sexual behavior of men. As a young girl with sexual feelings awakening, she became determined not to be responsible for causing the sexual sins of men: she entered religious life. In therapy she would ask what she must be doing wrong if another person found her to be attractive in any way.

The area of sexual response is framed by moral boundaries. For many people the morality of sexuality overshadows the psychological implications or social consequences of sexual behavior. To view sexuality exclusively from a moralistic stance leads to a kind of legalism. The legalistic attitude toward chastity is exemplified by the way in which eighth-graders often deal with the sixth and ninth commandments: "How far can I go? Can I kiss my boyfriend or girlfriend? How long? What if it gives me pleasant feelings in my genitals? Can we touch each other's genital organs? Is it seriously sinful if we don't 'go all the way'?" Confessors no longer have glib answers for all these questions, because moral theology has come to recognize the complexity of human motivations and human behaviors. Perhaps the best answers for such questions come from areas other than moral theology. Sermons about the sinfulness of alcoholism probably never helped an alcoholic reform or kept anyone from becoming an alcoholic. To enable individuals to appreciate the internal and external consequences of their behavior provides greater motivation than does threatening them with the eschatological outcome.

Teenagers make healthy decisions, which are also morally sound decisions, about sexuality when they receive encouragement to be healthy, morally sound young people. Their attitudes and decisions about sexual behavior represent only a part of their response to the world that expands within them and around them. One cannot draw sharp boundaries to mark off sexuality from the rest of life. When overzealous adults attempt to separate sexuality behind artificial lines, young people identify those lines as whitewash. If adults want adolescents to make sound decisions in sexual matters, then adults must support the process of healthy adolescent maturation. Adults must respect adolescents as individuals so adolescents may learn to respect their own individuality. Adults must respect the privacy of adolescents' minds, of their lives, of their conversations so they may be willing to demand that others respect their privacy. Adults must allow and encourage decision making in adolescents so they will experience both the satisfaction and the responsibility of this power. Adults must trust the ability of adolescents to think things through so they will come to rely on this ability within themselves. Adolescents value the good example and sound principles of those adults who treat them in this manner.

Religious celibates sometimes exhibit the same attitudes about sexuality that adolescents exhibit. "How far can I go and not violate my vow? What can I get away with and not feel guilty? Tell me where the boundaries are so I can get as close to them as possible. Tell me when my behavior becomes sinful so that I can stop just a little short of that." Their goal is not to enhance their celibate state by celebrating the spiritual virtue and personal value of it but to adhere to the letter, not the spirit. This is indeed legalism. At present, the letter of sexual morality is obscure. The moral theology of sexual behavior abounds with psychodynamic issues. The role of compulsion, the effects of anxiety, and the influences of depression require consideration. The delicate patterns of psychosexual development, now better understood than before, influence the application of theological principles to sexual behavior. Some abuse this development in theology to create loopholes through which to escape from personal responsibility.

Father Ed came for therapy at the insistence of his bishop. For twelve years he had maintained a sexual relationship with a female employee of the diocese. Apparently he had come to terms with his sexual behavior as a necessary part of his life. Ed held responsible positions and worked diligently in them. He reasoned that he could not do the work without the release and relaxation provided in his illicit relationship. Early in the relationship, Ed experienced some guilt because of his erotic involvement. This guilt troubled him for several months and interfered with his effectiveness as a priest. In therapy he recalled his decision to eliminate his sense of guilt rather than to eliminate his source of guilt. He told himself that he could not be sexually continent, because of the pressure of his work. The work needed to be done, and he had the ability to do it. He concluded that the work of the church was clearly more important than whether or not he remained celibate.

Ed's poorly conceived logic had not totally reassured him, however. He had a twinge of conscience once a few years prior to his brief encounter with psychotherapy. He had attended a spiritual renewal program at a major institution in the United States. The program lasted nine months. Ed worked at it intensely, but with his characteristic superficial sincerity. As was recommended, he chose a spiritual director and spoke with him regularly, but not candidly. He never discussed his sexual life with his spiritual director. Near the end, the program included a special workshop by a guest speaker. The guest speaker had written extensively on the subject of celibacy and intimacy and his writings presented a permissive point of view. Ed decided that now was the acceptable time to resolve his twinge of conscience. He chose the guest lecturer as his confidant and found spiritual solace in his hands. The visiting expert advised that, since this situation had existed for so long, it might do more harm than good to attempt to terminate it abruptly. Rejection of the woman might cause her psychological distress, and Ed must consider his obligation to her. He was advised that perhaps a time would come when a break in the relationship might be more opportune. In the meantime he should accept "the reality of his sexuality."

One should not conclude that Ed's sense of shame kept him from being more open with his spiritual director. He spoke quite freely about his behavior to several persons who had no need to know. He chose the visiting lecturer, not out of any sense of shame, but out of a desire for reassurance, however brief, that he was not fully responsible. When he came to therapy, he still clung to this reassurance even though other religious advisers had clearly recommended immediate termination of the relationship. The traveling expert did him a grave disservice. Based on a thirty- to forty-minute interview, the expert gave him the answer he looked for but not the answer he needed. That answer could not have been based on an understanding of Ed, his life experience, or the turmoil that lay restlessly deep inside him. The expert's answer could only have come from his prejudicial position that the thesis of his writing was correct.

Ed did not continue long in treatment, because it did not provide additional support for his position. He did not wish to look at, and even less to grapple with, the grave inconsistencies in his behavior, the serious lack of integrity in his own life, and the deep injustice in his relationship with his companion.

A married man requested psychiatric help because of his bisexual behavior. Erwin grew up as a devout Catholic and, until the previous five years, had maintained an active spiritual life. He had been married twenty-six years and had four children. Throughout most of his married life he participated in brief, superficial homosexual contacts. He struggled against this behavior and found support in personal prayer and the sacraments. Five years before his approach to psychiatric treatment, Erwin sought counseling. The therapist took the position that the bisexual behavior was "no big deal" and suggested that he "just relax and enjoy it." The therapist's attitude discouraged Erwin. He discontinued counseling, gradually stopped attending liturgical services, and became unable to pray. When Erwin sought help the second time, the psychiatrist took a different approach. Together they examined the compulsive aspects of his personality. They explored the origins of his sexual conflict and the consequences of his sexual conduct. He came to recognize that his homosexual forays related also to marital distance and disharmony. He discovered actions he could take in his marriage, in his social contacts, and in his work setting to aid him in controlling his homosexual behavior. He began to talk about his desire to revive his spiritual life. He accepted the recommendation that he see a spiritual director and gave permission for contact between the psychiatrist and the spiritual director. Through therapy, he became responsible for behavior that may previously have been beyond his control and thus beyond his moral responsibility. Acquiring responsibility for this behavior enabled him to renew his spiritual life and required him to revitalize his marital relationship.

Religious celibates who disclose sexual difficulty are often dismissed too casually. They usually come to the spiritual adviser asking one question: "Is this behavior morally wrong?" A yes or no answer to that question may provide moral guidance but deny psychological assurance. Other questions need consideration: What are the emotional components of this behavior? What are the psychological and interpersonal components of this behavior? Are elements of justice involved?

Spiritual advisers sometimes too readily dismiss masturbation as an area of concern. A compulsive element is often involved, with a consequent diminution of responsibility. The spiritual guide, recognizing the lack of formal sin, may advise the individual not to be troubled; religious in treatment often describe this attitude on the part of their confessor. Certainly one cannot question the soundness of the theological position; however, it is usually not psychologically satisfying. The individual typically views autoeroticism as incompatible with the vow of chastity, and correctly so. In principle, it is incompatible with the vow to lead a chaste life. Whether or not one is responsible for the behavior, the behavior is not consistent with the vow. Therefore, individuals caught in such a conflict feel some need to control this behavior. They should be encouraged to strive to minimize and if possible to eradicate the behavior, not as a moral issue but as a psychological issue. Although there may be no moral guilt attached to some masturbatory behavior, there is often morbid guilt, a feeling of guilt, and this offers motivation for change. The adviser or therapist should not foster the morbid guilt as a method of promoting sexual constraint. An increase in morbid guilt may only stimulate more frequent masturbatory acts. On the other hand, the morbid guilt often declines if the individual puts sincere effort into controlling the behavior. This decline in morbid guilt occurs even if the effort at controlling the behavior is unsuccessful.

Sometimes it is important to help individuals understand the dynamics of their sexual behavior. This is not the province of spiritual direction but belongs instead to psychotherapy. Unless a spiritual director has adequate training in psychotherapeutic techniques, he or she should refrain from attempting to treat the psychodynamic aspects of sexual behavior. These include distortions in psychosexual development as well as compulsions, anxieties, and other emotional disturbances that may contribute to sexual problems. If a spiritual director chooses to become a therapist for a person with sexual difficulties and is fully competent in the role, perhaps that director should ask someone else to take the role of spiritual director. Therapy is not spiritual direction, nor is spiritual direction therapy. The person who wishes to wear both hats may develop a head too large for either of them.

A young woman in a religious community sought psychiatric help because she feared that her habit of masturbation was causing emotional confusion and mental deterioration. She and her spiritual director had worked two and a half years on the problem; it only became more frequent. Her spiritual director apparently fancied himself a trained counselor. He made the same mistake many people make who have had three or four courses in psychology. In his attempt to be her therapist, he used some very questionable tactics that certainly contributed more to her emotional turmoil than her masturbation did. On one occasion, he had her masturbate in his presence in an attempt to increase her shame. One might legitimately question his motivation for recommending this. In psychiatric care she progressed rapidly and gained control of the masturbation, a behavioral counterpart of her repressed anger.

In therapy, Elizabeth, a forty-five-year-old religious, reported the problem of daily masturbation. It soon became evident that this problem represented considerable emotional pathology. It proved to be symbolic of much of her psychosexual development. When she was a child her father worked out of town most of the time. She regarded him as a kind, gentle man but absent from the home and therefore unable to demonstrate his caring in any regular manner. Her mother drank excessively and, in episodes of rage, verbally and physically abused her two children, especially Elizabeth, probably because she was her father's favorite. To assuage her loneliness, the mother frequently brought men home to spend the night with her. The two children went to Catholic schools; the more Elizabeth learned about religion, the less she understood her family. She had little opportunity to talk with her father. She became terrified of her mother, and not without reason. She could not talk to the sisters at school, because her shame about her home life overwhelmed her. The sisters seemed to assume that everyone came from an ideal Catholic home. It seemed to Elizabeth that everyone did, except herself. She became withdrawn and guarded carefully all the things she thought.

Elizabeth's menarche was traumatic. She had no prior knowledge of menstruation. Everything about sexuality, especially her own, seemed frightening and bad. She denied her own sexual interests as well as her sexual development. She could not prevent menstruation, but she could disown her feminine maturation. She mistakenly considered herself to be ugly. She never dated. She avoided associating with boys. She entered religious life at age twenty. She felt lonely in the novitiate. One day the novice mistress became angry with her and verbally abused her; that night Elizabeth masturbated for the first time.

In religious life Elizabeth became increasingly aware of her own sexual desires and was simultaneously more ashamed of them. She confused sexual feelings with sexual decisions and sexual behavior. The attention of men attracted but frightened her. She felt safe with priests who showed her some special attention, but over a period of several years she had become erotically involved with three of them. All the while the masturbation continued. She felt more guilt over that than over the heterosexual involvements, and, in fact, the masturbation was the more pathological behavior. It occurred nightly and included fantasies of physical and sexual violence that greatly disturbed her sensitive nature. The masturbation represented the loneliness she had experienced so keenly in her father's absence. It represented the violence she had experienced in her mother's presence. It represented her mother's solution to loneliness and Elizabeth's doubts about herself as an attractive person. Her masturbation depicted the emotional components of her psychosexual history: loneliness, fear, violence, shame, doubt, secrecy, unworthiness, ugliness. It gave her nothing but a line to the past. It brought her to despair and almost to suicide. Through insight into the evolution and meaning of her behavior, she gradually eliminated the morbid fantasies, although she could not completely control the compulsion.

With increased understanding of herself and her sexuality, she no longer sought or permitted heterosexual involvements. Most importantly, Elizabeth left behind the terrible self-image she had carried for years and became a secure religious, making an outstanding contribution to her religious community and to the church.

Religious women and men frequently have little appreciation of the power of sexual drives, either their own or that of others. Consequently, they exhibit naïveté regarding the hazards of physical or emotional closeness. Religious express themselves through physical contact more frequently and more easily than they did a decade or two ago. Embracing someone in a public setting may be totally different from embracing that person in the privacy of an office or the seclusion of a rendezvous. Failure to recognize the difference comes from lack of emotional sensitivity or sexual sophistication. Some persons will object strongly to such a position and say, "How ridiculous!" One confessor gave attractive female penitents, as their usual penance, the instruction to embrace and kiss their confessor. Certain spiritual directors embrace some of their directees. Certain counselors embrace some of their counselees. Certain psychiatrists embrace some of their patients. Usually these embracers do not caress all the people who come to them in this dependent relationship, only some of them. Why some and not all? Which ones? The more attractive ones? The ones who are somehow more vulnerable? More needy? More seductive? The embracers may protest that these statements imply wrongdoing on their part. They may insist that they have no sexual motives whatsoever in this behavior and maintain that these comments insult them. It might be advantageous to consider this behavior not from the point of view of wrongdoing but from the point of view of propriety. The fact that the conscious intention of the embracer may be innocent does not guarantee an innocuous result. Anyone who works with people should be aware that unconscious motivations play a role in the behavior of individuals, including oneself.

Even if the embracer has no sexual motivation, conscious or

unconscious, what about the one who is embraced? A person in need, coming to another for help, easily confuses what is communicated. Everyone is aware of the tendency to hear what one wants to hear, especially when one is troubled, frightened, or depressed. Therefore, the director, confessor, or counselor has an obligation to communicate carefully and precisely to the distressed and dependent person. Words, the most exact medium of our communication skills, can be misinterpreted. Tactile communication can certainly be misconstrued. An embrace can be a simple greeting with no more significance than a handshake. An embrace can also be a sign of friendship, a symbol of respect, an indication of affection, a gesture of sympathy, a statement of love, a mark of attraction, or a signal of erotic desire. What does the embracer mean by the caress or the kiss? What does the recipient understand it to mean? Even though the embracer's intention may be the purest, the embracer has responsibility for the consequences of the embrace. The possibility of misinterpretation is almost always present, especially when there is a mood of emotional closeness and an atmosphere of absolute privacy. The embracer carries the responsibility to consider the possible misinterpretations by the one who is caressed. Psychiatrists and other well-trained counselors remain very cautious in making any physical contact with patients. They are well aware of the transference and countertransference overtones of physical overtures. The embracer also carries the responsibility to consider very seriously his or her own motivations, allowing for the possibility of unconscious motivations.

Eric, a young diocesan priest, enjoyed wrestling with boys of junior high age. He liked athletics and spent time with this age group in promoting their athletic interests. He realized that, on occasion, while wrestling with one or two particular boys in the privacy of his room, he would have an erection. He decided that he did not need to be concerned about this, because he never engaged in any genital play during these exchanges. However, on one occasion when wrestling with a thirteen-year-old boy of whom he was particularly fond, he had an erection. The boy became aware of it and, in an anxious reaction, went home and mentioned the episode to his parents. They responded with alarm and went to the pastor. Escalation occurred at every turn, spurred on by a variety of apprehensions. The boy worried about his own sexuality. The parents worried that their son had been molested. The pastor worried about scandal. He notified the chancery office, and officials there worried about a lawsuit. The school authorities became involved, and they worried about their public image. The bishop, without discussion or investigation, ordered Eric to leave the parish that day with no good-byes and with no future contact with anyone in the parish. Eric's fleeting erotic contact had aroused anxiety in everyone and caused a number of precipitous responses.

In his new assignment Eric suffered from acute anxiety and marked depression. In therapy, he came to understand the sexual motivation of his wrestling and thus the indiscretion in his behavior. Prior to treatment he had denied the sexual significance of this behavior, although from his history, the significance seemed obvious. For years he had engaged in active sexual fantasies about boys in this particular age group. These fantasies always accompanied his acts of masturbation. He also revealed that earlier in his adult life he had on three or four occasions solicited oral sex from boys of this same age. Eric had imprudently not recognized the potential hazard of his wrestling contacts as precursors of overt sexual behavior.

The denial of where one's behavior may lead often results in unexpected sexual involvements. Sometimes individuals become so intent on the goal of helping another person that they fail to evaluate, or they excuse, the means they take to achieve that laudable goal. This is not a hazard only for celibate religious; it is a potential risk for anyone who works closely with others in a one-to-one relationship that involves the revelation of the private world of one person to the other. A minister, married twenty-two years, with two teenage sons, counseled

a woman in his congregation. She had gone through a traumatic divorce and subsequently experienced a great deal of
emotional distress. The minister did not have the training, the
experience, or, perhaps, the self-restraint required to deal with
this rather complicated woman. She gradually reached the
point of calling him every day for reassurance and solace.
Sometime later, he began calling her every day to express his
concern for her. Then they met occasionally, and later frequently, for coffee. Eventually they began meeting for lunch.
Soon suicidal threats brought him rushing to her house day
or night. His expressions of concern changed to expressions
of affection, then of love. Their rendezvous moved from coffee
to lunch to dinner to bed. At his recommendation, she sought
psychiatric care, and as a result of treatment she ended the
relationship.

A married man of forty-five described in therapy his close
relationship with his secretary. They had worked together for
three years. She had become his confidante, and he had become hers. He and his wife did not communicate well and had
some relationship patterns that were unsatisfactory to him.
He discussed his unhappy home life with his secretary; she
shared with him the tribulation of her ongoing divorce. His
therapist encouraged him to consider the direction in which
the relationship with his secretary seemed to be going. He
denied the possibility that anything more than a good friendship existed between them. Within six weeks, he and his
secretary entered an openly sexual relationship, which led to
severe guilt on his part and increased conflict in his marriage.

The morality of these relationships is not the point at issue
here. The psychological antecedents of sexual involvement and
the psychological significance of sexual behavior are under
consideration. A person may be encouraged to focus on the
morality of his or her sexual behavior and be led to disregard
the psychological significance of that behavior. Sexual behavior,
like other behavior, sometimes indicates an underlying conflict.
Although illicit sexual behavior may itself cause conflict within

the individual, it may also be the result of a more important unresolved conflict.

Eugene had been ordained fifteen years when he came for therapy. His superior insisted that he seek help. Eugene had been a good student, a compliant seminarian, and a promising newly ordained priest. He had an agreeable personality and got along well with others. Within the third year following ordination, he became erotically involved with a married woman in the parish who had come to him for guidance. Her husband discovered the relationship and reported it to Eugene's provincial. The provincial reprimanded Eugene and moved him to another parish. Unfortunately, that was only the beginning of his misadventures. One woman after another succumbed to his charm, including several female religious, one of whom became pregnant and had to leave her community. The provincial finally sent Eugene away to a renewal program with orders not to return until he solved his problem.

Eugene's therapy initially progressed well as he delved into the intricacies of his own personality and studied the psychodynamics of his adult behaviors. He reviewed his youth and the responsibility he had felt to keep his mother happy. His mother apparently had a martyr complex, and, of the five children, Eugene became her knight-errant. He described his father as loud, boisterous, uncultured, frightening, and "sexually hurtful" to Eugene's mother. His mother wanted Eugene to be a priest and rejoiced when he entered the seminary. During his formation years in Europe, Eugene adapted well. He enjoyed studies. He engaged in sports and found satisfaction in the competition. He never thought much about the future or what it would be like to be a priest. He knew he was making his mother happy. He thought he was making God happy. He never thought much about whether he was happy. Whenever he felt unhappy, sports provided a quick cure, and the feeling would go away.

Eugene expressed concern that he lacked control of his life: "I feel like something throws me around." He engaged in

secretive eating binges and hated himself for them. He fantasized himself as a "cool, calm man of steel, able to handle
anything." At the same time, he talked about his deep sense
of inadequacy and his fears of "being alone." "I need someone
out there, someone to care about me." He described a woman
as "a touchstone, a safety place." He had a strong feeling of
"wanting to be held," but compared his reaction to an embrace
with the reaction of an alcoholic to his first drink. He thought
of sexual intercourse as "the most I could hope for from a
woman, the ultimate in a relationship. . . . I don't have more
to give." He also saw himself as a little child. "I relate to
everyone out there as a child. I can get what I want and not
be held responsible. Being responsible isn't fun."

Therapy reached a stalemate. Eugene did not want to serve
as a priest, but neither did he wish to leave the priesthood.
Guilt over his behavior remained a constant theme. He became
increasingly indecisive about his life. He looked at reasons to
remain a priest and reasons to leave the priesthood. But he
could not move toward a decision. One day his therapist suggested that he consider his sexual behavior not as something
shameful and immoral, as was his judgment, but as something
genuine in his life, as a trustworthy response to his own life
history, and as valuable information in his discernment process. This approach startled him, but it got things moving
again. He worked through to a sound resolution of his quan-
dary. He applied for laicization and went on to establish a
stable marital relationship. Indeed Eugene did "need someone
out there," but he also needed to know that he had far more
to give to another than a mere sexual encounter.

On occasion, entry into religious life has virtually fixated
psychosexual development at an immature level or has caused
regression to an earlier psychosexual phase. In some instances
it seems reasonably certain that further psychosexual maturation cannot occur within the confines of religious commitment.
This was the case with Eamon, who came to therapy on the
recommendation of one of his religious superiors. Eamon, the

eldest of three children, apparently had had a normal psychosexual development until the time he entered religious formation. He played "doctor" with a neighbor girl at age five. At
age eleven he began masturbating, with fantasies about the
neighbor girl. When masturbation began, he did not know it
was wrong. His mother gave him a pamphlet to read, and
then he began to feel guilty about the masturbation. It became
a matter for confession every Saturday and a source of great
embarrassment. Nevertheless it continued unabated. He commented, "I never willed to stop." He engaged in sexual play
with a male friend over a period of several months at about
age twelve.

During eighth grade he wrote "love notes" to a girl who
infatuated him. In high school his interest in girls continued,
and he dated regularly. Shy and uncomfortable, he envied the
popularity and self-assurance of more athletic students. In
tenth grade he engaged in some genital fondling with a girlfriend, and, on one rather furtive occasion, they had intercourse. He lost interest in her after that. In twelfth grade he
dated another girl and continued this relationship for five years.
She was very religious and very proper. He thought he wanted
to marry her, but she did not allow any demonstration of
affection. Because of her, he began praying more.

Eamon's parents did not provide any positive sex information or attitudes except for the pamphlet his mother had given
him earlier. They made derogatory comments about anything
that might suggest sexuality, such as a low-cut dress or reference to anyone being pregnant. Although he dated regularly
in high school, no one in his family ever referred to the fact.
He would get dressed up, ask for the car, and leave the house.
He knew that his parents knew he was going to a school dance
or on a date. His relationship with girls never generated a
comment. What a powerful message his parents gave him!

After going with the one girl for five years, Eamon began to
think about entering religious life. He recalled, "I needed to
save my own soul." He went to confession one Saturday and

had nothing serious to confess. The confessor asked him if he had ever considered being a priest. That encouraged him, and within a short time, he made a "sudden decision to enter." In treatment he commented, "That decision always seemed suspect to me." He entered a religious community within six months and never questioned the decision afterward. Even during treatment, he refused for a long time to question the decision.

During his first year in formation, he experienced his first adult homosexual feelings. Two of his peers in their cassocks were kneeling in chapel ahead of him. He was sexually aroused, and, even though the thought was repulsive, it did not go away completely. His heterosexual fantasies grew less frequent and were replaced by homosexual fantasies. Two years later he had his first homosexual encounter. After ordination these experiences continued for ten years, typically with seventeen- to twenty-year-old males. This age group represented his own teenage years. "Their facial features are in some manner the way I wanted to see myself, innocent and gentle." He worked in an isolated region and took great risks in arranging these contacts, which always consisted of only one or two brief encounters. In his assignment he worked with all males. He commented, "I feel just as attracted to women if there are women around, but there are none." About his behavior, he said, "It feels like I can't do anything about it. It relieves tension, the way masturbation relieves tension. The tension is a feeling of loneliness."

He had excluded his homosexual behavior from confession or spiritual direction many years before "because it wasn't doing me any good." As a youth he had encountered guilt and humiliation in confession because of masturbation. He thought that entering religious life might end his sexual conflict. He apparently saw religious life as asexual. When he found new sexual conflicts within religious life, he lost hope of resolving his problems. He became superficially complacent and expended much emotional energy in ignoring the internal struggle that seemed to have no solution.

In the treatment relationship, he gradually accepted the fact that his life lacked integration. He acknowledged that his erotic involvements represented a source of inner turmoil for him, a potential for great damage to his community and to the work of the church, and an occasion of serious harm to his partners. As he began to examine his life more closely, he discovered the reasons for his inner unhappiness and his outer dishonesty. He began to consider the possibility of leaving the priesthood. During that period of treatment his prayer life took on new meaning and vitality. The homosexual fantasies decreased and heterosexual fantasies replaced them. He met a woman about his age and began forming a relationship with her. He left the religious life after considerable thought, prayer, consultation with superiors, and discussion with his spiritual director. His homosexual fantasies and inclinations ended. He returned to what he had left behind when he entered religious life. Had Eamon remained in religious life, it is unlikely that his sexual behavior would have or could have been modified. A strong element of compulsion in his homosexual behavior stemmed from the unconscious conflict created by trying to live a commitment he should not have made, a commitment that he had refused to examine prior to entering psychotherapy.

Many moderns believe that a celibate life is an anachronism and totally irrelevant; others criticize the celibate life as fraudulent and impossible to achieve in reality. Some may argue that the case histories in this chapter prove the impossibility of a life of vowed chastity. But failure on the part of some to achieve a goal does not make the goal unattainable. The incidence of conjugal infidelity does not establish the impossibility of fidelity. Nor does the difficulty of preserving marital fidelity in our culture provide any argument for suggesting it is impossible. Celibacy, like marital fidelity, is preserved only by working at it. If a married person studies how many corners of communication can be trimmed and how many approximations to unfaithfulness can be made, then fidelity represents a constant burden, a restrictive environment, a yoke of law and not of love. There is only one good way to be a faithful spouse or a faithful celibate, and that is totally, constantly, and whole-heartedly. Cutting corners detracts from the complete picture. Looking over one's shoulder decreases one's motivation. Investigating other possibilities diminishes one's focus. If a married person is cutting corners, reconsidering the involvement, and wondering about others, something is missing in the marriage. The celibate who is determined to sustain the integrity of commitment by not cutting corners, by not walking the problematic paths of risky relationships, by not watching for some better alternative, that authentic celibate will find chastity a possible and rewarding goal.

Celibate religious are not asexual beings devoid of sexual feelings and sexual responses. However, their sexual attitudes and behavior may show various kinds of confusion and restlessness. Sometimes this sexual turbulence is caused by fixation at or regression to an immature level of psychosexual development. For other religious, sexual disharmony is caused by their unwillingness or inability to acknowledge or to accept the restrictions they have placed on themselves in regard to their adult sexuality.

In the assessment of their sexuality religious must consider not only the moral aspects of their sexual inclinations and behavior but also the emotional antecedents and psychological consequences of their sexual attractions. Theological considerations and moral advice do not usually resolve the affective conflicts and concerns that religious may have about their sexual responses. Some religious err by denying the presence of their own sexual drives or by ignoring the force of others' sexual drives. At the other end of the spectrum, some religious are keenly aware of their own and others' erotic desires and sexual seductiveness, and they choose to engage in games of sexual jeopardy. Religious who intend to keep the commitment they made in their vow of chastity must be willing to analyze their motives for and the satisfaction they gain from intimate emotional encounters and close physical contacts.

For many decades concerns about sexuality have dominated moral theology at the expense of other topics that relate more to justice. Recent social developments and new theological thought have stimulated a healthy trend in religious communities to move away from a preoccupation with "sins of the flesh" and to attend to "sicknesses of the flesh," as evidenced in the poverty of the world. This transition has brought religious communities to re-evaluate their vows of poverty.

7. Conflicts Relating to Poverty

Stewardship has become the term associated with the vow of poverty as a re-evaluation of this vow takes place throughout religious life. Religious communities examine their stewardship of material goods, and individual religious reflect on their personal interpretation of poverty in response to changes in living styles and money management.

Conflicts arise in this area for several reasons. The old interpretation of the vow of poverty continues to permeate most religious communities. Although community policies no longer dictate the harsh frugality of the past, a pall of privation often overshadows the enjoyment of material goods. Adults who grew up during the Great Depression frequently have an attitude of parsimony that prevents their enjoying the use of money or even relaxing in the possession of it; religious who are moving from the past interpretation of poverty have a similar struggle.

For some people, knowing how to spend money can be more difficult than knowing how to get along without it. Competency in the use of money requires more than a knowledge of arithmetic, just as the management of one's schedule requires more than an ability to tell time. Children and adolescents should have an increasing interest in and control over their use of time and money. They learn from example; they learn from guidance; but they also learn from experience. The young person in an independent living situation may have considerable difficulty managing money unless she or he has had some prior experience in personal budgeting. The young adult with no previous responsibility for programming the day, the week, and the month usually has difficulty controlling the time-related independence of college or of living alone. The reality of autonomous living demands personal proficiency in money and time management. These are the worldly goods over which people have stewardship: money and material things that are acquired and time that is allotted.

The adolescent who has the opportunity to make decisions regarding the use of money, whether earned or given as an allowance, learns financial responsibility. Teenagers in psychotherapy sometimes oppose the recommendation that their parents give them an allowance. They argue that they do better financially with the "ask as you need it" method. By this method they may do well economically, but they do not do well developmentally. They miss some training in responsibility. They intensify their dependent relationship to parents at a time when that dependence should decrease.

Teenagers often have difficulty completing their schoolwork and family chores on time. Anxious parents quickly correct the deficiency by establishing schedules for the adolescent to follow. Homework must be done from four to six in the afternoon, chores from seven to eight in the evening. Bedtime is ten P.M., and the time of arising is six A.M. Major jobs around the house must be completed on Saturday morning, and major school projects on Sunday afternoon. So it goes. The adults manage the adolescents' time. Grades improve. Everything runs smoothly. However, in these arrangements adolescents lose ownership of their most valuable possession, time. Soon after graduation from high school, these young people move into an independent living situation, and then, because they have never learned personal responsibility for scheduling time, trouble occurs. For these emancipated young adults, getting to class or getting to work seems easy at first because others schedule these routines. Difficulty comes in arranging their personal time in order to be prepared for class or ready for work. They become increasingly ill prepared for school or for the job, and then they begin to skip class or work to gain more time to do those personal things that seem so difficult to accomplish. But they manage this additional time poorly and then increase their neglect of the schedule imposed by others in an attempt to compensate for their inability to schedule private time responsibly.

In treating marital conflicts, therapists find that mismanagement of things and of time are recurring themes. A husband buys expensive tools he does not know how to use. A wife spends money for hobbies she never has time to enjoy. A wife always arrives late when she and her husband have agreed to meet. A husband consistently sleeps too late, while his wife spends the first half hour of her day trying to awaken him. These patterns of behavior represent immature attitudes toward the stewardship of time and money.

Individual religious have had, until the last fifteen or twenty years, little autonomy in the use of time and less in the use of money. Increased independence in these areas brings two questions, How much freedom do I have? and How do I handle the freedom I do have? The situation of some religious resembles that of a middle-aged widow referred for psychiatric evaluation by her attorney. She and her husband had been married thirty-six years. They lived on a farm, twenty miles from a city. She never wrote a check, never had any knowledge of their finances, and never was allowed to go with her husband to the accountant's office. Her husband did all the grocery shopping and totally controlled all the money. She rarely left the farm, and when she did, it was only to go to the nearby town with her husband. After his death she was quite unable to understand, much less manage, her financial affairs. Within two years she sold her farm for one tenth its value. The psychiatric consultation was for the purpose of evaluating her competency in business affairs.

Although many religious adapt reasonably well to the new interpretations of stewardship, some find the changes burdensome. Some experience difficulty in buying for themselves from their monthly stipend items that the community previously provided. Silently and secretly they endure deprivation, because their interpretation of their vow makes it impossible for them to purchase for their personal needs. Spending money seems to violate a contract they sealed with God long ago.

More frequently the difficulty with temporal stewardship revolves around the prudent allotment and use of funds. Personal budgeting requires some experience, some flexibility, and some foresight. Religious communities cannot establish a monthly allowance that is equitable for all, so they make provision for unusual needs; however, the individual religious must request the exception. Some hesitate to present their legitimate requests for additional funds, but they may resent others who petition for extra amounts. Other religious characteristically press against the limitations of religious vows no matter how broadly defined. They search for exceptions to every rule. They interpret every policy liberally and leniently. In regard to poverty, they pride themselves on being responsible for material goods, and they strive to acquire control over as much of the community money as they possibly can.

In the past religious sometimes stretched the boundaries of poverty by using the principle of "occult compensation" (surreptitiously taking from an employer who unjustly underpays the employee). They took more than their allotted share of community goods, but they did it quietly and secretly. The resultant material gain may have troubled their consciences at times, but it did not disturb community tranquility. Today, a few religious practice a kind of excess compensation that not only violates the spirit of poverty but also destroys the spirit of trust within the community. Their ready access to money perplexes other community members. At times they obtain community funds through unsubstantiated requests, and the actual use they make of those funds may be questionable. Since most religious are honest in their statements as well as in their use of money, those in authority find it difficult to suspect the honesty and thus impugn the integrity of individual religious, even though human weakness may cause even a religious to lie and to steal. Sometimes these affluent religious obtain their money from relatives or friends outside the community. Although community rules usually require that they turn over these monies to the community, they find reasons why such rules do not apply to them. Whatever the source of their abundance, they use it to live well themselves, and sometimes to curry favor with others. Community disharmony results as confidence in community leadership decreases and cooperation with one another deteriorates.

Sister Florence was an example of the personal struggle some religious have with the possession and use of money. Florence campaigned for every respectable cause that came along. She espoused the rights of the poor, the underprivileged, minorities. Although everyone acknowledged that she labored unstintingly for the destitute and the downtrodden, some thought that she lost perspective at times. As her work increased in scope and in notoriety, the demands she made on her community increased in volume and in intensity. She attempted to justify all her demands in the name of those whom she served, but as time passed it became increasingly obvious that a portion of what she requested served her own needs. She traveled in style. She wined and dined rather sumptuously. She regularly spent several days away from her assigned duties inaccessible to everyone. Her unwillingness to account for the use of funds as well as for the use of her time increased. Florence practiced a self-deception that occurs among some of the Lord's laborers. They believe that those who do the Lord's work deserve special privileges and those who care for the undesirables of the world need to care for their own desires in special ways. Some who know poverty intimately in their daily tasks exempt themselves from the rules of poverty that bind other religious. Perhaps their discomfort with the ugliness and pain of extreme poverty makes them excessively fearful of encountering it in their personal lives.

Though some religious struggle with poverty in their temptation to have wealth and to use money, other religious have difficulty with this vow in their temptation to know the wealthy and to use them and their money. Most religious quickly recognize the scandal they may give to everyone when they use money in a prodigal manner. They are not as quick to acknowledge the scandal they may give to the poor when they cater to the rich. The person with means often becomes an object of their special interest, their special courtesy, their special awards because they expect some monetary gain from the relationship. In some instances, religious justify the development of these relationships as a source of financial support for their community and the work of the community. Because they do God's work, they overlook their prejudicial treatment of God's children. In other instances, these relationships are used to provide a source of personal financing for the individual religious who finds the yoke of stewardship too burdensome. The vow of poverty forbids the accumulation of wealth, but the spirit of poverty forbids the cultivation of the wealthy.

The majority of religious conscientiously and prudently administer the money and material goods assigned to them. It is no small sacrifice in a society of relative luxury always to buy clothes on sale or at the Salvation Army store. For most professional persons, a basic wardrobe of one good dress or one good suit would be absurd. For active people, traveling long distances by bus rather than by plane usually represents economic distress. Choices of this kind bring the vow of poverty to the level of virtue. These choices, no longer imposed by the edict of authority, are made freely if not always gladly by individual religious. The vow of poverty is surely more difficult to observe today than in pre–Vatican II days. Now it expresses a personal decision. Before Vatican II it represented a community attitude.

Some religious have problems in budgeting their funds. Occasionally the use of a personal credit card creates complications for religious who forget their human frailty. Temptations with regard to sexuality and power regularly remind most religious of their moral weakness, and sometimes religious in positions of power and prestige have been tempted by avarice. However, it is a new experience for most religious men and women to confront their human weakness in the temptation of worldly goods, particularly when those worldly goods are so easily available with a credit card. At least the bill at the end of the month may force them to consider whether or not they have an excessive attachment to things and may renew their belief that a day of reckoning does eventually come.

Money often represents an extension of the individual, and its use becomes an expression of emotional need. Some people have a cache of "mad money" to spend recklessly when they are irritated or unhappy. Obsessive-compulsive people have difficulty spending money and typically are dissatisfied with what they buy. Persons in an expansive mood may spend impulsively and thus extravagantly and imprudently. One depressed religious in treatment incurred a sizable debt through the use of his credit card. In his depression he reached the point where the unrestrained use of his credit card did not disturb him, because he did not care what happened to him. People who are overworked, with little opportunity for relaxation, may use money unwisely in an attempt to compensate for their feeling of emptiness. The unemotional outline provided by a personal budget helps most people avoid the "mood-management" of money.

In dealing with money adults may exhibit competitiveness and jealousy related to early sibling rivalry. Religious sometimes justify their use of funds not on the basis of legitimate need but on the principle that all should share in equal fashion. Some adults still watch to discover who receives the largest piece of cake. They identify all those who own a more expensive car than theirs. They are keenly aware of what others possess and constantly compare that with what they themselves possess. Their sense of entitlement supposes that they should have at least as much as others have. Shadows of the past may cloud the perceptions of religious also and bring them into this cold world of envy and distrust.

Father Frank reported in therapy how angry he felt toward his superior, whom he acknowledged to be a good and just man. He commented bitterly, however, "My superior doesn't love me. But I know he loves two of the other clerics in the house because he talks to them more than he talks to me." Frank had one sibling, a brother two years his senior, who surpassed him in everything they did as children. His brother excelled in sports, in academics and in popularity. Most important of all, Frank believed that his mother loved his brother more than she loved him. In adult life his brother built a successful business, but Frank entered religious life, partly to please his devoutly Catholic mother. He continued to perceive himself as inferior to his brother. Throughout his life in community he battled with superiors over his share of everything, whether it was material things, time, or affection. Constant rivalry with his peers kept him in inner turmoil and outer conflict.

In treatment Frank revisited the scenes of his childhood and discovered the positive elements in his relationship with his brother. He acknowledged the conflict that had existed between his parents and recognized how he unwittingly became a pawn of his alcoholic father. The strain between Frank and his brother arose primarily from the marital disharmony rather than from sibling rivalry. With the development of deeper understanding his lifelong jealousy toward his brother abated. As a result, Frank mastered the realities of disproportion that exist in community life.

Members of religious communities now pursue varied careers, multiple activities, and disparate apostolates. This diversification imposes a drain on certain temporal assets. The community car has become a focal point around which temporal needs converge. In the past community members could usually walk to work, because the work place was the school, the hospital, or the special institution, and these were close to the community residence. If community members traveled some distance to work, they could go together since they generally worked together. Under those conditions, only a few needed to know how to drive. Now, in terms of transportation, community life resembles family life. Many families face on a daily basis the question of how to transport simultaneously two parents and two or three children in five different directions with one or two family cars. This problem takes on new magnitude when the children become two or three adolescent drivers. Many religious resolve the matter of personal stewardship of temporal goods quite well until it comes to the community car. It is not important to own a car, but it is extremely important to have the use of one. Rank within religious communities no longer depends on the date of one's profession of vows but rather on the frequency of one's access to an automobile. The keys to the car have become a new symbol of power, and the standards of stewardship become tarnished in the struggle between the haves and the have-nots.

Another source of status in religious life is the earning power of community members. Those whose work brings money into the community sometimes demand special privileges because of their financial contributions. Superiors may support these individuals in their claim to extraordinary treatment and thus help establish a covert system of rank based on individual income. The college professor may refuse to take a turn helping with the dishes after the community meal because he or she considers it an undignified chore. The religious earning thirty or forty thousand dollars a year may insist that she or he has already contributed sufficiently to the community when a request comes to help with the spring cleaning, to participate in the community open house, or to pack for a move to another building. Some communities continue to foster the attitude that those among them who do the menial domestic tasks are, if not second-rate religious, at least second-class citizens. A particular hardship of aging in religious life is to fall into the category of "unproductive" members, where one often experiences a sense of rejection and unworthiness.

In a discussion of the vow of poverty, the stewardship of time must be considered, since a list of worldly assets includes time. Religious characteristically exhibit more deficiencies in the use of time than in the use of money. The problem is not that they waste time, but that they do not spend it well.

Religious often require psychiatric care as a result of their neglect of time management. The schedule of the day controls them instead of their controlling the schedule. Each time segment, from early morning to late night, demands certain responses from them. They always hurry to meet the next dictate of the commanding clock. They fail to make choices about their lives and thereby lose their sense of autonomy. In this regard one seminarian remarked that his only decision in the frenetic schedule of his day was which television channel to select for the late news. Even then, other community members often curtailed his moment of freedom.

As religious succumb to the increasing burden of schedules, which are usually of their own creation, they attempt to recapture some free time by curtailing certain activities. They decrease their involvement in spheres that are not regulated by the direct demands of others or by definite, prearranged schedules. They reduce the time they spend in spiritual exercises on the premise that their work keeps them in contact with God. As a result, their spiritual life becomes arid and their primary source of motivation fades away. They continue to shorten the time spent in spiritual exercises until they meet only the minimum obligations. After they squeeze their spiritual life dry in an attempt to gain more time for their active ministry, they turn next to their recreational life in search of additional time. They give up leisure time in the evenings, then on their days off, to catch up on their work. They practically abandon community interaction. However, each time they take an hour or two from prayer or from recreation in order to meet the demands of their work load, those additional hours somehow do not appear to reduce either the volume or the urgency of their work. These are people whose work load seems to increase in direct proportion to the amount of available time. Extra time is fuel that makes their merry-go-round go faster. Just as financial overexpenditure or imprudent investment of money can lead to bankruptcy, so can the unwise or profligate use of time lead to emotional insolvency.

Father Francis worked hard in the many assignments given

him by his religious superiors. He had a half-time assignment in teaching, a quarter-time assignment in administration, and a quarter-time assignment in parish ministry. Initially he thought this arrangement would offer him a pleasant variety and a desirable balance in his work. Francis spent considerable time in class preparation, for he was determined to be a good teacher. Students responded to his enthusiasm, and his classes at the college became popular. He was pleased and consequently devoted more time to class preparation. Students approached him in increasing numbers and took up larger amounts of his time. His college work soon occupied thirty to forty hours each week.

His superiors expected that the duties of administration in a small house of seminarians would only take a few hours of Francis's time each week. Their time estimate was reasonable for a person who accepted the position as a duty to keep the facility operating in a perfunctory fashion. Francis did not have the personality to adjust to such a plan. He had a drive not just to do things well but to expect continuing improvement in himself and in others. The administrative assignment as interpreted by Francis required at least twenty or thirty hours each week.

His parish assignment seemed routine enough, since it consisted of some well-defined duties assisting in a local parish. In his usual fashion Francis approached this task with vigor and imagination. His interest in liturgy developed as he discovered changes that could be made and additional services that could be provided. The pastor and the parishioners appreciated Francis's efforts and encouraged him to spend extra hours in the parish. Before long, his involvement required at least twenty hours each week.

During his first year in these assignments Francis came for psychiatric help. His primary symptoms were anxiety and insomnia. He experienced episodes of tremulousness, rapid heartbeat, chest pain, and light-headedness. He began to worry about having a heart attack or a stroke. He became preoccupied with his physical health and developed a variety of physical symptoms. When he went to bed at night, he mentally reviewed the day, wondering if he had left anything undone and evaluating the things he had done. Before going to sleep, he mulled over the next day, trying to devise a formula to fit the myriad tasks and multiple problems into the hours of a day that was never long enough. During this mental activity he thrashed about in bed, unable to get to sleep. Finally exhausted, he slept, but he often awakened with a start remembering some unfinished task. Dreams of contests, of examinations, and of failure troubled his sleep.

Prior to coming for therapy Francis tried to compensate for his time deficit by neglecting those private, invisible, and unspecified schedules that provide periods for recreation and times for prayer. He erroneously decided that his parish duties fulfilled his spiritual needs and that his contacts with students fulfilled his recreational needs.

In treatment Francis quickly became aware that schedule conflicts were what precipitated his anxieties and insomnia. However, this initial insight did not relieve his symptoms, for his behavior patterns originated in earlier developmental phases. When he was eleven, his parents were divorced. He and his older sister and two younger brothers remained with their mother. She turned to Francis as the most dependable and stable of the children, and he assumed the role of surrogate father. He had been psychologically primed for this role prior to his parents' divorce when he did his utmost to keep them from quarreling. He experienced their divorce as a failure on his part, and their continued hostility after the divorce kept that failure vivid in his mind.

During therapy Francis recalled how overwhelmed he had felt as an adolescent by the problems of his family. He tried to support his mother emotionally, but his attempts to moderate her antagonism toward his father were unsuccessful. He tried to maintain family contact with his father and felt defeated when his father, remarried and moved away. He perceived

himself as responsible for one brother's poor grades, for his other brother's involvement in drugs, and for his unmarried sister's pregnancy. He viewed all these events as failures on his part, and he commented, "I do not take failure gracefully." He acknowledged that he had "a compulsion to please people and to make everything right for everybody." He also came to recognize that his sense of self-worth depended on "how well I do things."

As treatment progressed Francis gradually extricated himself from the emotional entanglements of his earlier years. He freed himself from the burden of guilt that had been generated by the failures of his family members but that he had intercepted and made his own. He demarcated the true boundaries of his past responsibilities as a youth and then moved on to set some limits on his responsibilities as an adult. With this newly discovered ability, his treatment advanced rapidly. He placed some distinct limits on the time he allotted to each of his assignments. He successfully presented to his superiors some sound recommendations modifying various aspects of his work. They cooperated in altering his time commitments for the following year. His anxiety symptoms gradually ended, and his sleep patterns returned to normal.

Religious as well as others often say, "I do not have enough time." In fact, everyone has enough time, or at least all the time that she or he is going to have. One lifetime is all the time anyone can have, and it is foolhardy to behave as if one can expand the allotted time by stuffing it with activities. To perform good works does not give the righteous person more time, any more than the performance of wicked deeds decreases the time available to the wrongdoer. A lifetime provides all the time one needs to live one's life and to live it well. The complaint that one does not have enough time involves, in a sense, a psychological deception. The statement suggests that more time exists but one simply cannot find it or cannot get possession of it. To look for more time in a day that is the length of every other day, or in an hour that is the length of every other hour, is an idle quest.

The notion of stewardship includes not only the proper use of temporalities but also the preservation of goods. Community members are the most important resources in a religious community. To encourage them to preserve their physical health and their emotional well-being promotes the exercise of stewardship. This is more than just a theoretical notion, for it has practical applications. Many religious contribute to their own physical and emotional illnesses by not organizing their time to allow for adequate spiritual enrichment, sufficient exercise, appropriate recreation, and necessary relaxation and rest. In place of these healthy, stress-reducing activities, they are likely to substitute too much alcohol, too much food eaten too quickly, and too many pills to help them relax and sleep. Psychosomatic illnesses and psychiatric problems develop from such neglect and create a heavy financial burden for some communities, a burden that could often be avoided if individual religious followed sound practices of mental and physical health. In a healthy marital relationship, one spouse may say to the other, "You are overworking. Slow down. You need to relax a little more. It's important to both of us." Members of religious communities rarely voice such concern for one another or to one another.

Sister Felicita expended all her energies in her dedication to work. She regularly taught in a college that her community owned. She gave workshops and lectures throughout the United States. She had written many articles and several books. She served on various committees and boards. Her community acknowledged her diligence and awarded her high praise for her work. She obtained several outstanding awards and achieved some national prominence. No one in her community ever took note of the manner in which Felicita lived. She shunned community recreation and rarely attended community liturgies. She never exercised. She had no hobbies or interests outside her work. Occasionally she went to a movie, but always alone. She drank excessive amounts of coffee and soft drinks containing caffeine. When she had deadlines to meet, she used diet pills to stay awake and work longer hours. She had taken two different sleeping pills every night for four years. She had periods of anxiety, for which her doctor prescribed tranquilizers, and periods of depression, for which her doctor prescribed antidepressants. On some days Felicita took five different mood-altering medicines.

In psychiatric treatment Felicita evaluated her stewardship of her inner resources. She made some changes in her lifestyle, changes that came slowly and painfully. Finally she was able to function without the use of medicines. She learned to recreate and to relax. She renewed her spiritual life. She increased her involvement in community relationships. She became less "productive" but happier, less prominent but healthier, less praised but holier.

The conservation of community members as valuable resources demands a high standard of care for their physical and emotional problems. Religious sometimes select physicians because they are Catholic rather than because they are competent. Superiors may recommend physicians who have made generous donations to the community, who send their children to a Catholic school, or who have a daughter or son who is a religious. An inept physician or an unqualified therapist may be chosen for any one of a number of irrelevant reasons. Such attitudes may prove costly in health care. Similarly, religious who postpone care because they wish to avoid the expense often aggravate their condition, which later requires more care and more expense.

One Catholic university conducted a one-year program of education and spiritual renewal for religious. Many religious attended the program as a sabbatical year away from their communities. A number of them had significant emotional conflicts that clearly needed some assistance in their resolution; program policy recommended that these emotional conflicts be resolved through spiritual direction. When this failed, as it almost invariably did, the troubled religious were referred to the university counseling program to be seen by a student trainee. When this failed, as it usually did, referral

might at last be made to one of the local professional therapists. By the time this referral process with the intervening
treatment attempts ended, three fourths of the year had passed.
The religious then faced the dilemma either of entering treatment with the possibility that it might not be completed before
time to return home or of postponing treatment and perhaps
never having the same opportunity again. Whatever the reasons were for the program policy, it did not produce the best
use of money or of time or provide the best care for the
distressed religious.

Just as it is important to conserve oneself in relation to time
and thus prolong the benefit that time provides, so it is important as part of stewardship to conserve material goods and
thus prolong their period of usefulness. Private ownership
provides the best psychological motivation for vigilant conservation, but religious communities must depend on an awareness of corporate ownership to induce members to preserve
community possessions. In administrative consultation with a
psychiatrist the provincial of a religious community expressed
grave concern over the irresponsibility of the community members. They drove the cars but never arranged to change the oil.
They used the summer house but never hired anyone to repair
the leak in the roof. They watched the paint peel off the houses
in which they lived but never suggested that anything be done
about it. Their attitude of detachment hardly seemed virtuous
as the property of the community deteriorated around them.
This was not the spirit of detachment that spiritual writers
praise; it was a spirit of indifference.

The vow of poverty brings still another emotional conflict to
some religious. The possession of personal goods stimulates
the creative abilities of many people. A religious woman of
deep spirituality and great inner peace once said that the
greatest sacrifice she had made in the religious life was to
renounce personal possessions. She had a great desire to possess beautiful things. Their monetary value did not attract her,
but she found satisfaction in their beauty. Perhaps women

especially have a need to possess beautiful things. It is not so much a need to own things as it is a need to make some small corner of life more attractive, more graceful, more enchanting through their artistic choices and creative arrangement of fine objects. Some men also experience this kind of sacrifice in their lack of personal possessions. One man who left the priesthood fashioned with remarkable skill exquisite tapestries that adorned his home as magnificent works of art. One might speculate about whether the warmth of his spouse and the embrace of his child did not open in him a creative dimension that might never have blossomed in his community life. The sacrifice of things that make life beautiful weighs more heavily on some religious than on others.

A few decades ago religious rarely had problems with stewardship. Community schedules organized their time and included periods for prayer and times for recreation. While their few personal possessions gathered dust in the community trunk room, their attachment to worldly goods faded under the harsh light of ascetic poverty. New directions in religious life facilitate access to the trunk rooms where material possessions are stored as well as to the hidden recesses of their minds where desires for worldly gratification lie. The locked door of the trunk room, the restrictive boundaries of the community horarium, and the inflexible regulation of funds no longer protect the individual religious from avarice or indolence. Persons who had to ask if they could have a postage stamp may find it difficult to manage the elusive bounty of a personal budget. Persons who organized time by the sound of a bell may find it difficult to manage the transient abundance of an ordinary day.

Some of the most difficult personal conflicts brought on by changes in community life focus on the vow of poverty. In past years members of religious communities lived as subordinates in a system that provided for their material needs in an impartial manner and that regulated their time in a prescriptive fashion. Religious now face new challenges as they accept personal responsibility for managing material goods and time, even though many of them have had no previous experience to prepare them for these tasks.

Some religious find it difficult to use money blamelessly and effectively. Others are startled to confront their own avarice as they demand more than is appropriate and thus increase the inequities that exist in communal living. Today, in contrast to the past, financial matters have become the concern of all community members. This increased interest and awareness sometimes make productive work with good pay a mark of prestige, and occasionally a source of privilege, within a community, relegating domestic work to a lesser status and implying rejection to the aging and infirm.

Characteristically religious have experienced difficulty managing their time well as they surveyed large vineyards and few laborers. In the past, communities rather artificially arranged long periods of private and common prayer and short periods of common recreation. Prayer and recreation now represent unstructured portions of the day of a religious. Consequently they are the least likely areas to be preserved by the disorganized religious or by the religious who feels overburdened by all sorts of demands.

Those religious who fail to maintain their own physical health by timely, reliable, and sometimes costly medical care, who fail to protect their own emotional well-being by proper exercise, recreation, and relaxation, and who fail to keep their spiritual dedication by regular prayer are likely to succumb to unhealthy supports such as alcohol or prescription medicine misuse to maintain their functioning.

8. The Turmoil of Substance Abuse

In years past the "whiskey priest" exemplified for most people the struggle of religious personnel with substance abuse. In response to their Catholic rearing, the laity tried to look the other way if the local priest made a spectacle of himself. They explained to their children that "the priest is not well today." The laity tried to avoid talking about the priest's alcoholism. His superiors tried to avoid embarrassment. His religious confreres tried to avoid confrontation. He tried to avoid help. For decades alcoholism was typically dealt with in this manner when it affected a family member, a personal friend, or the local priest. Avoidance perpetuated the problem of alcoholism: To avoid talking about the priest's drinking, the parishioners avoided the priest. To avoid embarrassment, his superiors avoided him. To avoid confrontation, fellow religious avoided him. To avoid help, the priest avoided others. Thus he became increasingly isolated from his superiors, his community, and other people. In his isolation, he found consoling companionship in his bottle.

Programs to treat this problem began to take shape as the treatment of alcoholism gained acceptance, if not respectability. Programs such as that at Guest House provided treatment and rehabilitation. The problem of alcoholism among male religious was beginning to be confronted openly by religious authorities with the support of their religious communities. The problem of alcoholism shifted from the confessional to the consulting room as moral theologians released their hold on the alcoholic priest and acknowledged the hold that compulsion had on him.

On the surface alcoholism seemed to be the extent of substance abuse among religious communities twenty or thirty years ago. However, another problem existed then and still exists among religious men and women: that of abusing prescription drugs. In some ways it is an iatrogenic problem. Most physicians conscientiously maintain a wary attitude in prescribing all medicines, but especially analgesics, tranquilizers, and sedatives. The physician who is otherwise scrupulously cautious often loses his or her habitual vigilance when facing a religious as a patient. The physician may know all the tricks of those who obtain prescriptions fraudulently, but that store of knowledge is not even considered when Father George or Sister Gertrude sits across the desk smiling innocently and explaining how a particular medicine is the only thing that gives any blessed relief. This is an excellent example of what is known in psychiatry as countertransference. The physician has a set of attitudes about priests and sisters. Those attitudes suppose that religious would not abuse drugs, because they are religious, that religious would not resort to deception or fraud, because they are religious, and that because they would not abuse drugs and would not resort to deception or fraud, there is no need to be cautious in writing prescriptions for them for habituating medicines.

The more clever religious may never mention the desired drug. It is enough to list the right symptoms and wait for the prescription to come out the pay window. Many years ago a psychiatrist treated a sister who enjoyed the use of amphetamine compounds, later known on the street as "speed." Sister Genevieve could successfully "hit" any doctor in town for a prescription of Dexedrine without ever mentioning the drug itself. So that her community would not receive bills for her office visits, she chose physicians who did not charge religious. She deduced that physicians who did not charge religious held them in high esteem and therefore would be unlikely to suspect them of drug abuse. In those days of religious poverty Genevieve sometimes had difficulty obtaining the money to pay for her prescriptions. In her own ingenious way she eventually solved that problem too. Genevieve taught college chemistry and in her spare time learned to make amphetamines in the college laboratory.

Occasionally it is necessary for a psychiatrist to contact another physician regarding the misuse of prescriptions by a religious. The other physician usually responds with incredulity. She or he finds it difficult to believe that any religious, and especially this religious, would abuse drugs. Psychiatrists who have little experience in treating religious may fall into this same error. Psychiatrists and other physicians who have a traditional view of the impeccable integrity of all religious overlook the possibility of this kind of problem.

The abuse of drugs is an occupational hazard for those who work in the medical field. Availability, familiarity, and an exaggerated sense of personal control in relation to medicines are important factors in their abuse by medical personnel. Religious who work in the medical field have the same inviting reasons to abuse drugs. In spite of newly established freedoms within religious life, the variety of relaxing experiences for religious remains limited. In medical work settings religious encounter the same kind of pressure and the same kind of tedium that laypersons encounter. In addition, religious may be isolated emotionally, and sometimes physically, from their communities. Recreational opportunities are restricted, and relaxation is difficult. To leave work is not enough. They need to leave it behind but cannot, because nothing else fills the void. They begin to sleep poorly, and sedatives are the simple answer. They become increasingly tense under the pressure of work, the absence of close companionship, and the lack of recreational outlets; tranquilizers are the easy answer.

In the role of physician or nurse, the religious is as much at risk for drug abuse as any other doctor or nurse. Sister Geraldine worked as a nurse in hospitals for over twenty years. She was fifty years old when she came for psychiatric treatment, referred by her regular physician at the insistence of her superior. Eighteen years earlier she had had an operation and following the surgery used narcotics for an appropriate period. Twelve years before coming for treatment Geraldine was having some conflict with her local superior, and her physician prescribed phenobarbital to help her maintain her calm. Because of easy access to drugs at work, she began self-medicating. Initially, phenobarbital sufficed to relax her and help her sleep. Over the years she added and abused other medicines. Just prior to coming for therapy she worked as a nurse in a large nursing home. For several months she had been self-administering four to five intramuscular injections of Demerol during her eight-hour shift. She obtained the narcotic by substituting sterile water for the Demerol prescribed for her patients. During her off-duty hours she had a supply of brandy and vodka that kept her calm.

Geraldine's father died of alcoholism when she was twelve years old. He was a strict man who physically abused her and her older brother. She feared him and knew no affection from him. Her parents quarreled frequently, and occasionally her father physically abused her mother. After the father's death, the mother did not remarry but worked to support her two children. Geraldine's mother had not successfully protected either of her children from their alcoholic father; however, she had provided for them considerable tenderness and affection to offset the harshness of their father's behavior. Following the death of her husband, the mother began to favor her son and became even more affectionate toward him. Perhaps he provided a male counterpart in her life. At the critical period of Geraldine's entering her adolescent years, her world of family disintegrated. She realized that she loved her father in spite of his unkindness, and she grieved over his death. She was unable to resolve her grief, because she had no opportunity to express it outwardly. Her mother suddenly seemed uncaring toward her and unapproachable. Her mother's rejection prevented a healthy resolution of her grief and magnified the first loss by adding a greater one. As she approached the insecurity of her early adolescent years, she found no solace from others and turned inward to nurse her hurt. Previously she had known harshness from her father, tenderness from her mother, and faithfulness from her brother. These feelings, which had been relatively constant in her life, changed abruptly. Her father, whom she had thought she hated, now became an object of her love, although he was gone and love was too late. Her mother, whom she had depended on for comfort, now became a source of unhappiness as Geraldine experienced her rejection. Her brother, who had been an ally in their common fate, now became her foe as she viewed him with jealous animosity. Geraldine became socially withdrawn and emotionally guarded. She felt she had been betrayed and refused to trust again.

Geraldine attended a Catholic school. The sisters consoled her when her father died, and she responded to their attention as a substitute for her losses at home. She began to consider the possibility of becoming a sister. Her mother was devoutly religious and strongly approved of her daughter's entering the convent. At age seventeen she became a postulant.

Geraldine never trusted her religious superiors and remained guarded with them. She was congenial toward community members but never close to anyone. She never caused problems, because she never revealed that she had any. She participated only in those community exercises that were obligatory. As the years passed there were fewer and fewer of these. She followed the tradition of many in her community and became a nurse. Her work became her primary interest and provided her principal source of relationships. She maintained a good but superficial rapport with staff and co-workers, but she had no friends within her community. She used her work as an escape, but it offered her little relief and no rewards. In therapy her psychiatrist often thought of her as an orphan, lost in the big world, trying to smile at the right time for the right people, searching for warmth, physical comfort, affection, and security. Through therapy Geraldine decided not to return to work in the nursing profession. She worked as a bookkeeper in her community and performed some volunteer work for a social agency. She learned to live without drugs and without alcohol. Her search ended, not because she found what she sought, but because in therapy she came to terms with the deprivations of her life and the limitations of her personality. She renewed her spiritual life and restored her belief that one day she would find her true home.

In past years, the structure of life for women religious made access to alcohol difficult, and prescription medicines or drugs pilfered on the job became the principal sources of chemical dependence. Therefore, the incidence of drug abuse was probably higher for female religious than for male religious, who had easy access to alcohol. With the dissolution of conventional barriers and the abandonment of distinctive religious dress, it is now an easy trip to the liquor store for religious women. Although their monthly allowance from the community may not be great, it is sufficient to permit direct purchase of alcoholic beverages. Changes in community structure, community schedules, and community stability provide opportunity and perhaps incentive for an increase in the incidence of alcoholism in communities of women religious.

Social drinking has long been a regular practice in many religious communities of men, and to gather for a social hour before dinner is traditional. In addition to the custom of alcohol use in their communities, male religious have typically moved about freely in a social world where alcohol is in common use. Research clearly indicates that hereditary factors, psychological forces, and physiological makeup contribute to the disease of alcoholism. However, an additional component must be present, and that is opportunity or occasion. If one hundred people are exposed to the regular use of alcohol, one can safely assume that at least a few of them will eventually misuse alcohol. Culturally, an ability to "hold one's liquor" has been a symbol of masculinity. In such a cultural background it is especially difficult for a man to accept the fact that he cannot consume alcohol with impunity. Some male religious because of their early psychosexual development have an increased need to establish a masculine identification. The manly qualities that they associate with alcohol encourage its use and make acknowledgment of abuse difficult.

Father Gus sought psychiatric care six years after his ordination. His presenting difficulties were depression, obesity, and abuse of alcohol. He regularly had three mixed drinks before dinner, wine with dinner, and three or four drinks after dinner. He had recently begun having one or two drinks before lunch. During his first few weeks of therapy, Gus associated his use of alcohol with a variety of negative feelings including loneliness, tension, anger, depression, resentment, and confusion. He admitted that he used alcohol to lessen his anxiety in social situations, and when he avoided social situations, he drank to excess in his loneliness.

Gus came from an economically deprived background. His father, a coal miner in Appalachia, died of a cerebral hemorrhage while at work. He had passed the age of retirement, and his physician had advised him to stop working because of his poor health. He had chosen to continue working because he "enjoyed his work and was happier there than anywhere else." Gus's father was ordinarily a quiet man who sometimes exploded at Gus in anger and at other times teased him for being a sissy. Gus had five older siblings who were more athletic than he and who joined with the father in playing ball and in teasing Gus. When his mother was present, she rescued Gus from his tormentors, but her participation in church activities frequently kept her away from the house. His mother appreciated Gus's intelligence and his interest in music and poetry, and she encouraged him to escape from their style of life, which she considered bleak and purposeless.

At age sixteen Gus left the small town where they lived and went to a Southern city to live with his paternal grandparents and attend a Catholic high school. Although he never fit in with his peers, he enjoyed the academic challenge and did well in school. In treatment he commented about this period,

"I never felt like a normal teenager." The possibility of attending college seemed extremely remote until Gus thought of becoming a priest. With that idea, doors to the future opened for him, and he went through them with enthusiasm and energy. He was determined to take advantage of every opportunity and to succeed.

In college and seminary Gus quickly developed leadership abilities and assumed leadership roles. At the same time, he acknowledged the authority of others and worked to gain their approval. In treatment Gus recalled that his mother had always depended on him to help her make decisions because his father was unable to make any decisions. Although Gus had regarded his father as ineffectual and resented his passivity, he had always tried to please him. Gus's motivation to excel and his high intelligence resulted in superior performance during his academic years. His teachers and religious superiors encouraged him, and for the first time in his life, his peers respected him and befriended him.

Following ordination Gus was assigned to parish work, which he approached with his typical eagerness. The heavy work load soon tired him, and he sought relaxation with friends and relatives who lived nearby. He discovered that these relationships increased his feeling of exhaustion because "my friends unburden themselves on me" and "my relatives come to me with all their personal and family problems." He began to feel defenseless and subject to attack as he had in childhood, but his mother could no longer protect him, because she had died the year before he was ordained. Gus had perceived his mother as a very nurturing person, feeding him those values and attitudes that had brought him to his present state. His mother had not only fed him emotionally but had also baked special treats for him to compensate for the harassment from his father and siblings. Food continued to be a source of consolation in his mother's absence, and then as he began to use alcohol, he discovered a comforting effect that even his mother had not been able to provide. The more he felt psychologically abused by others, the more he looked for relief in food and alcohol. He had repressed his anger toward his father and sisters by crying and running to his mother. He buried his anger toward those who took advantage of him by drinking or eating alone. At least unconsciously, he recognized the self-destructiveness in his behavior when he reported a dream in which he was in a grocery store and shoppers were killing each other with their loaded grocery carts.

Food and alcohol consumption symbolized maternal support to Gus. Alcohol use also represented a masculine identification. A male teacher in high school had involved him in a homosexual relationship that had lasted for about six months. In addition, Gus had engaged in some brief homosexual encounters during his college years. He said that because of these encounters he had "never been aggressive with women." He silenced his doubts about his masculinity by using alcohol to bolster his courage with male peers. He once said to his therapist, "I know I need to discover quiet time in which to pray and think, but I'm afraid of what I might find there." His father had never used alcohol, but Gus viewed his father as a weak person. In an unguarded comment during therapy, he said, "Alcohol makes me feel like a man."

The initial insights Gus gained in treatment were not enough to curtail his excessive eating and drinking. The pressures of work and the expectations of friends and family prevented him from achieving his goal of abstinence as an outpatient. A period of hospitalization and the nurturance offered there enabled him to stop drinking and to control his eating patterns. He continued to need the supportive relationship of psychotherapy for another three years before he could let go of his therapist whom he had viewed as his protector.

Social drinking is becoming a common element in the lives of female religious. Communities of religious women serve wine with increasing frequency at their social gatherings and with dinner on special feast days. Some suggest that as wine became associated with dinner on special occasions, there appeared to be an increase in special occasions in some communities. Mixed drinks followed the advent of wine in some houses. Communities where social events regularly involve alcohol consumption often display a wide selection of alcoholic beverages.

These comments are not intended as criticisms of the practices mentioned. Religious should surely celebrate life and its significant moments. The festival of life and the warmth of relationships can be complemented by the appropriate use of alcohol. It would be naive, however, not to recognize that the increased accessibility and the greater acceptability of alcohol dispose a certain percentage of susceptible individuals to its abuse. Sisters now associate more freely with laypeople, not only professionally and personally but also socially. In social settings they are often invited to have an alcoholic drink. Most female religious are comfortable in these situations and handle them well. They feel free to decline alcohol or to accept it. If they accept it, they are aware of the need for responsibility in its use.

A few religious, both male and female, resemble adolescents who have waited several years to reach the age when drinking is legal. Alcohol was forbidden before and now is no longer forbidden. For some of them drinking represents a sign of emancipation. It symbolizes freedom, adulthood, independence, self-determination. Sister Grace had been a secret drinker for years. She found great satisfaction in her ability to obtain alcohol and to use it without detection. In a distorted fashion it represented independence. She used alcohol to defy authority, even though her religious superiors were unaware of her drinking. In therapy she was able to reorient herself in relation to her vow of obedience as she came to understand her need to rebel. She became aware of her emotional conflicts relating to dependence and independence and, in their resolution, gained control over her alcoholism. Some people drink primarily because someone else objects to their drinking; this behavior is an example of a whole range of behaviors in which individuals harm themselves in order to hurt someone else. This reasoning enters into the drinking behavior of some emotionally immature religious men and women. They are like children who frequent the cookie jar not because they are hungry or even because they love cookies but because their parents have told them not to do so.

Persons with a family history of alcoholism, depression, or suicide are at greater risk for developing alcohol problems than are those without such backgrounds. Physicians often advise persons in certain life situations to curtail their use of alcohol or to avoid its use altogether. People who have suffered emotional loss are more vulnerable to the abuse of alcohol, particularly if the loss undermines their self-concept. Thus the loss of a job may be more significant emotionally than the loss of a friend or relative, because the loss of a job may be more damaging to the ego and thereby increase the individual's susceptibility to the nurturing effect that alcohol seems to provide. If an individual experiences considerable stress at work and finds it difficult to relax, the use of alcohol may be ill advised. An individual who travels and is intermittently separated from family and friends should be more cautious about the use of alcohol while away from home. Persons who are physically exhausted or emotionally drained are more susceptible to the effects of alcohol. An angry encounter may influence a person to overindulge in alcohol use. People who are lonely, depressed, anxious, angry, or fatigued should exercise caution in their use of alcohol; the caution they exercise should be directly proportionate to the magnitude of their negative feelings. One might sum this up by saying, "When you think you need a drink, it is not the time to have it. When you are feeling good and do not need a drink, you may enjoy one with little risk."

Religious who use alcohol, no matter how moderately, might exercise prudence by occasionally reviewing the circumstances that increase the risk of alcohol abuse. Unfortunately, religious, because they experience themselves as separated from the world, sometimes feel a false sense of security regarding alcohol use, and the fallacy of self-exception is often an insidious element in alcoholism. The lives of many religious contain emotional ingredients that mix poorly with alcohol: A religious may be given an assignment that is incompatible with his or her education and experience. A religious may be removed from an assignment in an arbitrary manner or in what appears to be an arbitrary manner. A work assignment may be especially stressful, but the sense of commitment of the individual religious might prevent her or him from seeking a change of assignment or a re-evaluation of the work load. The scheduling requirements of some ministries may keep religious out of contact with their friends in the community. At times some ministries appear quite foreign to the rest of the community and seem to take the individual into another world. Most communities also have some irritating members who readily become involved in angry exchanges with others. The superior can rarely be a support to everyone, and some may mistrust him or her. Circumstances such as these produce an ominous setting: personal loss, marked stress with no source of relief, lack of emotional support from others, distrust of the person in charge, and irritating exchanges with associates. In such settings the use of alcohol brings increased hazards for misuse.

At age sixty-three Sister Georgia was ordered by her provincial to consult a psychiatrist. Her superiors had been concerned about her alcohol and drug abuse for over twenty years. Instead of insisting that Georgia receive professional help, previous superiors had tried to hide the problem from everyone outside the community. This particular religious congregation took pride in the fact that many of their members came from prominent families in the region. Their primary ministry was teaching, and their schools catered to the affluent. Obviously Georgia's problem would have been an embarrassment to them if it had become known outside the community, so it was necessary to hide Georgia within the community. A number of restrictive maneuvers on the part of superiors finally brought

Georgia to the status of a virtual prisoner in the community infirmary. She could not leave the area unaccompanied, and any medicines, including aspirin and cough drops, were doled out by infirmary staff. Even with these limitations Georgia managed to obtain alcohol or pills from time to time. At various times she had endured periods of "house arrest," and at other times she had been transferred abruptly from one assignment to another in an attempt to allay the suspicions that arose concerning her behavior.

Assured of complete confidentiality, Georgia came to trust her psychiatrist and openly discussed her problems of abuse. She had misused alcohol and drugs for over thirty years. Her problem began following several surgeries when she was younger. Georgia was born with a spinal defect that impaired her gait and that finally necessitated surgery because of increasing disability and pain. She had ten operations in seven years and then spent eighteen months in a complete body cast. She used crutches for an additional four years. A week following one of the major operations Georgia returned to her teaching and other duties, "working ten hours a day." The doctor had recommended that Georgia rest three weeks before resuming any activity. It was at this time that she began using wine at night to help her sleep. In treatment, Georgia commented, "I never would have abused alcohol and medicines if I had been allowed time to recover from the surgeries." However, her superiors could not be held entirely responsible for Georgia's premature return to duty. Georgia had always tried to prove her worth by her productivity and had undoubtedly pressed her superiors to put her back to work. In spite of her physical disability and the multiple operations, she described herself as having been "a very strong young nun."

Georgia's father and several paternal relatives were alcoholics; probably Georgia had a predisposition to substance abuse. She was the youngest of six children. Her parents divorced when she was nine, and because of her mother's emotional instability, Georgia was sent to a boarding school. She was lonely there. Being teased by the other children because of her awkward gait intensified her insecurity. In the manner of some insecure children, she tried to please adults and worked hard at every task to gain their acceptance. The sisters at the boarding school responded warmly to her industry, and Georgia decided that she wanted to live as they did.

Her community life became an extension of her boarding-school existence. She tried to ingratiate herself with superiors, although she inwardly resented their demands. She would work to the point of exhaustion and then be unable to relax or to sleep. At the time Georgia began therapy, she was retired because of physical incapacity, but she retained a number of small jobs and activities, which she approached with her characteristic intensity. She said, "If anyone asks me to do something, I can't say no." At the same time she described herself as "stubborn, quick-tempered, independent, and rebellious." This inner disposition had never been revealed to her superiors, who regarded her as a placid and submissive religious except for her addictive behavior.

In fact, Georgia's addictive behavior had become an expression of anger and resentment toward others. At one point she admitted that she "drank wine just to spite the superior" in one convent where she lived for six years. Although she was not teased in community as she had been in boarding school, she encountered some indignities. Prior to her spinal operations one of her superiors told her she was "babying" herself and that she "just needed exercise" to improve her walking. When confined to her room to keep her from alcohol or pills, she felt humiliated, frightened, and resentful. She stated, "It drives me crazy to stay in my room." No one remembered that she had been confined in a boarding school for seven years and in a body cast for eighteen months. Some community members who knew about her addiction accused her of substance abuse when they noted her unsteady gait. They did not know that her physician had encouraged her for several years to use a cane or that she had stubbornly refused because it made her feel helpless. On one occasion another sister called her "an old drunkard." One of her superiors, in exasperation, said to her, "You act smart, but you look so dumb." Georgia resented the times she had been transferred without warning and without explanation. She resented the times her room had been searched, sometimes secretly and sometimes openly. She felt she had been treated "like a fool" by her community.

Georgia talked frankly about the accessibility of alcohol and drugs through the years. During one period the wife of another teacher mailed her sedatives in gift-wrapped packages that the community did not suspect because of the return address and the gift wrapping. In one of the high schools where she was the librarian a lay teacher brought her wine regularly. A hired woman who did the cooking in a convent where Georgia lived brought her wine and hid it under her pillow when the sisters were out of the house. One physician whom she saw for several years "gave me a brown bag of pills every time I went to see him." He never knew she had a substance abuse problem. At one time she had several different physicians prescribing a stimulant, and she took as many as twenty of them in one day. Sometimes when shopping, chaperoned by another sister, she stole bottles of aspirin and antihistamines from stores to support her need for pills. She summarized these stories as follows: "When a person is an addict or an alcoholic, there are always ways of getting things."

Georgia found resolution of old conflicts in the therapeutic setting. She reviewed the psychological wounds of her community years and rediscovered in them the heartaches of her childhood and adolescent years. Once her substance abuse began, she never felt at peace within herself or with her community. She had been unable to talk freely to anyone inside her community, and she had always believed, "We can't talk to anyone outside the community about community affairs." In treatment Georgia talked at length about community affairs. She talked about the behavior of her superiors, the behavior of her peers, and her own behavior. At one point in therapy she worried because "deep in my being I have not forgiven them." She came to forgive them for their deficiencies when she was able to forgive herself for her weaknesses. She learned to say no when she felt overburdened or overtired. As a child she had never been allowed to complain. She had practiced the same stoicism in community life but had self-medicated to alleviate her unspoken complaints. In therapy she learned to accept her own limitations and to expose them to others. She learned to accept the fact that complaints need to be made in order to let others know how much one can do, how far one can go. Georgia made peace with the errors of her past; she made peace with the mistakes of her community. In return she found a spiritual peace within her vows and an emotional calm within herself independent of artificial sources of tranquility.

Sedatives and minor tranquilizers, also called antianxiety agents, have an appropriate place in helping people cope with stress. Their use as temporary aids during periods of emotional strain may prevent deterioration in adjustment and prolonged psychological impairment. However, their use requires judicious management. Normally the prescribing physician has that responsibility. The point has already been made that many physicians tend to be less direct, less forceful, with religious than with other patients and sometimes less careful about the sedative-tranquilizer drugs prescribed for them. Because of the growing awareness of possible harmful side effects of medicines and a greater interest in consumer rights and responsibilities, many patients exercise personal caution in accepting prescription medicines. Religious might benefit from this consumer trend and maintain their own vigilance in using medicines, especially those that may be habit-forming.

With long-term use, sedatives, tranquilizers, and analgesics can be habit-forming. Physicians in psychiatric practice encounter religious who have taken Valium or Librium or one of the many related tranquilizers for a period of four or five years. Father Gregory, a diocesan priest in the Midwest, had conquered a twenty-year problem with alcoholism. During the following ten years various physicians regularly gave him prescriptions for sleeping pills and an assortment of tranquilizers. When Gregory finally sought psychiatric care, he was taking two sedatives at night and five tranquilizers during the day, but these did not stabilize him emotionally. Gregory needed to confront the emotional conflicts that were causing his substance abuse and resolve them in a healthy manner. The alcohol, and later the prescription drugs, had delayed that confrontation for nearly thirty years.

One of the important disadvantages in the long-term use of tranquilizers and sedatives is that such use perpetuates the problems. Use of these medicines provides a temporary support but not a permanent solution. They reinforce the individual's avoidance defenses. Tranquilizers taken during stress of short duration have no harmful effects. Some problems are of short duration and are resolved just by the passage of time; sedatives and tranquilizers may decrease a person's discomfort while the time passes. To use sedatives and tranquilizers to cope with problems that are not going to go away presents genuine hazards. Persons who encounter prolonged periods of unrelenting stress should seek professional help to evaluate the situation thoroughly and to undertake a satisfactory resolution of the stress. Tranquilizers obviously do not solve problems, and people who take tranquilizers regularly may become less motivated to solve problems. Taking tranquilizers regularly and for long periods may make a person more comfortable but not more capable. Years pass, but the problem remains, and at the age of fifty or sixty a person is less flexible and may have fewer options for resolving a conflict than at the age of thirty. With age people become less resilient, less energetic, less bold, and less adaptable. The long-term use of tranquilizers may be emotionally debilitating not because they cause weakness but because they prevent people from using their strengths to resolve conflicts and to cope with stress.

Occasionally individuals cannot resolve certain conflicts or relieve certain stresses, either because they do not have the required psychological skills or because there are no salutary solutions to the problems. The continued use of tranquilizers may be necessary for them to maintain a stable adjustment. Such use should be accepted as a last resort both by the patient and by the doctor, and careful control of medicine by both the patient and the doctor is essential.

The extended use of sedatives, however, is rarely appropriate. Somnologists, or sleep experts, claim that the prolonged use of sleeping pills is the commonest cause of insomnia. Sleep, a psychophysiologic function, is influenced by a person's physical health as well as by a person's emotional state. Brief periods of sleep disturbance respond to the use of sedatives. Prolonged periods of sleep disturbance require careful investigation for physical or emotional causes.

The abuse of alcohol and drugs by sisters, brothers, and priests represents one extreme of behavior in relation to these substances. Another extreme occurs in those religious who assume a critical attitude toward anyone who uses medicine, however appropriately, or alcohol, however temperately. They object to the use of alcoholic beverages as a matter of personal precept and moral principle. These individuals are reminiscent of bishops in former days who insisted that everyone receiving the sacrament of confirmation take a pledge of temperance. They regard the use of sedatives, tranquilizers, and analgesics as a sign of personality weakness and as bordering on a lack of faith. In them, faith does indeed seem antithetical to reason. Such individuals particularly suspect psychotropic medicines because they presume that people can correct their own emotional problems by praying better and by being more strict with themselves. Their own virtue seems questioned if their physician suggests a sedative, an antianxiety agent, or an antidepressant. They tend not to comply with the dosage or schedule of a prescription. Physicians often do not suspect religious of noncompliance, assuming that religious will respond to the doctor's authority and will carefully take medicine as prescribed.

Religious are not exempt from the potential for drug and

alcohol abuse. They are also vulnerable to the illegal use and abuse of marijuana, cocaine, and various hallucinogens. As they move about with increased freedom in the secular world and choose not to be separated from the demands and conflicts of the secular world, religious need to recognize the pressures of that association and to review the reasons for their own vulnerability. The stress of their schedules, their frequently experienced loneliness, their limited opportunities for recreation, and their increased interaction with the secular world all converge to increase their susceptibility to substance abuse. As religious become less distinguishable from laypersons in their dress and in their deportment, health providers may stop perceiving them as persons who are somehow immune to the damage and waste of substance abuse.

But religious communities themselves should support sensible attitudes about the appropriate use of alcohol and prescription medicines. Their use does not automatically constitute abuse. Persons who drink alcohol moderately, whether they are laypersons or religious, are not violating propriety. Similarly, persons who use sedatives, antianxiety agents, analgesics, or antidepressants judiciously, under careful medical supervision and for suitable periods of time, are not thereby being psychologically unstable or spiritually derelict. However, each person must accept the grave responsibility for determining the boundaries of propriety and the limits of prudence. The discriminating use of alcohol neither advances nor detracts from emotional stability but requires a certain level of emotional maturity. Psychotropic medicines do not of themselves produce emotional progress, but they may be helpful in a treatment program designed to advance personal growth.

9. Confusion About Personal Growth

The term *personal growth* has become popular in religious communities during the past twenty years. As religious communities began to confront the psychological conflicts and emotional unrest within their membership, they caught on to the idea that the personal growth of community members would eliminate their difficulties. They made this assumption because they accepted the notion that personal growth is synonymous with progress and betterment and, for some, even the equivalent of virtue. Individuals who are not growing are considered unimaginative, apathetic, and reactionary, whereas those who are growing are considered creative, enthusiastic, and visionary. Before judgments are made about the people who are growing or not growing, there should be some agreement about the concept of growth.

One subtle psychological attitude about growth must be remembered: A great deal of research has established that change contains a disturbing aspect for everyone. Human beings tend to cherish and maintain the status quo because the familiar makes them feel secure. Change, the introduction of something new, causes tension, which results in some anxiety. Persons who are undergoing changes find them less unsettling if they can perceive those changes as beneficial events and as growth experiences. Many religious have been quick to place the changes in religious life under the umbrella of personal growth because that gives those changes the mark of integrity and virtue. They assume that the changes taking place are all positive and do contribute to personal growth. That assumption is far from proven. To claim that a behavior or an experience advances one's personal growth does not make it true in reality. In a religious community, at times such a claim is only a defensive posture taken by a particular religious to thwart a restrictive definition of the rule or an inhibitive statement of religious authority.

"Growth" has always been a priority for most religious communities, but in the past, growth meant community expansion through increased numbers, additional institutions, and mission stations in remote areas. However, growth in numbers and expansion geographically slowed down and then stopped. Some novitiates built in the fifties and sixties never opened. Houses of study, seminaries, convents, and schools closed and were sold to seculars. The mean age in religious communities rose rapidly as the number of aspirants declined markedly. The growth of the community numerically and geographically could no longer represent the excellence of religious life, even though in the past it had been viewed by some communities as a sign of God's special favor. (In the beatification process of the foundress of one large community of religious women, the grounds for beatification included the rapid numerical growth of the community. However, at the time of her beatification, that same community could not attract sufficient novices to offset the number of those who were being laicized. In addition, the mean age of the community had risen to sixty-four, and several members died each year. Unless a strong increase in vocations occurs, canonization of their foundress can hardly depend on numerical growth of the community.) Religious communities have not lost their enthusiasm for growth. They have transferred some of their energy for expansion into new ministries that touch many who were never served by the institutionalized religion of a few decades ago. Most religious communities, undefeated by the decline in new members, encourage old members to obtain the kind of education and experience that will equip them to serve in the growing diversity of new apostolates.

The human-potential movement has sold the idea of personal growth to a technological society that yearns for some personal values. Growth seminars flourish throughout the country. Large corporations provide workshops and training classes for personal growth. Experts on personal growth peddle their wares throughout the land, claiming that growth will solve people's conflicts, improve their lives, and make them whole and happy. Participants in the weekend seminar and the marathon growth session come home convinced but not cured. The techniques of salesmanship are extremely refined and persuasive: The personal magnetism of the presenter, the facilitator, and the healer charms the audience. People find inspiration and hope for change. They become believers and effusively praise the leader. Their euphoria attests to the excellence of the growth seminar. The value of the experience should, however, be judged on the amount of personal growth or improvement that takes place in their lives. The great majority of participants acquire no lasting benefits from such programs, but they remember the euphoria and search for it again in the next seminar that comes along. The cycle then repeats itself.

The entrepreneurs of personal growth often emphasize the stages of life that people go through and exaggerate the significance of these steps. The timetable of growth begins at birth whether one follows Freud, Erikson, Spock, or Gesell. Although authorities carefully demarcate the developmental periods of infancy, childhood, adolescence, adulthood, and old age, they acknowledge that the individual may only approximate these time periods of physical, intellectual, social, and emotional development. Overanxious parents ignore the latitude that is recommended in assessing individual growth and push their young children and their adolescents to keep in lockstep with the schedule of life. They can accept a youngster who moves ahead of the developmental schedule but not one who lags behind.

Popular books such as *Passages* and *The Seasons of a Man's Life* extend the schedule of life into adulthood, and as a result, individuals develop expectations of themselves and of others. A career choice should be made by age eighteen. Education must be completed by age twenty-six. There is an age to marry or a time to have children. There are menopause, the empty-nest period, the prospect of aging, the time of retirement. The publicizing of these time posts of life helps people prepare for them but also creates apprehension about them, since their negative aspects usually receive the most emphasis. Cultural expectations affect religious too and raise their concerns about the timetable of their personal and professional lives.

At age sixty-two Sister Henrietta became depressed and requested psychiatric care. Her depression seemed to develop after she attended a three-day community workshop that focused on the "growth potential" of community members. Following the workshop Henrietta felt that life had passed her by and that various opportunities for growth had been denied her throughout her years in community. She had entered religious life at twenty-four and had been relatively happy until the last four years.

In therapy Henrietta reviewed her early life. She had grown up on a small farm in Iowa, and her family had always been poor. When she was twelve, her father died of a heart attack. Her two teenage brothers took over the farm and eked out a meager living for their mother and four siblings. Her mother was in poor health, and Henrietta quit school in the eighth grade to help with the housework and the care of her two younger siblings. She continued in this role until her younger siblings became self-supporting. Then Henrietta chose the life she had always wanted and entered a community of teaching sisters. Because of her lack of formal education, she became a kitchen helper, later a cook, and finally the kitchen supervisor.

Henrietta had developed arthritis at age fifty-five and found it increasingly painful to do her work in the kitchen. Her physician recommended less strenuous work, and her superior placed her in parish ministry. This did not go well. Being in charge of the kitchen at the motherhouse gave Henrietta some prestige and authority as well as a certain respect within the community. The last stronghold of visible power in some communities lies in the domain of the kitchen, an area that everyone needs to rely on but no one wants to manage. Outside her own territory Henrietta felt unequal to others and very conscious of her lack of education. She knew that she possessed a good native intelligence, and she began to contemplate how life might have been had her community provided an education for her.

The workshop on growth intensified Henrietta's desire for a new career. Although her imagination stretched to fresh horizons and new beginnings, her age, her arthritis, her uneducated status, and financial limitations within her community reminded her in clarion tones that it was too late for her. Her spiritual director and her superior had encouraged her to take a sabbatical year to study in a renewal program. They implied that she might discover a career change as a result of this growth opportunity. During that year Henrietta obtained psychiatric care for her depression. Because she expressed dissatisfaction with the course her life had taken and because she resented her community for their part in her life's direction, for a time she doubted her fidelity to her vocation and considered herself unworthy of God's love. In treatment she came to terms with the deprivations of her past and accepted the reasons for them. She acknowledged the realities that limited her future in religious life and concluded that her disappointment with religious life did not detract from her spiritual values or weaken her relationship with God. She recognized that it was too late to start over, that she had traveled too far down the path to turn back, and that growth may occur in conceding to life's events as well as in struggling to change them. Her depression lifted, and she returned to her community to work part-time taking care of the special diets for the ill and the elderly.

Although popular articles propose a strict schedule for life events in adulthood, most evidence shows that adult periods of transition are becoming less well defined. Some marry early; others marry much later. Some go to college immediately following high school; others begin college in their fourth or fifth decade. Some enter religious life after high school (if the religious community will accept them then); others enter after college and a prior career involvement. The late vocation is no longer an anomaly in religious life. Persons in their twenties and thirties manage businesses and serve as executives, while others in their sixties study for graduate degrees. The life cycle has become more fluid and less fixed. The theory of clearly delineated periods in adult life comes from the blending of data to produce statistical averages. The adult escapes the normative boundaries more easily than does the infant or adolescent. At age five all normal children approach the same level of development within a time span of twelve to eighteen months. At age fifteen, the great majority of healthy adolescents approximate a developmental norm with a deviation of two or three years. The variation around a statistical norm increases for those at age thirty. At age sixty, one person may have slipped into old age, whereas another may have remained quite youthful. The variation around the norm increases in direct proportion to advancing years.

There is something artificial about the idea of seeking specific growth experiences. Life is an unfolding succession of years and experiences. To assume that growth occurs only with certain experiences, under specific conditions, and at particular times disposes an individual to overlook the enrichment that may come from an ordinary event in a casual moment. Persons who search for particular growth experiences are similar to the six-year-old who asks mother or father, "How do I grow up?" A parent cannot tell a child how to grow up, how to become an adult. It is a process of inner development and outer experience that permits and sometimes obliges a movement toward greater maturity. Adults who recognize, on the one hand, their own inability to explain to a child how to grow up, how to become mature, may, on the other hand, be first in line when the promoter of magic formulas for personal growth arrives at town hall.

The psychological themes of coping with stress, dealing with interpersonal relationships, setting priorities in life, and responding to conflicting demands recur throughout the periods of childhood, adolescence, adulthood, and senescence. The supporting players change; the stage setting varies; the lighting sharpens certain scenes; but the play runs endlessly. Individual growth does not depend on being the only player in center stage under full lighting. Growth occurs throughout a lifetime in a unique pattern as the special personality of the individual interacts with the particular experiences of his or her life.

Personal growth is a popular term that lacks precise definition. Religious comment to one another, "I need a personal growth experience. I'm stagnant," "I'm not able to grow in my community," "My community isn't growing," "My spiritual director says I'm not growing," "My superior hasn't grown since the day of election." Religious superiors advise uncompliant community members to take some time off for personal growth; in times past they more likely would have missioned them to some isolated area. Big business makes promotion contingent on personal growth. Married persons tell their spouses that they want a divorce because the spouse is not growing. Parents develop guilt because their children have inadequate growth experiences. Laws against discrimination may one day include not only race, sex, and creed but also level of personal growth. More and more people talk about personal growth—getting it or doing it or advising others to get it or do it. As a result, experts on personal growth have appeared throughout the country selling personal growth experiences like snake oil from the back of a covered wagon. One can legitimately ask the question, Did the demand create the product, or do the sellers of the product create the demand?

In this adult craze for growth experiences the question should be asked, What is meant by growth? Obviously it does not mean increasing one's height or weight or age. Does it mean becoming wiser or more mature or achieving greater inner peace? Or does it involve increasing the number and variety of experiences? Is it related to more education or a new career? Does it require new relationships or different patterns of relating? What are people looking for who are caught up in the pursuit of personal growth? Personal growth must have something to do with understanding oneself better. The ancient Greeks said, "Know thyself." They did not mean, "Get in touch with your feelings. Know where you're coming from. Know where you're at." They more likely believed that people should know themselves by understanding their abilities, their limitations, their imperfections, their strengths, and their weaknesses, and that people should know when to push themselves and how far, and when and how to rest, relax, recreate. This kind of growth in self-knowledge guides the individual to an understanding that brings stability and to an appreciation that brings peace. Personal growth takes place from within and not from without. It comes from expanding oneself, not from experiencing others. It occurs in stretching self to understand others, not in struggling with others for their understanding. Education does not produce growth, but insight does.

The story is told about a New England farmer who was encouraged by the county agent to attend the forthcoming meeting at the county seat. The farmer asked, "Why should I attend the meeting? What benefit will I get from attendance?" "Well, the meeting will teach you how to be a better farmer," replied the agent with enthusiasm. The farmer was thoughtful for a few moments and then commented, "Why should I learn how to be a better farmer when I'm not being as good a farmer as I know how to be now?" People search for growth experiences to help them be better people when they are not being as good as they already know how to be.

Personal growth does not result from getting in touch with one's feelings. The human-potential advocates bypass cognition and focus only on immediate sensory and affective experience. Their rallying cry is, "Don't think, feel. Lose your mind and come to your senses." Too often personal growth is equated with increased awareness of feelings, both tactile and emotional. Touch becomes the pre-eminent sensory modality simply because it is associated with the concept of feeling. Although the sensory experience of feeling with one's fingers is limited and cannot compare to the broad affective experience of emotional responsiveness, some experts in personal growth attempt to use experiences of touch to gain access to an individual's affective life.

Some human-potential experts will not only help the individual contact and clarify all immediate feelings but will also lead the individual back through all the unpleasant emotional events of the past in a process presumed to heal those painful memories and free the individual to grow, to move forward. The theoretical posture in this approach implies that negative emotions and painful memories prevent psychological growth and only positive or pleasant emotions enhance psychological and spiritual development. This theoretical position is not supported by the realities of emotional life. Distressing experiences can contribute to psychological maturation, and the unpleasant memories of those events may reinforce their earlier benefit. It is important to weave those experiences and those memories into the final fabric of a well-integrated life.

Feelings tell people very little about themselves. Feelings are primarily relational. They are responses to the world outside, to others. Individuals learn something about others through their affective responses to others. Feelings of fear indicate that others are threatening. Feelings of anger suggest that others are hostile. Feelings of love show that others are attractive. Feelings of sadness signify that others have moved away. Feelings involve people in life but do not direct that involvement. Feelings move people but do not guide them. Personal growth depends on decisions, directions, and choices, and therefore on thought and judgment. The random experience of kaleidoscopic feelings does not produce personal growth.

Occasionally a religious will express a need for a particular affective experience in order to promote personal growth. Often this experience is an affectionate relationship with a person of the opposite sex. Formation directors and spiritual directors sometimes support such a relationship as a growth experience. Some people defend the proposition that individual religious cannot develop fully without such an experience. They take this position even if the religious in question has experienced a close, loving relationship with parents, siblings, other relatives, and friends. If in fact a person has never experienced an affective relationship of this kind, then the emotional development of that individual is handicapped and entrance into religious life should be questioned. Loving relationships are necessary for an individual's psychosexual growth and maturation, but those affective experiences do not require a relationship between two adults based on erotic or romantic attraction. The only growth likely to occur when a person vowed to celibacy seeks the experience of a sensory and sentimental love is a growth of desire for more of these experiences.

The first area in which to grow is within oneself. Knowledge and understanding of self and of the experience of one's life come from thoughtful self-evaluation. Most individuals could probably spend a lifetime becoming as good as they already know how to be. Most people avoid the task by researching the techniques. Everyone already has criteria by which to measure growth. From their family background and early experience religious women and men have a definite picture of what it is to be a good person. As a result of their formation years they have a clear representation of what it is to be a good religious. During their years of training each has formed a reliable view of what it is to be a good educator, a good social worker, a good administrator, a good parish minister, a good professional whatever is the chosen field. These are the criteria by which they can evaluate their growth. To become a good human being, a good religious, a good professional takes a lifetime. Inner reflection about these goals produces new insights for improvement. By reading the self-help books, listening to the cure-all tapes, attending the growth-experience workshops, many individuals confound the issues and lose sight of their inner knowledge of themselves and of their goals. They learn new techniques that reputedly produce change, but they fail to change, because they forget the essentials of introspection, motivation, and will power. The religious who rushes to attend every available "growth event" might do well to contemplate the question, Am I now being as good a person, as good a religious, as I know how to be? If the answer is affirmative, then that individual has apparently reached a state in which no further growth is necessary. If the answer is negative, then that person can begin to strive for that goal without seeking some new enlightenment from others. Prayerful self-evaluation, continued contemplation of goals and shortcomings, and a renewal of dedication to virtuous living can produce motivation for change and strengthen the force of will to effect change. All the growth experiences in the world will not obviate the need for these internal processes.

Father Hal came to a psychiatrist because he felt that his life lacked growth experiences. At the time, he was attending a university-sponsored renewal program for religious. The faculty and the other participants frequently talked about personal growth, and guest lecturers came regularly to reinforce the human-potential aspect of the program. Hal had worked in parishes for the twelve years since his ordination, but his bishop had recently asked him to work in the marriage tribunal. Hal came to the renewal program seeking some intellectual stimulation and spiritual enhancement in preparation for this new ministry. However, as the months passed, he began to wonder about his maturity and competence, because everyone seemed to be saying that a person must find growth experiences in some explicit, organized fashion to become fully human and completely effective.

In a few sessions with the psychiatrist Hal discussed his family history, his psychosexual development, the evolution of his vocation, and his years in the priesthood. He seemed to be aware of his personality strengths and weaknesses. He knew that he had difficulty expressing anger, but he had successfully coped with a cantankerous pastor in one of the parishes to which he had been assigned. He was extremely lonely at times and found that he was more sexually aroused during these periods. On the one hand, he regarded his celibacy as "a gift God has given me," and he persevered in his vow. He discussed his fears of rejection by others and his reticence in revealing himself to others. On the other hand, he had a strong sense of reverence for people and generally got along well with others. Hal belonged to a support group of priests in his diocese and found this helpful. He regularly took one day off each week and enjoyed a variety of leisure activities. He set aside time for prayer and spiritual reading no matter how busy his schedule became. It was apparent to the psychiatrist that Hal did not need psychiatric care, but he did need reassurance that he was growing from within by striving in a realistic manner to be a productive person and a worthy priest.

One religious community of about seventy members experienced severe disharmony and turmoil for many years. They sought help from various outside professionals. They had lectures, workshops, consultations, visitations, seminars, and retreats in endless array. Each new expert that anyone discovered was invited to take a part in resolving the conflicts within this community. The community even developed new conflicts about which experts to invite and which ones to champion for a return visit. The experts included psychologists, social workers, educators, psychiatrists, growth facilitators, group leaders, and spiritual leaders with various backgrounds and credentials. So many experts visited over the years that if they had all been gathered in one room, they would have outnumbered the community. And if all the experts had gathered at one time, they would have agreed on a number of truisms about conflict resolution, truisms that had always been evident to the community members. Once they set forth the basic platitudes, the experts would probably have found some disagreement. In other words, the principles on which the experts would agree were already known to the community members, and the novel ideas or particular techniques would have been matters of controversy for the experts themselves. The most striking aspect of the situation was that each person in the community already knew how to be a better person, a better religious, and a better community member. They chose to see their conflict as a community task, and they searched for someone to make the task easy. By this approach they avoided the fact that each one had a personal task to be a better community member and to make the private sacrifices this task entailed.

Another very large religious community became enchanted by a certain kind of growth workshop. Those in authority gave strong support to community members who wished to attend these workshops. Over the course of a few years several community members began to give the workshops, at first for community members and later for the public. Because of official support and the aggressive attitude of workshop leaders, the popularity of the workshops became difficult to resist. The original workshop expanded into a series of workshops designed to produce growth in specific areas. Community members who attended the most workshops achieved a certain prestige within the community and a clear approbation from superiors. Those who defied the community trend and refused to become involved in the "growth movement" encountered considerable criticism from other community members for being uncharitable, unchristian, and opposed to building community. However, these growth workshops seemed to produce very little real growth. Members of the community continued to have the same conflicts within themselves, with other community members, and with those outside the community. Several religious who had participated in the workshops sought psychiatric help. There was no evidence that the workshops had produced useful insights or advanced the growth of any of them, and a few had found the experience disturbing and detrimental.

Sister Helen, one of the principal workshop facilitators, sought psychiatric assistance. Helen had been a grade school teacher and local superior for about twenty years. Several years previously her spiritual director had encouraged her to attend some of the growth workshops. When the classroom and administrative duties became burdensome for Helen, she decided that she would like to become a facilitator for the growth workshops in her community. She did so by her own fiat. She needed no further training than the few workshops she had attended. No credentials were required. There was no one to question how well prepared she was, to evaluate her abilities, to supervise her work, or to judge her competence. Helen created a new career for herself.

In their first meeting, it became obvious to the psychiatrist that Helen was incompetent in her work and that this kind of work contributed to her emotional turmoil. She had had a chaotic childhood. Her parents quarreled frequently and violently. Her mother was a severe alcoholic; and in drunken rages was abusive to Helen and her four siblings. The family members never discussed the mother's alcoholism even after her death from cirrhosis when Helen was only seventeen. On the day of Helen's graduation from eighth grade her mother arrived in a drunken state and embarrassed everyone. In reviewing her early years with her mother, Helen remarked, "She ruined my life." In discussing her adult years, she commented, "Emotional messiness disturbs me greatly." For several years Helen had been trying to use the workshop principles to enhance her personal growth. She admitted that her career as a workshop facilitator was motivated by her own needs and not by a dedication to the work or a desire to help others. She said, "The need to be perfect is always with me. I have to look good all the time. I can't make mistakes." Her role of facilitator gave her a sense of psychological superiority, a position of apparent perfection from which she looked down on others. With considerable candor she acknowledged that she "became hostile" toward some of those who attended her workshops, that she often "overreacted," and that she was "not sensitive to the feelings of others."

Her spiritual director, who had originally advised attendance at the growth workshops, was now recommending psychiatric care. A psychologically more astute director would have recommended psychotherapy in the first place. At this point Helen refused to continue in treatment and gave the excuse that it would jeopardize her status as a workshop facilitator. The true reason for refusing psychotherapy was probably Helen's awareness that a review of her life would lead to an examination of her own inadequacies and finally to a self-evaluation that she was incompetent in her chosen career. She could not start the journey, because she knew where it would take her. She continued to provide growth workshops for religious and laity for many years. The techniques of personal growth that she taught were not sufficient to bring about growth in Helen. Her work brought continuing acclaim from those who responded with brief exhilaration to the idea that change can happen without personal struggle or deep understanding. Others, however, responded to Helen's insensitivity and underlying hostility and quickly denounced her. She became a controversial figure in her own community and in the city where she worked, although her superiors continued to sanction her work and attest to her effectiveness. One can speculate that Helen's involvement in the workshops kept her from seeking the help she truly needed; one can further speculate that others were defrauded of genuine growth for the same reason.

A career change can be an opportunity for growth in terms of experience, education, or professional status. Of itself, however, such a change does not produce personal growth. Yet, religious sometimes promote a career change as an answer to their own growth needs. Becoming better at what one does brings more internal growth than transferring one's interest and talents to another field. Those who seem to plod along at one life's work, honing the tools of their trade or profession, studying their productions with an eye toward improvement, strengthening their best skills and purifying their worst, those individuals may not be exciting or stimulating for others, but they come to a depth of understanding and a richness of life that is inspiring. They have ripened from within and demonstrate a wholesome maturity. Others, who have difficulty taking root, who pursue external change with the expectation of internal transformation, who doubt their own abilities before they fully develop them, these individuals are likely to find that aging brings withered hopes and empty dreams.

Growth in self-knowledge and self-perfection produces a stability from which one can reach out to others. The deeper a person grows internally the further he or she can extend self to someone else. The tree that has extensive and healthy roots supports widely spread branches. The more content people are with their own life-picture the more content they will be to view others kindly. Everyone has psychological bruises, scars, wounds. Individuals can search these out and expose them with all their affective attachments. Indeed, this sometimes must be done in a treatment situation. It is not enough to believe that these psychic traumas are significant elements in "who we are" or in "where we are coming from." Individuals who may need to look at these traumas also need to leave them behind. They must be relinquished in order for growth to occur. They may be brought to the surface, but they must be buried again with the past. Anger, hurt, hatred, revenge tie people to the past and separate them from others. Love, hope, enthusiasm, joy link people to the future and bind people to others, who become more important than themselves.

As a person grows more deeply within, he or she becomes capable of growing more deeply outside of self in love for others. Growth can occur every day in areas where growth is ever possible: a kinder response to another, a small surrender of one's own will, better preparation for the work of the day, return to a neglected task, an enhanced celebration of leisure, a study of one's failures to be as good a person as one knows how to be. The religious who seeks continuing personal growth in some external experience should instead ask, How can I judge my superior less harshly, react to others in community more generously, perform my tasks more faithfully, view my imperfections more gently, love others less selfishly?

Personal growth is a popular but often misunderstood concept among religious today. It suggests that external experiences such as educational opportunities, growth seminars, interpersonal relationships, or career changes automatically produce positive psychological changes. Growth becomes falsely associated with something new, something different, and something that stimulates affective responses. In reality, personal growth primarily involves internal response and intellectual conviction. For the most part, feelings respond to the external world and are shaped by that world, but judgment and decision partially shape that external world and are the basis for personal growth. Growth requires regular self-evaluation and continuing endeavor to measure up to already-known standards of goodness, gentleness, and responsible living. Growth does not come from an accumulation of experiences of life but rather from an acceptance of one's life experience. It may necessitate some private concessions of will and some public admissions of error. It may demand that past traumas of injustice and injury be left behind and that present and future conflicts of loss and aging be faced more realistically.

•

10. Problems Involving Loss and Aging

The importance of emotional loss depends not so much on the magnitude of the loss as it does on the attitude of the one who suffers the loss. The loss of one dollar means nothing to the millionaire unless he or she is also a miser. The loss of one dollar to an eight-year-old is catastrophic unless the eight-year-old has no appreciation of its value. Attachment provides the foundation for emotional loss, and the significance of the loss relates directly to the intensity of the attachment. The miserly millionaire may be as attached to each dollar as the eight-year-old is. Both may experience the loss with the same force, even though their losses are not of the same relative magnitude. The millionaire may find no consolation in abundant residual funds to alleviate that sense of loss. The eight-year-old may wonder for years where that dollar went and secretly expect it to be found and reclaimed.

Religious who leave everything to follow Jesus, as the young man in the gospel was invited to do, sometimes wonder at their own inability to accept loss. They try heroically to entrust the course of everything to Jesus whom they follow, but the force of their affection for creatures and things disturbs them. They fail to understand that detachment is not the same as lack of attachment. Attachment binds individuals to other persons or objects in a manner that makes those others emotionally meaningful. Detachment requires individuals to accept separation from others even though they remain very attached to those from whom they are separated. A newlywed may accept separation from family and friends to accompany the spouse to another area. The separation may be accepted willingly but sadly, and there is no decrease in attachment because the separation occurred. The experience of detachment does, however, cause a sense of loss. On the other hand, if the newlywed had no emotional ties with family members, then the move to a distant place would involve only physical separation from family but not detachment and thus no sense of loss. Detachment implies attachment. The experience of loss does not come out of indifference.

Religious sometimes fret because their spirit of detachment does not eliminate their sense of loss. In fact, if there were no emotional loss, there would be no basis for detachment. Religious sometimes deny their feelings of loss, because grieving over the loss of creatures seems to contradict their commitment to the Creator. They reason that by their choice to become religious they have accepted God as completely sufficient for them, and therefore any person or thing should not assume enough importance to cause them grief in the loss. They think that they violate their fidelity to God if grief makes them want to say, "I cannot go on living without my friend or my parent. I do not want to go on living without that person."

Some religious find a basic inconsistency in grieving too much. Their faith is not tested by their loss, but it is threatened by their need to grieve. The depth and force of their feelings of grief seem to separate them from the vitality and power of their faith. In reality, these forces are not contradictory to each other or incompatible with each other. Since human beings function at different levels simultaneously, they may experience feelings at one level that seem inconsistent with beliefs at another level. Feelings and faith do not need to be reconciled in their view of the same life event, because they operate with different response systems. But conflict necessarily results if feelings and faith are accepted as sources of equally valid conclusions coming from the same response mechanism. Feelings of inconsolable grief cannot weaken faith as long as they are recognized as feelings about a loss and not viewed as intellectual ground for determining the existence of a loving God. Nor can faith prevent feelings of grief over loss, unless faith deteriorates to nothing more than a series of platitudes to assuage the pain of life but with no intellectual assurance of reward in a better life to come. Faith and feeling may not always be in harmony, but their discord is part of the music of life.

Life as a religious does not decrease the number of losses a person is likely to experience, nor does it lessen their impact. Emotionally healthy religious have as many attachments to other people and to objects as laypeople have. However, the lifestyle of religious often requires them to practice detachment in regard to the subjects of their affection more frequently than laypeople are required to do. Religious life seems to demand a special capacity for detachment. The sacrifice made by the religious novice in leaving family and friends involves heartaches but rarely causes prolonged grief, because the separation is freely chosen. Anticipation of a loss and preparation for it tend to mitigate the strength of its effect; the process of detachment is less difficult when the separation and consequent loss were initiated voluntarily. Persons who have experienced a number of losses in their lives, losses that were apparently accepted uneventfully, may be overwhelmed by the addition of one more loss, particularly if it occurs without warning, without preparation, and with no element of personal choice.

Sister Ingrid sacrificed family, friends, and native land to enter religious life. In the novitiate she experienced homesickness and loneliness for a few members of her family. She gave generously of herself in her initial sacrifice, and she continued through the years as a nurse to give generously to those whom she cared for and to the members of her community. She seemed not to count the cost in all that she did and all that she gave. She never complained and rarely expressed any of her own needs. At work Ingrid met a divorced woman who gradually became her closest friend. About four years after the friendship developed Ingrid was transferred to work in a rural area. She and her friend exchanged frequent letters and occasional phone calls. Since Ingrid was financially unable to return to visit her friend, the latter came to see her on a couple of occasions. During the last visit her friend seemed unusually affectionate at first. She found an excuse to kiss Ingrid on the mouth three or four times and embraced her with surprising warmth. At the time Ingrid instinctively withdrew from this physical closeness. Then her friend became distant and preoccupied. By the time she left, her manner toward Ingrid was extremely cool. Ingrid wrote to her friend shortly after the visit but received no reply. Then she telephoned. It was obvious to Ingrid that something was wrong, but her friend would not discuss it and indicated that additional phone calls would not be welcome. The friendship had undoubtedly ended, but Ingrid had no idea why. She was devastated by this sudden change in her friend, and she became morose.

The other seven members of Ingrid's community were neither understanding nor supportive. Possibly they resented her close friendship with someone outside the community. Their attitude was, "Snap out of it. Pull yourself together. Don't take it so hard." Ingrid became increasingly despondent. She slept poorly and lost weight. She developed a severe dermatitis. She wept without provocation. She withdrew socially from the community. The others complained to the provincial about Ingrid's lack of community participation. When the provincial tried to talk to her, Ingrid expressed irritation at the provincial's interference and at the behavior of her companions in reporting to the provincial. Ingrid's work deteriorated in spite of her efforts to maintain high quality performance as a nurse. She developed severe gastrointestinal symptoms, and the doctor indicated that they were due to her emotional state. Her provincial ordered her to obtain psychiatric care.

Therapy revolved around the concept of loss. After Ingrid was born, her mother was ill at home for about two years. During that time the paternal grandparents lived in the home and took care of Ingrid, her two older brothers, her father, and her sick mother. During the first two years of her life Ingrid had little contact with her mother but became very attached to her grandmother. After the mother recovered from her lengthy illness, she gave birth to another girl. The mother gave all her attention to the new baby and remained uninterested in Ingrid. The mother continued to favor the younger daughter and the older of her two sons. After she regained her health, she again showed herself to be a strong-willed, querulous woman who let everyone know her likes and dislikes.

When Ingrid was four, the paternal grandparents left the home and moved to their own house a few miles away. Ingrid felt abandoned because of this, and occasional visits to them did not adequately console her. When Ingrid was eight, the paternal grandfather with whom she had had an affectionate relationship died. She remembered missing him greatly after his death. Because of her grandfather's death, Ingrid stayed with her grandmother intermittently from age eight to age fourteen. She preferred being at her grandmother's house. As she discussed this part of her life in treatment, she commented, "My mother never liked me." Her mother never showed Ingrid any signs of physical affection but was excessively affectionate toward her sister and the older brother. At a small family gathering when Ingrid was fourteen, she overheard her grandmother say to the other relatives, "All the children will be successful except Ingrid, who is just a good worker." Ingrid fought back tears so no one would know that she had heard, and she sat in sadness for hours thinking about what her grandmother had done. She never went to stay with her grandmother again and never shared a private thought with her after that.

Ingrid's father was fond of her, and she loved him, although they were not close. Her father and mother fought bitterly most of the time, sometimes because of his drinking but mostly, Ingrid decided, because her mother wanted to dominate him. She could not recall that her father ever won an argument. Secretly Ingrid took his side. Her mother probably sensed her allegiance and rejected her even more strongly. Ingrid knew that she could not depend on her father, because her mother controlled him. Ingrid dated at age seventeen and eighteen. She liked one young man but broke off their developing relationship because "I didn't want someone to turn his back on me again."

Ingrid summed up her childhood and adolescence by saying, "I had to learn to get along on my own because there was no one to turn to." The physical and emotional separation from her mother, the feeling of abandonment when her grandparents moved, the death of her grandfather, and the emotional betrayal by her grandmother caused Ingrid intense suffering. Throughout those years her father never provided Ingrid with a dependable relationship. Ingrid had incurred a series of momentous losses during her developmental years, and she carried the unsettling aftermath of those losses into her adult life. When as an adult she formed her first close relationship with the divorced woman, the latter turned against her without apparent provocation and without any reason that Ingrid could understand. For a time there had been someone "to turn to," but then suddenly that someone "turned her back on me again." This event recalled all her previous losses and was emotionally devastating. Her community intensified her grief because they too turned their backs on her. The thunderous echoes of abandonment, rejection, betrayal, isolation came crashing down around her. All the losses of her past reawakened and reverberated with their original violence because she had never consciously acknowledged the outrage of those years, the turbulence they had caused her, or the fury she had felt.

Initially in psychotherapy Ingrid wept a great deal but only at home by herself, not during the therapy sessions. She would not expose her grief to the therapist, because he might turn away from her. She dreamed about her friend; she composed unmailed letters to her; she constructed in her mind conversations between the two of them. She was like a child pounding on the door of her home, begging to be let in, with no one answering her cries. Symbolically the therapist took her by the hand and walked back with her through the empty house of her childhood, to examine her mother's behavior, to review the relationship with her grandmother, to watch the struggles of her father. She came to terms with the reality of her emotional deprivation as she relived those experiences and bit by bit extricated herself from their destructive impact. She realized that her emotional needs had been lost in the unfolding course of others' lives. She grieved more openly during treatment sessions and in her tears absolved those who had neglected her. After this was accomplished, she examined the relationship with her recent friend and accepted the friend's freedom to change her mind. She continued to view the loss of her friend as a painful experience and one that she could not completely understand, but the desperation and denial that had characterized her reactions to the loss were gone.

Loss accumulates during a person's life, and each new loss retraces the pathway made by prior losses. The loss of a parent during early adolescent years represents one of the most enduring privations that a person can experience. This loss seems to create a pool of sorrow that tears can never drain. Ignatius, a priest for ten years, found himself immersed in depression during the snowy winter months in his parish in the Northeast. His winter depression precipitated excessive use of alcohol, and the latter released sexual inhibitions. During treatment he discussed the sudden death of his father when Ignatius was twelve years old. As he walked home from school one December day, he saw an ambulance at his house. His father had come home in mid-afternoon not feeling well. He had become more ill in the next two hours, and his wife had called for the ambulance. By the time it arrived, he was unconscious, and he died of a cerebral hemorrhage in the hospital that evening. Ignatius vividly recalled his father's funeral. He remembered distinctly the sound of the crisp snow crunching under the feet of the pallbearers. For weeks after the funeral the widow and her three children walked to Mass each morning to pray for their spouse and father. Each morning the snow crunched beneath their feet with that awful muffled thud that sounded to Ignatius like the beat of death. As treatment continued, Ignatius recognized the lasting imprint of sorrow that his father's death had made on his life. His life in a religious order made him lonely and intensified his sadness. His homosexual lapses only deepened his isolation. After prayerful consideration and appropriate consultations, Ignatius left the priesthood and later married. He became better able to cope with an adolescent loss that would never leave him, but the winter snows no longer covered him with depression.

Religious confront the same kinds of loss that laypeople encounter. Loss of position, loss of prestige, loss of power, loss of efficiency, loss of vigor, all of these can be important to religious. A change of assignment sometimes causes serious loss for religious. Transfer from one location to another may mean separation from important friends either within the community or outside it. One of the hardships in contemporary life is the mobility of society. A large percentage of families move every two or three years. They usually talk freely about changing jobs, leaving their neighborhood, packing their belongings, and selling their home. They are less likely to discuss openly the loss they experience in separating from their close friends and familiar surroundings. However, when a family moves, they have each other, and some families say that frequent moves have brought them closer together. Religious typically move as individuals, not as groups or with companions. No matter how resigned they are to the will of God and the requirements of the community apostolate, there is emotional loss in transfers that disrupt emotional attachments. If religious could openly discuss their feelings of loss, the process of emotional separation and detachment would take place more smoothly and more stably. But it is often difficult for them to admit these feelings to themselves, and it is even more difficult to mention them to others. They fear that the superior might interpret their comments as opposition. Community members in the old assignment may construe any complaints as subversive to authority. Community members in the new assignment may understand these feelings of loss as antagonism toward them. Laypersons might regard expressions of grief over a transfer as unbecoming for a religious. As a result, religious often suppress these feelings, and the reservoir of loss fills with sadness.

Even though a different assignment does not always include a change of residence, it normally requires a period of emotional readjustment. A change in work may be as simple as a transfer from one school to another or only from one classroom to another and involve teaching other subjects. Recently, changes in assignment have become more complex for religious and often involve different kinds of work. An individual religious may be transferred from parish work to teaching, from retreat work to campus ministry, or from social work to spiritual direction. In contemporary communities, the religious superior rarely makes these decisions unilaterally. Dialogue and discernment assure the individual religious of participation in the decision-making process; however, no matter how fully the individual participates in the decision or how willingly he or she accepts the change, there is a feeling of separation in such reassignments. One invests a part of self in work accomplished, in associations at work, and in people who are served. Therefore, in leaving an assignment one leaves behind something of self and experiences a sense of loss.

There may be a loss of prestige or position. School administrators do not remain school administrators. Religious superiors, with some few exceptions, are not elected for life. Even pastors have lost some rights of tenure. Because of changing apostolates and fewer personnel, religious communities have withdrawn from some institutions, and as a result many religious have lost positions of authority. Schools have closed. Hospitals have been taken over by large corporations. Lay faculty compete with religious in Catholic colleges and universities. Departments of religious studies and schools of theology are no longer the unchallenged domain of religious. Although religious communities in many cases initiated these changes, the changes have nonetheless brought a grave sense of loss to many individual religious and to some whole communities of religious.

Different individuals within the same community may manifest one or another stage of the grieving process. Some exhibit the stage of denial, disbelief in the community decision and direction, and they refuse to accept the community changes that starkly confront them. Others experiencing anger and resentment are harshly vocal in their objections to the changes or sulk in the quiet wrath of obstructionism. Others appear despondent about the changes and seem unable to find the energy or motivation to contribute in any constructive manner to new community endeavors. These components of grieving overshadow some communities and seem to drain their vitality. Disbelief and despair, rage and rebellion echo throughout these communities. Slowly the process of healing begins, and patches of resolution gradually appear. Increasing numbers of religious, each in his or her unique way, progressively are able to appreciate the social and cultural changes that make adaptation on the part of religious communities necessary. This understanding brings about a resolution of emotional conflict, so that personal choices can be set aside for community goals and societal needs. After this psychological acceptance has occurred, statements about the will of God and the needs of the people of God become meaningful and motivational.

There is another way in which religious avoid their emotional reactions, especially in the area of loss. They have encountered the pain of loss as they separated from family and friends to enter religious life and as they moved from place to place within religious life, leaving friends, unfinished tasks, and sometimes personal items behind them. It is not uncommon for a fifty- or sixty-year-old religious not to have lived longer than four or five years in any one place since leaving home at age eighteen. In order not to continue experiencing the pain of separation, some religious become emotionally aloof, although they remain superficially friendly. Their affability makes

them attractive to others, who move to establish warm, genuine, and enduring relationships. Then one day the hospital
board meets, and the religious member is absent. A brief
announcement of assignment in another city is all there is. The
parish bulletin brings the first news that the pastor of five
years has been transferred to another parish and has already
departed. In some instances the religious who is parish coordinator, hospital pastoral care worker, administrator, teacher,
nurse walks away with no good-byes, with no indication that
others have been left behind, with no apparent regret. A feeling of emptiness settles over those who remain. That emptiness can gradually be filled, but the emptiness that goes with
the departing religious becomes greater with each additional
departure. Religious who have difficulty saying farewell have
problems dealing with loss.

Religious sometimes dedicate themselves to a cause or a
project that takes on great personal importance. Sister Irene,
a college professor, had done some scholarly writing and had
received considerable recognition for her accomplishments.
Rather suddenly, she became depressed and sought psychiatric
assistance. One of the reasons for her depression was her
concern that a book she had written several years before was
going out of print. Even though there was no longer a market
for the book, she tried desperately to persuade the publisher
to keep the book in print. She considered this book to be her
best work. She commented, "I feel as though I am watching
my child die." Just before coming for treatment she celebrated
her sixtieth birthday—or, rather, endured it.

Irene was experiencing a mid-life crisis. She discovered that
she was looking at the downhill slope of life, counting not the
years she had lived but the years she had yet to live. She
began to doubt her ability to accomplish the amount or quality
of work she had produced in the past. Through treatment, she
was able to put into words her doubts about herself and her
uncertainties about the future. She was able to acknowledge
the losses that had occurred and that would occur, but she

learned to accept them and to circumscribe them with the positive realities of the rest of her life.

Religious sometimes suffer the loss of their idealism. This may occur so subtly that they are unaware it is happening. The investment of self in relationships that promise great returns but end in emptiness, in work that demands high dedication but provides no fulfillment, in causes that slip from faultless levels to baser planes, this kind of self-investment slowly brings disillusionment and ultimately loss of idealism. Improvident belief in one person or groundless optimism about one subject can shatter idealism. The loss of idealism is not the same as emotional or physical fatigue, although they may appear to be identical. Physical fatigue and emotional exhaustion leave intact the value system of the individual. Loss of idealism involves a collapse of that system. When ideals are gone, the integrity of the individual is easily compromised. This loss is like the loss of innocence. The person can go on but can never return. Some lose not only their idealism but also their memory of it as a desirable approach to life. Others experience a continuing sadness, a nostalgic remembrance of greener fields and brighter mornings that have disappeared forever. Psychiatrists who work with married couples hear them describe behaviors that wore away at their initial gift of self and gradually eroded the fabric of love that held them closely together. Married persons should preserve the idealism of their married commitment against the seduction of other relationships and other involvements. Similarly, religious should not allow relationships with others or involvements in routine work or in great causes to obscure the vision of their commitment as religious. The loss of idealism is an irretrievable loss.

The process of aging brings people face to face with irreversible loss and confronts them with the inevitability of death. Aging probably causes as many conflicts for religious as it does for laypersons. As individuals become aware of decreased energy, diminished vigor, failing physical stamina and health, they fully realize that they too are finite. Failing eyesight, impaired hearing, stiff joints, flabby muscles, wrinkled skin remind them, unkindly at times, that the world must prepare to go on without them. The work orientation among religious assigns a greater value to those who are productive members of the community. They esteem activity so highly that inactivity produces a sense of guilt. Aging community members cling tenaciously to previously assigned tasks, stubbornly refusing to acknowledge that those duties now exceed their capability or endurance.

Many religious do not accept retirement gracefully but construe it as a declaration of their uselessness. Retirement programs for elderly religious will never be successful until religious become convinced that they have a right to retire. Religious communities often exhibit unrealistic attitudes toward their aging members, attitudes that suggest that those who labor in the vineyard of the Lord do not grow weak or tired or old. In recent years some communities have adopted retirement programs and have shown interest in preparing their members for retirement years. However, the common practice of the past continues in most communities, whereby religious are expected to work until they are released by the injunction of illness, the impairment of senility, or the disengagement of death.

It is emotionally debilitating to witness the weakening and to attend the dying of those who have been important in a person's life. The aging and the dying of community members causes strong emotional reactions in those who stand by during the process. In talking to a psychiatrist one seventy-five-year-old sister described her uncomfortable feelings as she watched a former provincial of the community play with dolls outside her bedroom door in the infirmary. Religious communities frequently maintain their senile, their incurably ill, and their terminally ill within the community setting. This laudable practice causes feelings in community members that they have difficulty acknowledging or expressing. The care of these individuals is burdensome, no matter how willingly it is accepted. To acknowledge to oneself and sometimes to others the strain of such responsibility is healthier than to pretend that it is a joyous task. The care givers may see the role as a blessing, but it can be an exhausting one. To view it as hard and unpleasant work, emotionally taxing, sometimes frustrating, and often unrewarding, does not lessen the virtue of the work or the value of the blessing. It is not unusual for a psychiatrist to be asked to see in consultation a person who has been hospitalized because of emotional and physical collapse after the lengthy ordeal of caring for a dying spouse, parent, or child. The emotional and physical demands of such care are often overwhelming, but the care givers may deny the burden until they reach the point of exhaustion. Those who care for others during prolonged or terminal illnesses should be encouraged to acknowledge their negative feelings and should take positive steps to compensate for the emotional and physical strain they undergo.

Sometimes religious communities excessively ritualize dying and death. Community members, and at times even visitors, file through the terminally ill patient's room in a kind of predeath viewing. An obsessive quality appears in the meticulous recounting of details of the sick person's previous night. A morbid preoccupation surrounds each word of the doctor or the nurse and each utterance or movement of the patient. Community functions take on an atmosphere of expectation. The routines of daily living continue but seem to be detached from the overpowering reality of imminent death. There is a need to predict the moment of death so that the superior can be present. There is an expectation that the dying person will give some last word of extreme significance. Do they await a word of reassurance, a sign of forgiveness, a statement of faith, or an indication of love? This intense absorption in the process serves to distract from the outcome. This behavior is similar to that of the worried mother who keeps cleaning her child's room and making her child's favorite dishes while the child lies dying in the hospital. By becoming engrossed in the process, by concentrating on the details, by busying oneself with the unimportant, a person can minimize the importance of an event and postpone or even avoid its emotional impact.

It is quite possible that many religious respond to the process of dying with increased activity and endless absorption in details in order to avoid the fact of death. Everyone has strong feelings about death, and those feelings are intensified by the death of others. Feelings of fear, of doubt, of mystery, of abandonment, of guilt, of anger, of loss, feelings of all kinds encircle the reality of death. Strong faith, a virtuous life, and a sense of completion can contribute to a peaceful death and to the anticipation of a peaceful death. However, these intellectual convictions do not shield most individuals from a wide range of emotional responses in the presence of death. Religious do not violate their spiritual convictions if they fear death any more than they abandon their faith if they feel pain. Life entails a series of losses, death the last; and loss stirs the emotional responses of anger, resentment, denial, fear, and a sense of abandonment. A person may intellectually believe there is gain in dying, but emotionally loss stands stark and final.

Religious experience a gamut of emotional losses that begin when they leave family and friends to enter religious life and end when they leave this world to enter eternity. They encounter loss in the closure of community institutions and apostolates, in the loss of position and prestige, in changes of assignment, in the failure or completion of projects, in the death of relatives and friends, and in their own aging and dying. The intensity of their grief depends on the degree of their attachment to those persons, places, and positions that become the source of their loss. It is important that they allow themselves to mourn these events in their lives and not view their emotional impact as indicative of a lack of faith. Although they may practice spiritual abandonment and intellectual acceptance, their emotional reactions to these losses are likely to follow the normal patterns of denial, anger, and despair before coming to resolution. The experiences of loss accumulate throughout life, and some religious learn to defend themselves against these experiences by abandoning their attachment to others. However, this psychological maneuver separates them from the supportive relationships that friends and relatives can provide.

11. Relationships with Relatives

Most religious communities, in evaluating the fitness of a candidate, consider a good family background to be an important element. They prefer applicants from stable families that are not only free of psychopathology and aberrant behavior patterns but that also demonstrate high ethical and religious principles and provide a warm and supportive relationship to their members. Such families offer a secure beginning for their offspring and provide a sound base for their development into healthy adults.

Family environment provides the ground for psychological development in the formative years from birth to late adolescence. The maturation that occurs during that period of time establishes deeply entrenched attitudes, fixed patterns of behavior, and permanent personality characteristics. The modification of these attitudes, patterns, and characteristics in adult life is a difficult task and is seldom accomplished without the application of some powerful and persuasive force. Psychotherapy aims toward that very undertaking. However, it is not the only means to adult change; the corrective experiences of life also motivate adults to reshape those responses that they learned early in life. These corrective experiences involve highly significant persons or events that prompt the individual to reevaluate an attitude or response pattern, to recognize its ineffectiveness or its offensiveness, and as a result to make a change.

The intimacy of courtship and the entwining of marriage provide corrective experiences. Attachment to and involvement with offspring cause modifications in long-standing attitudes and behaviors. In family life the realistic responsibility of providing for others and the consequent necessity for accommodating to life's demands often impose personal changes. Religious have no exposure to these sources of psychological influence. As a result, these experiences that are often powerful and personal enough to effect permanent alteration in psychological responses are absent in the lives of religious. Because experiences of religious life are less likely to modify early family influences, it is important that the family background of the religious be a stable and supportive one. For the most part, the psychic structure that the novice brings to religious life establishes the psychological attitudes, the response patterns, and the behavioral characteristics that will continue throughout her or his religious life.

Religious communities do unknowingly accept candidates with troubled family backgrounds. Such families often conceal their pathology from the scrutiny of community questions or investigations. Committees or individuals who are responsible for the acceptance of candidates usually take people at their word. They neither search for hidden facts nor suspect duplicity. They ask questions and assume that the candidate and other informants give straightforward answers. Even when a religious community is willing to accept some candidates from disturbed families, it is nevertheless advantageous for those who do the formation work to know about that background. Such knowledge gives them a broader base for understanding and better insight for guiding the novice. However, the religious community does not always adequately investigate a candidate's family background. Perhaps those in authority hesitate to pry. Because their position as religious supports the sanctity of the family unit, they respect the privacy of family relationships. They may be reluctant to probe too deeply because they are uncertain about the significance of the information they might obtain. It may be more comfortable not to have information than to have it and be uncertain about what to do with it. Their lack of information may also result from not knowing what kind of information might be helpful and from not having the expertise to obtain it. Number of siblings, age and religious preference of parents, and physical health of family members tell nothing about family interaction. Questions about how decisions were made, what family gatherings were like, what happened on vacations produce considerable insight into family dynamics.

Candidates and their families may not strive deliberately to deceive the religious authorities: Families do not habitually reveal their secrets to strangers. They usually try to conceal them even from friends. Sometimes they practice concealment so well that they conceal even from themselves the disintegration that surrounds them. In a psychiatrist's office a married person may initially speak of his or her marriage as a perfect union and later come to recognize and finally admit that it has serious shortcomings. A teenage patient may at first insist that life is pleasant and productive and later uncover deep feelings of helplessness and despair.

Sister Joanna had been in community five years when she began therapy. She complained of suffering severe insomnia for the previous four months, and, although she thought her insomnia was stress-related, she was unaware of any source of tension in her life. Joanna was a full-time student and lived in a house of studies, where she got along well with the other eight sisters. She kept in close contact with her family, writing letters at least once a week and telephoning once or twice a month. Both her parents were Catholic, and both supported her religious vocation. Her father spent several hours each week in parish work and was highly respected in the community. Her one younger sister lived away from home, and her one younger brother still lived with her parents. Joanna had completed two years of junior college before entering religious life. She had dated occasionally in high school and more regularly in college but had never formed any close attachments.

Initially during interviews Joanna described her home life in positive terms. Her parents got along well together, although they had, as she put it, "the usual marital squabbles." She described her father as "a very religious man but quite strict." She described her mother as "a saintly woman, always giving of herself to her children and to others." Her brother still at home had "the usual adolescent problems," and her sister was "working and doing well on her own." Her therapist was not satisfied that these brief descriptions gave an adequate account of family relationships. After the therapeutic alliance became stronger, the therapist began to pry open the storehouse of family secrets. The picture unfolded slowly, and at times Joanna seemed startled by what she saw. It was as if she knew things that she had refused to acknowledge. Her father behaved like an absolute tyrant in the home. He had been verbally and physically abusive to his wife throughout their married life. Joanna had witnessed some of that abuse and had seen him severely punish her younger sister. Joanna grew up in fear and submission. She tried never to cross her father or mother. On one occasion at the age of seventeen she disagreed with her father. He struck her with his fist, and she went to school with a black eye and a fabricated story about how it had happened. Her fifteen-year-old brother was in bitter conflict with his parents and was exhibiting some very delinquent behavior. Her twenty-three-year-old sister had been alienated from her parents since she was twenty-one, when she left home to live in an apartment with two girlfriends. Her parents believed that she should live at home until she married.

Joanna's mother devoted herself to her children, and she expected their devotion in return. She took good care of them as they grew up. She cooked whatever they liked; she nursed them when they were ill; she kept their clothes clean and in good repair. She never asked them to do anything around the house, and on the rare occasion when they did help with the work, what they did was never good enough, and she would do it over. Mother shopped with the three children and chose all their clothes for them. She told them what to wear every day of the year throughout grade school and high school. She was a perfectionist and expected perfection from her children.

She often reminded them that she stayed with their father only for their sake. Joanna felt too guilty ever to be angry at her mother and too frightened ever to be angry at her father.

Joanna was poorly equipped emotionally for the close contacts of community living. She could not recognize her own angry feelings and became completely unnerved by the anger of others. If anyone in her community seemed annoyed or unhappy, Joanna felt guilty and was compelled to try to discover the cause and correct it. She had difficulty making decisions without prior approval from everyone. She tried to do the right thing all the time. A lengthy period of psychotherapy enabled Joanna to separate herself from the distorting experiences of her early life. In this process of growth she necessarily established independence from her parents, which they failed to appreciate. Joanna had suppressed the painful experiences of her early years in order to preserve a relationship with her parents; had she openly acknowledged her mother's domination and her father's brutality, she would have needed to escape as her sister had done and as her brother was about to do. Joanna had not deliberately deceived her community when she presented herself as a well-balanced young woman from a stable family. However, her choice of the religious life may have been the escape from family that she unconsciously sought.

Although in theory religious leave family to follow Jesus, the character of their family relationships follows them into religious life. Entrance into religious life no longer requires forsaking family ties but seems still to require a purification of family connections. Religious communities have unspoken norms for relationships between community members and their families. These norms require the individual religious to be devoted to his or her parents, who in turn are expected to be emotionally supportive, devout, well-balanced, and generous people. These norms require the individual religious to have deep affection for siblings, who in turn are expected to be understanding and upright, good parents, and devoted to their children. Religious communities place a premium on dedication to aging parents or troubled siblings. A few decades ago, religious associated virtue with restricted visits to family. Now there appears to be an attitude of reverence toward those community members who visit their families most frequently. Expressions of concern for the welfare of family members permeate the casual conversation and dominate the collective prayer in many communities. The significance attached to good family backgrounds and healthy family relationships creates problems for those religious who cannot boast such origins or demonstrate such contacts. Some religious are more frightened of their parents than concerned about them; they are more embarrassed than pleased by visits from their families; they are filled with hostile feelings toward relatives, making it difficult to pray for them.

During his psychotherapy, Jerry, a seminarian, discussed a recent three-day visit from his mother. She behaved in her typically seductive fashion toward two of his classmates and at the same time treated him like a little boy. Although he felt humiliated and extremely angry, he was unable to confront his mother regarding either facet of her behavior. He could discuss neither his feelings nor his mother's behavior with his friends. He maintained an appearance of calm but raged internally. Jerry gradually recognized that his mother had behaved like this as far back as he could remember, charming his friends and treating him in a condescending manner. This realization provided the impetus for him to tell his mother not to visit for a while. After several more weeks of therapy, Jerry talked frankly to his mother about his discomfort with her behavior. Although she did not acknowledge any validity in what he said, she altered her behavior carefully when visits were renewed.

Most people find it difficult to admit to others and sometimes even to themselves that they do not get along with one or both of their parents. Social norms decree that adult children have good relationships with their parents, no matter what kind of people the parents are or what kind of parenting behaviors they have exhibited. The biological production of a child establishes legal rights for the parents over the physical custody of that child, but it does not grant them inviolable claims over the affection and respect of that child. A child's affection for parents does not come at birth but rather develops as a response to parenting behavior. Adults who were abandoned in infancy by their biological parents cannot be affectionately attached to those parents. Individuals whose biological parents have seriously obstructed their development into mature adults cannot have an unblemished relationship with their parents. Persons whose parents have shackled them through guilt, subjugated them through fear, or demeaned them through humiliation cannot love and honor their parents without the contaminants of guilt, fear, or humiliation.

Emotions have an independent existence within the individual, and they cannot be eliminated by reason, controlled by will, overturned by social standards, or directed by community edict. However, the way in which individuals express emotions must be subject to all these influences if people are to escape from the primitive responses of raw emotional life. Emotionally rejected children, as well as physically abandoned children, cannot feel affection for their parents, although they often engage in fantasies of such a loving relationship. Emotionally abused or physically abused children cannot feel tenderness toward their parents, although they may pretend love and deceptively express it. Reason, social norms, cultural expectations may cause an individual to develop a sense of obligation and responsibility toward such parents, but emotional love cannot be there unless a new relationship develops that is positive enough to support affectionate bonds. Some adults cannot emotionally love their parents, because they have found them unlovable. Individuals must have the freedom not to love—at least in an emotional sense—family members. If religious communities maintain an attitude that all healthy and holy adults must love their parents and other family members, they automatically pass judgment on those within their community who do not, or indeed cannot, love their parents. It is not unusual for psychiatrists to hear religious patients struggle with this conflict. "I dread having my mother telephone. She makes me feel terrible. But I have to pretend it's great to hear from her when I talk to the community." "My father was a drunk who beat my mother. How can I love him? But I wouldn't dare let the community know how I feel." "Some of the community members are good friends with my parents. They don't see them as they really are. They wouldn't understand how I feel."

Religious who have spent years in community life sometimes continue to fear the power of their parents. Sister Joan had been a sister for fifteen years when she sought psychiatric care. Although she appeared composed and competent in her work as a nurse and in her relationships with others, Joan experienced severe emotional insecurity. She slept poorly and had recurring nightmares of failing examinations, of finding herself in embarrassing situations, and of being shunned by groups of people she knew. She had various physical complaints for which doctors could find no physical causes. She had begun having attacks of anxiety when anything unexpected happened.

In therapy Joan discussed her conviction that her mother, if she became determined to do so, could persuade Joan's superiors to put her out of the community. Although that fear seemed irrational, for Joan it was a reality. Joan's mother had systematically undermined and eventually destroyed every relationship Joan could remember having. Her father had been affectionate toward her when she was a small child, but her mother's constant nagging drove him to seek companionship and recreation outside the family home. In therapy Joan wondered why her mother never interfered when she and her two siblings engaged in fights, which Joan usually lost. Her mother always intruded in Joan's relationships with peers, participating in their activities, becoming involved with their parents, or disapproving of them if they were not attentive to her. Joan's mother established a close and confidential relationship with each of Joan's teachers. As a result, Joan remained aloof from them. As Joan progressed in the convent, her mother visited regularly, first with the director of postulants, then with the mistress of novices, then with the superior of the juniorate, and finally with the superior in each mission where Joan served.

During treatment Joan became increasingly aware of the anger she felt toward her mother. She recognized that she became physically ill following each visit by her mother, who would treat her like an unworthy child. She realized that many of her anxiety episodes were precipitated by unexpected telephone calls because they might be from her mother and require the litany of muffled responses, "Yes, Mother. Yes, Mother. Yes, Mother." When she received a letter from her mother, she would leave it unopened for days because she knew it would be critical of her. Joan's anger toward her mother initially made her more frightened of her mother, because she reasoned that if her mother and her superior became aware of her anger, they would judge her to be unfit for religious life and cause her to be dismissed from the community.

Although the kind of fear Joan had is unfounded, because canon law and community constitutions protect the individual against such parental interference, psychotherapists hear religious express this fear. When a religious has a strong fear of parental meddling, the parent is typically one who is highly respected by community members and who strives for a confidential relationship with the local superior and a special affiliation with the major superior. This kind of parent always supported the teacher, always took the neighbors' word about what the child did wrong, and always had to have a private word with the doctor after the child's visit. These parents give their children the impression that adults, the really responsible people, the people in authority, must always work closely together to keep undisciplined and unruly persons in line.

Father Joseph had worked hard in his community. He had always been conscientious, obedient, and untiring. His father was a personal friend and confidant of several of Joseph's confreres. He also contributed generously to the community and dedicated much of his time in retirement to charitable work for the church. Joseph was experiencing considerable difficulty dealing with his father and came for a period of brief psychotherapy in an attempt to understand his father better. Joseph and his father had quarreled a few months earlier, and his superior had come to Joseph with a firm recommendation that he apologize to his father and be reconciled. The superior did not know that the father had always been an inflexible despot within the family and that the recent quarrel had resulted from another of his unreasonable demands. Joseph believed, and not without supporting evidence, that his father had neglected Joseph's mother when she was gravely ill and that his father's failure to obtain proper medical care contributed to her death. The father had disowned Joseph's sister because she married a man of whom he did not approve. He had not spoken to his daughter in five years. Joseph's brother was divorced because his wife would not tolerate the father's intrusion into and control over their lives. One can speculate about the superior's motives for advising Joseph to make peace with his father, but the superior treated Joseph unfairly in attempting to influence his attitude toward his father without knowing anything about the relationship between them or the reasons for the quarrel. Sentiments such as Joseph had regarding his father are not soothed by the reverent but empty platitude "After all, you only have one father in your lifetime." Some people are not at all happy with the one father or one mother they have. A superior who assumes that all family relationships are as they seem to be might gain a great deal of information by asking, "What is your father really like as a father?" or "What was it like to be raised by your mother?"

Families sometimes take advantage of the relative in religious life. Family members often assume that the son or daughter, nephew or niece, cousin, uncle, or aunt who entered religious life necessarily develops certain superior abilities in dealing with other people's problems. Everyone in the family expects to unload his or her troubles on the family's private spiritual leader and personal counselor. Religious often find it difficult to refuse relatives who approach them for everything from a direct loan to taking custody of their children. The difficulty in refusing the requests of relatives is increased when the community encourages the individual religious to cooperate with these requests. The religious in this situation must at times feel like the married person who suspects that the spouse and the in-laws collude to make life difficult.

Father John suffered from anxiety attacks and used alcohol to excess to quell these episodes. His attempts at self-medicating increased in frequency as his anxiety intensified. John had never liked his father, whom he regarded as a weak and indecisive man. As a youth he believed that the financial situation of the family could have improved if his father had been more assertive and dynamic. His mother made all of the decisions, and during John's adolescent years she shared most of those decisions with John. John was bright, highly motivated, and determined to make a success of his life. He worked diligently in his early years of ministry and as a result attained some status within his diocese. This led to high expectations on the part of his bishop. His drive to accomplish every assigned task and the increase in requests from his superiors combined to create a heavy work load and a high level of psychic tension. However, demands from family were what caused his emotional overload and brought him to seek psychiatric treatment. His family members regarded him as their rescuer. Unfortunately, John viewed himself in somewhat the same manner. His family had remained behind in the impoverished area from which he came. His parents, six siblings, aunts, uncles, and cousins approached him by letter, by telephone, and in person when they had problems, whether those problems were financial, marital, legal, psychological, physical, or spiritual. Typically he tried to respond with money, advice, consolation, time. He never felt successful, because their circumstances never improved. He was haunted by the feeling that he was like his father because he could not lead them to a better life.

On one occasion John brought a fifteen-year-old niece to live in the city where he was stationed. Her parents had found her unmanageable, so they appealed to him for a solution. He persuaded a family whom he knew to give her a place to live. He used his influence to gain her admission to one of the local Catholic high schools. He arranged for psychiatric care for her. In reality, John had assumed a responsibility that he could not carry. His niece refused to go to the psychiatrist unless he accompanied her, and John could not afford this additional demand on his time. Before long, the family placement failed, and he hurriedly searched for another home. Her schoolwork deteriorated in spite of his help with her homework. John could not recognize the absurdity of his situation. He was a celibate male with a full-time job and several other responsibilities that left him little free time. He had on his hands a rebellious adolescent female without a fixed residence, failing in school, reluctant to receive counseling, and consuming time, money, and emotional energy, none of which he could spare. Angry and frustrated, he increased his alcohol consumption. His psychological condition worsened, and finally he required hospitalization. The girl had to return home to live with her parents.

Religious, to be mature, cannot be responsible *to* their families and, to be committed, cannot be responsible *for* their families. When a person marries, she or he must relinquish primary attachment to the family of origin and give first priority to the spouse and offspring. If this does not happen, there is conflict in the marriage. A husband who continues to be "mother's little boy" or a wife who continues to be "daddy's little girl" seriously impairs the marriage commitment and eventually destroys the marital relationship. Several decades ago there was a harsh and uncompassionate separation of the religious from family. Visiting was extremely limited; even correspondence was curtailed. The terminal illness or death of a close relative was sufficient reason for an unscheduled home visit, but if the religious visited during the terminal illness a return for the funeral was often not permitted. Present policies in regard to family contacts are radically different; now, some religious seem not to have left their families at all as they participate in both worlds, appearing not to belong fully to either. Sister Judith, a college professor, drove to the country every Sunday to spend the day with her parents. In addition they visited her three or four times during the week to go shopping, to go to dinner, or just to take a drive. Emotionally Judith continued to be their little girl, and this dependency on her parents adversely affected both her professional life and her community life. Father Jim escorted his widowed mother to all the social functions in town. He ate at her house several nights a week, and occasionally they had lunch together. On weekends he took her shopping and helped her with things around the house. At age sixty-two his mother was in good health and perfectly able to take care of herself. However, she feigned a degree of helplessness and at the same time drove her friends away. She had her little boy to look after her, although by doing so her son failed to look after a number of his pastoral duties.

Strong attachments to family members provide emotional sustenance for religious as long as these involvements do not interfere with their attention to professional duties or compromise their community commitment. It can be very beneficial for a religious to find a supportive, special relationship with a reliable relative, a relationship of mutual trust and affection in which each one respects the psychological integrity and personal priorities of the other. The unrest, the disharmony, and the uncertainty within community life undoubtedly contribute to an increased need for such associations outside community life, and the radical changes in regulations regarding contact with family come at an opportune time. However, some religious behave like those married persons who cling too closely to their families because of the insecurity, doubt, and conflict they experience in their marriage. Other religious do not have family physically near or emotionally available and thus are deprived of this source of support. Their parents may be deceased, aged and ill, far away, or emotionally inadequate for nurturing. Their siblings also may be geographically distant, psychologically inattentive, or emotionally inaccessible.

Religious communities have begun to acknowledge that not all family contacts are characterized by harmony and happiness. Some communities recognize that a vacation at home may not be a time of rest or relaxation. Instead it may be a time of hard work for the religious who finds a disordered house that has been neglected by elderly parents since last year's vacation. It may be a time of severe emotional strain for the religious who in going home confronts feelings of guilt generated by possessive parents, feelings of anger created by rejecting parents, or feelings of anxiety induced by demanding parents. A religious vacationing at home may be expected to fill in for another family member who needs an opportunity to get away for a while from the burden of caring for an elderly parent or a chronically ill spouse or child. Religious who go home on vacation out of a sense of obligation and who spend the vacation period trying to solve family problems and soothe family distress are not actually having a vacation, because they are not able to use the time to decrease their own tensions, escape their own worries, and restore their own enthusiasm. Some communities provide additional vacation time for those members whose visit home is physically tiring. There is ample evidence that visits home can be psychologically exhausting, and communities should recognize this in arranging vacation time. To do so, however, requires acknowledgment on the part of the individual religious and on the part of the community that family visits can be emotionally painful, debilitating experiences.

Although families sometimes take advantage of the relative who has entered religious life, on occasion it is the religious who takes advantage of the family. By reason of their vowed state some religious acquire a special place within the family. Parents may demonstrate a role reversal and regularly seek advice from the son or daughter who has entered religious life. Although siblings may resent this special position that seems to evolve from religious vows, they often submit to this change in family organization. These family attitudes may entice the individual religious into becoming unduly impressed with his or her own importance. These religious behave like the overindulged children of wealthy parents who grow up with a sense of entitlement. Their families treat them with great deference, so they expect the world to hold them in high esteem. They quickly forget the basis for their families' overindulgence and assume that special privileges are their birthright. They claim unfair advantages and expect unwarranted favors, to which their families characteristically respond. These religious often experience difficulty in dealing with others on a basis of equality. If their work places them in authority over others or gives them a position of prestige, they may succeed on a professional level. However, they have trouble making friends, because peers are not likely to acquiesce in their sense of superiority. They have trouble socially because the general public usually does not give them the respect to which they feel they are entitled, and rarely do they find people in the post-Vatican II church who grant them the full honors which they feel they deserve.

Individuals in religious life have complex expectations of others, and many of these expectations originate in their early interactions with parents and siblings. The term *transference* is used to indicate this facet of emotional life whereby the response of an individual is partially separated from the stimulus of the moment and takes some direction from the emotional signals of earlier times. Close relatives enter into the lives of religious not only through these cloudy windows of the past but also through the open doorways of ongoing association. There is no single pattern of family interaction that motivates a person to become a religious, nor is there any typical response of family members to the one who has become a religious. Persons in religious life should recognize that a wide variety of family configurations and family communications exists, and that these family characteristics may cherish, support, antagonize, nourish, reject, frighten, or overwhelm the individual who has left this family of origin to join a family of faith.

The influence of family background remains with the individual throughout adult life. Good childhood experiences prepare people for healthy adult lives. Those entering religious life may consciously or unconsciously conceal derogatory information about their families from the scrutiny of religious communities. Once individuals enter, religious life often fails to provide the intensity of relationships and the impact of life events that can sometimes serve to correct deficiencies in earlier emotional development.

Individual religious need the opportunity to relate to their parents and other family members in terms of their own experiences within their own family unit and not based on social expectations about the psychologically healthy family or community expectations about the spiritually united family. Some religious may find that they are physically exhausted or psychologically debilitated by visits with their families and require additional vacation time for their personal renewal. Others may need to avoid or to confront family members who make exorbitant demands on their time, their funds, their energies. Some religious may need the freedom to express negative reactions to family visits or unloving feelings toward family members. Those religious are fortunate who have supportive, understanding, and noninterfering families.

Occasionally religious and their families continue to be intermeshed excessively with one another. This can occur if the religious remains too attached to and too dependent upon parental support, either financially or emotionally. The religious may also hold onto family ties because family members grant exceptional status to the religious. On the other hand, family members can foster inordinately close bonds in a variety of ways with the one who has entered religious life. One of the most intrusive things that parents can do is to establish a special relationship with the superiors of their son or daughter and thereby continue to exert parental control through their manipulation of religious authority.

12. Conflicts of Religious Authority

One of the most difficult tasks in the world today is that of the religious superior. Three factors combine to make this position complex and unwieldy: First of all, religious superiors at the present time bridge a broad span of historical development. They must respond to those in their communities who continue to think in pre–Vatican II fashion. They also need to reply to those in their communities who have caught the authentic spirit of Vatican II, as well as to those who tend to carry the direction of Vatican II to extremes that are more personal than apostolic. Secondly, the job of religious superior is never defined in realistic terms of psychological qualifications, administrative duties, required expertise, working hours, or necessary stamina. The third source of difficulty lies in the fact that religious superiors typically have no individual or group to whom they can go for confidential advice, personal support, or affectionate companionship.

Most religious communities have been polarized, and some have been fragmented, by the changes resulting from Vatican II. Changes in the religious habit, for example, at first produced conflict and serious hostility in most communities of religious women. Although the use of secular clothing no longer causes open dissension among the majority of religious, some still harbor a deep sense of loss and a feeling of betrayal over the change. One or another issue has emerged to dominate the scene of community conflict during the past two decades. Sometimes religious communities have focused on and fought over topics that were quite incidental to religious life. At other times their controversies have revolved around matters that touched on the central values of religious life. Religious have quarreled over their cloister, determining what new boundaries should be established for strangers, friends, families, and associates. They have argued over admission policies and formation programs. They have disagreed about interpretation of their vows. The importance of common prayer, changes in liturgical form, and the process of electing superiors have been topics of dispute, along with changes in corporate ministry and collegial authority. These topics, as well as others, remain unresolved in many communities. The controversy is at times plainly visible, and the community is painfully aware of its courageous struggle to reach a consensus. But some controversies are more subtle and resemble the dysfunctional secrets that sometimes disturb families. Everyone knows the distressing secret, and everyone knows that everyone knows it, but a conspiracy of silence blocks any reference to it. It is as if the family, or in this case the community, has tacitly agreed not to talk about the issue because they find it too painful or too complicated. In this way a family may ignore the behavior of an alcoholic parent or of a delinquent adolescent. Or they may ignore a serious financial loss and continue a lifestyle that each one secretly knows they can no longer afford. Similarly, the members of a religious community may pretend not to notice the physical deterioration of their buildings, the psychological impairment of their leaders, or the decreased demand for the services they have traditionally provided. Dysfunctional secrecy regarding important matters creates a pall that affects the interrelatedness of community members and drains their emotional vitality.

The wide range of disharmony that exists in religious communities requires the attention of each newly elected religious superior. If the superior needed only to deal with a variety of opinions and a diversity of approaches, the task would be complex but not overwhelming. It is not just ideas that are at stake; it is life's blood. Those who take religious vows believe they have received a special call, and each one has responded boldly and magnanimously. For them, religious life involves firm dedication and high resolve; it should not be lived apathetically or dispassionately. Is it any wonder that religious cling so zealously, then, to their individual visions of what that life should be?

Religious communities do not always select superiors because of their leadership abilities. Some communities are in such chaos that they cannot identify their needs for leadership or recognize those who have leadership ability or potential. There are now consulting firms that specialize in helping religious communities diagnose their leadership requirements and determine their leadership potential. It is unfortunate that some communities prolong their own conflict and confusion by burdening themselves with inadequate superiors because they will not confront their own leadership needs. When the members of a religious community wish to avoid some of the problems that confront them, they may choose a superior precisely because she or he does *not* possess strong leadership qualities.

Sister Karen became a major superior when she was nominated by her community and appointed by her superior general, even though she objected vigorously to taking the position. Her community had been in severe discord for several years, and there was open animosity everywhere. By nature, Karen was a placid person and socially reticent. She had remained emotionally removed from the seething conflict within her community. Although her placidity, her shyness, and her dispassion appealed to the angry and disorganized members of her community, they chose her for their superior not because of those qualities but because they knew she lacked the psychological fortitude to call them to task. Her term of office was a disaster, not for the community, but for her. The unwavering dissidents within the community left during Karen's term of office, neither because of what she did nor because of what she did not do. They had simply used up their time and exhausted their indignation. Those remaining continued to avoid the problems of the community, and they functioned poorly in their various jobs because of their anarchic community life. Karen became depressed and was at times suicidal. After completing her term of office, she took a sabbatical year but could not regain the peace and detachment she had know before. She began therapy and continued her separation from her community for an additional year. It was difficult for Karen to absolve her community from the injustice of recommending her appointment as their provincial, and it was difficult for her to be reconciled with the superior general who had appointed her in spite of her protestations. Her religious family had exposed her to more than she was able to bear, and they did so without regard for her. Their hostility toward one another was so great that the sacrifice of one person seemed inconsequential to them.

Karen became a provincial because her superior general ordered her to accept the position. Karen's interpretation of obedience left her no alternative. Although religious superiors occasionally accept the position as a matter of obedience to those in authority over them, fortunately this procedure of mandatory appointment is becoming rare. The complexity of the position, the emotional strain involved, the need for good leadership skills all support a process of selection that allows the individual religious to accept or refuse consideration for the position of superior.

Some religious encounter a different problem of obedience in considering a leadership role: They are willing to accept the position of superior, and even to seek it, because they have concluded that God wants them to do so. They have prayed about it and believe that such a course is God's will. It is obviously fitting that religious pray for guidance in considering the role of community leader, in accepting that role, and in carrying out the responsibilities of that role. However, the religious must surely be presumptuous who prays to know God's will regarding an important leadership position but attaches to that prayer a request for the necessary talents to meet the demands of such a role. Before attempting to discern the will of God as to whether or not one should assume a leadership role, it would be appropriate first to do a careful and honest self-evaluation as to whether or not one is, in fact, leadership material. On occasion the question of God's will in the matter need never be taken to prayer, since the answer may become quite obvious after judicious introspection. Sister Kathryn was a capable young religious with a poor self-image when she entered psychotherapy. She worked hard in the treatment setting and in a few months had resolved some personal conflicts, markedly improved her evaluation of her own worth, and settled some serious doubts about her vocation. Before completing therapy, as she contemplated her future ministry in religious life, she expressed her belief that she should avoid major leadership roles because she did not have the ability to analyze complex situations or to organize extensive planning. This accurate self-appraisal bolstered her sense of personal worth rather than detracting from it and gave her a good perspective from which to view the authority of others.

Not too many years ago, religious considered the guidance of the Holy Spirit as their basic security in the selection of religious superiors; all religious communities can attest to the guidance of the Spirit in the providential selection of certain holy, wise, and courageous leaders. During this period, religious believed that they should not seek office openly or covet it secretly. To do so seemed sacrilegious, a repudiation of the Spirit. Radically new approaches to the election process cause some religious to be concerned that the voice of the Spirit will no longer be heard. Some communities freely examine and discuss the qualifications of those who consider becoming superior and subject them to questioning in open forums. This resembles the practice of leadership selection in many professional organizations. When community members file solemnly into a hushed room in the presence of the Ordinary, each one absorbed in private thought, prayerful attitude, and a sense of grave responsibility, the presence of the Holy Spirit seems apparent as they cast their votes for a new superior. But the Spirit must also be near when community members sit in open discussion of critical issues, community needs, and the credentials of contenders for community leadership, thus preparing themselves to cast ballots based on informed judgment and prayerful enlightenment.

Though the use of political process in choosing superiors is usually beneficial, there will always be a few religious who try to separate the selection of superiors from the wishes of the community and from the guidance of the Spirit and make it a raw political process involving graft and power. A monsignor undergoing psychiatric care for a reactive depression gradually disclosed one of the reasons for his depression. He felt betrayed by an influential clerical friend in Rome when he discovered that his friend had other clients as well as the monsignor who were paying him large sums to obtain for them an appointment to the office of bishop. In the past there have been some religious who sought the office of superior cautiously, subtly, surreptitiously. Today those who believe in their own leadership abilities are freer to let others know of their aspirations, and this permits those others to evaluate their qualifications. Those who believe they have leadership qualities must now allow the community members, through discussion and discernment, to determine what benefit their particular skills and gifts might bring to the community.

Someone wisely remarked that a good leader must have the ability to inflict pain. People are sometimes hurt when a leader refuses their requests, but a good religious superior cannot say yes to everyone. There are too many conflicting opinions, too many opposing issues, too many incompatible goals. Religious superiors often like to see themselves in the role of the benevolent father or mother; the titles "Mother Superior" and "Father General" emphasize that character of their office. A superior who adopts a strongly parental attitude may be deeply hurt when an angry community member verbally abuses the

CONFLICTS OF RELIGIOUS AUTHORITY / 183

superior as heartless, ruthless, insensitive, and incompetent. For the superior who tries to assume the role of a loving parent, such behavior seems like personal aggression. However, the religious who attacks the superior rarely does so out of personal animosity. The religious superior not only represents immediate community authority but also symbolizes all the authority figures from each individual's recent and distant past, including overstrict parents, overindulgent grandparents, heavy-handed babysitters, punitive teachers, harsh formation directors, unsympathetic previous superiors, or a cold and demanding deity. Although superiors obviously cannot answer for either the mistakes or the misdeeds of these others, community members sometimes treat them as if they were responsible. Those who endured maltreatment from authority figures in the past transfer their resentment to authority figures in the present, and their consuming desire to right past wrongs may precipitate them into frequent and bitter confrontations with their superiors.

After three years in office, Father Kevin, the major superior of a large community, sought administrative consultation with a psychiatrist. Kevin was experiencing marked fatigue, uncharacteristic irritability, and occasional tearfulness. Kevin was an energetic forty-two-year-old man with a stable family background, sound personality traits, and excellent leadership qualities. When he was elected by a unanimous vote of his community to be their provincial superior, he presumed that this represented a clear indication of their trust in his mature judgment, leadership capabilities, and personal integrity. In regard to most of the community Kevin's assumption was valid, but a few had unrealistic expectations of him, as they had had of every superior before him. These petulant community members initially regarded each new superior as offering a regime in which the community would finally recognize their true worth and emotionally compensate them for the injustices they had experienced from prior authority figures. Like the other superiors, Kevin did not measure up to their requirements, nor did the community awaken to their special needs. Soon after taking office Kevin became aware of their disappointment in him, and he watched this disappointment turn first to anger, then mistrust, then contempt, and finally enmity. Even though they never took a united stand to oppose him, he began to think of them as a cohesive group and was always surprised when they did not all vote on the same side on community issues.

During psychiatric consultation Kevin gained some important insights into his role as superior. He learned that there were significant differences between those who attacked him and those who disagreed with him. Those who disagreed with him did so because they understood the issues differently than he, and his personality or style of administration did not influence their judgment. They tried honestly to evaluate problems and took positions based on careful consideration. They respected Kevin whether he agreed with them or not and acknowledged his authority as provincial no matter which course the community recommended. In discussing the behaviors of those who regularly attacked him, Kevin discovered that issues were not of importance in their interaction with him. They criticized him whether he agreed with them or not. Since they were not united on matters in dispute, they rarely voted as a solid block. The only thing they had in common was an emotional problem with authority figures, but this common ground did not unite them, because it represented a private, personal, individual conflict. Kevin came to accept the fact that he could not satisfy the expectations of these individuals, because he could not remove the pain of their past or repair the harm that had been done. It was of benefit to Kevin to learn that it was the cloak of his office, not the fabric of his character, that made him their target.

In past years, when the vow of obedience carried with it an aura of reverential docility, it was not difficult for a superior to maintain a parental role. Cultural attitudes toward legitimate authority have changed greatly, however, and with those changes have come new interpretations of the vow of obedience. As a result, the position of religious superior has become more administrative and less maternal or paternal. Although this transition in role definition is at different stages in different communities, it is moving rapidly toward defining the superior as administrator. There are advantages for the superior who shifts from a parental attitude to an administrative stance: Good parenting involves considerable emotional investment and a readiness to assist with the burdens of the children. Each child requires individual emotional attention, and the emotional return to the parent is rarely commensurate with the emotional outlay. The religious superior who assumes a parenting attitude must make a number of emotional disbursements that are endless and that are inconsistent with one another. One cannot go to the racetrack and bet on every horse to win without suffering a serious loss. Superiors who become emotionally involved with their community members in a parenting fashion these days experience a serious drain on their emotional resources. As they become emotionally depleted, they think less clearly, perform less ably, and administer less competently. Members of religious communities no longer behave like good children, obedient, respectful, grateful. They behave more like independent adults, defending their legal rights, protecting their psychological integrity, and expressing freely their opinions as well as their emotions.

The religious superior who takes an administrative rather than a parental stance responds to the present realities of religious life. The business affairs of religious communities are increasingly important. Financial solvency is essential to survival and often depends more on keen business ability than on good personality traits. In the past, religious superiors often depended on their personal charm, their persuasive manner, or the affection of others to elicit large financial contributions to the community or to serve as a base in negotiating favorable business arrangements with others. Charitable contributions, which were a major source of income for religious communities, are no longer as plentiful or as generous. Previously religious entered the marketplace as mendicants to ask alms from the rich and as servants to care for the poor. Those in the marketplace treated them well and not only met their requests but also gave them advantages in business dealings. Now religious come into the marketplace as entrepreneurs selling their services like other professionals and demanding salaries in return for their ministry. As a result, those who conduct business with religious are more apt to conduct it in a firm, unyielding manner. Under these circumstances, religious superiors must often be strong-willed and shrewd business persons in order to anticipate the loss of certain sources of community revenue and to develop new sources of revenue.

New attitudes about financial remuneration for the services of religious have brought a shift in sources of income. Some years ago people considered religious to be universally and uniquely self-sacrificing, dedicated to the service of the needy, and poorly compensated for their labors. They identified religious as generous individuals caring for the sick, providing for the poor, teaching the word of God to the young, and working to improve the spiritual life and general well-being of all. This popular view of religious created an appealing base for liberal financial support from the laity. Though it is fiscally more sound to have religious adequately paid for their services as teachers, nurses, social workers, counselors, and parish workers, this change to a base of adequate salaries decreases the incentive for donations. Payment for the services of a religious may at times be difficult to distinguish from payment for religious services. As salaries for the former become more common, donations to the latter may tend to fall short. The coordinator of education programs in a parish usually receives a salary, whether that person is a religious or a layperson. Should a priest who brings the sacraments to an isolated area of the diocese charge a fee for his services? No one questions the appropriateness of paying for the services of a licensed counselor who is also a religious. Should one then pay a religious for the time spent in spiritual direction? What if the sacrament of reconciliation is part of the spiritual direction? As religious move from a fiscal base of charity to one of professional remuneration, they must guard against simony and maintain a careful distinction between the sale of their temporal expertise and the gratuitous ministry that flows from their special call.

There are other reasons for a decline in contributions to religious communities. Communities no longer attract large numbers of novices whose families gratefully share their worldly goods with the communities that their daughters and sons have joined. The commitment of some to the religious life no longer serves as an inspiration for the generosity of others. In addition, religious must compete with the high-pressure techniques of all the other people who work for their share of "the charitable dollar." In such competition, few in religious life have the stature or the flamboyance to inspire philanthropy. Many worthy causes appeal for financial assistance, and the cause represented by religious communities no longer has a high priority for most people.

These monetary matters are only a part of the administrative problems facing religious superiors. Superiors also need to be familiar with various federal, state, and local regulations. There are tax issues, legal implications of community policies, and benefits of Medicare and other government programs. These topics and similar ones expand the duties of the religious superior and demand certain aptitudes in that person. Over the years it has not been unusual for priests, well trained in dogmatic and moral theology, canon law and Scripture, and working effectively in parishes, to be appointed as pastors and discover that they had no training and no expertise in the responsibilities or tasks of administration. Legal issues, financial matters, and personnel management were not part of their experience or education. These administratively naive priests not only became pastors, they also became bishops and major superiors. Many serious, and some notorious, financial disasters ensued.

Those religious communities that cling to the concept that

the superior needs primarily to be a benevolent maternal or paternal figure court poor leadership in a complex economic and political society. Religious superiors need strong administrative abilities to cope with the new attitudes of their constituents, to guide their communities through the changes that continue to occur in religious life, and to lead their communities through the intricacies of the contemporary political, social, and economic realities that increasingly impinge on the religious community. Dynamic leadership in any sphere today requires a great deal of exchange with and response to the subjects of that leadership. The majority of young people in contemporary society will not accept an authoritarian model of leadership, no matter how benevolent. Everyone demands his or her rights. Everyone wants to be heard, wants a part in decision making. This is true in all areas of life. Patients want to be informed about medical procedures and about the medicines they take so that they can participate in an informed fashion in decisions about their own bodies. Citizens demand information about their water supply, about waste disposal, about increases in utility bills so that they can agree or disagree with what is done. Students want to play a part in making policies in their institutions of learning. Workers' unions have prospered because employees want to share in the decisions made by employers.

Until recently religion remained an area in which an authoritarian approach was still acceptable to most believers, and many churches maintained an autocratic hold over their members. These two trends, the secular demand to participate in decision making and the believers' need to follow a religious authority, oppose each other in the religious community. Some religious, usually although not exclusively, the older members of the community, want to maintain the traditional view that extended the authority of dogmatic theology into the daily life of community and established the superior's word as the voice of God. Other religious, usually but not exclusively, the younger members of the community, regard the superior as a person whose authority comes not from God but from the community. In their view, therefore, that authority continues only as long as it represents the best interests of the community. Unfortunately the individual's interpretation of the community's best interest may sometimes involve the individual's best interest more than the group's best interest. In the present state of flux in religious communities, there are variations of both these views.

There are three principal ways in which the role of the religious superior is defined: the legal definition, the social definition, and the psychological definition. The legal definition is found in church law and community constitutions. Most communities are revising their constitutions and, in the process, redefining or clarifying the position of superiors. This legal interpretation of the superior's role provides a precise and explicit description of the parameters of religious authority without recognizing the diversity of persons held within those parameters. The social definition of the superior's position originates in the attitudes and responses of community members to religious authority. This view of the superior is variable and provisional because it arises from the diversity of community members, their past contacts with authority figures, their psychological conflicts surrounding dependence and autonomy, their competitive interactions with one another, and whatever anxieties they may have arising from events inside as well as outside the boundaries that mark community. Because this community definition arises from such divergent attitudes and is influenced by so many factors, it is imperative that the religious superior not allow himself or herself to be patterned by it. However, as the superior resists the stereotype established by the community, he or she must remain attentive to, but not necessarily responsive to, the expectations and limitations imposed on the leadership role by the community.

In spite of the legal definition and the social definition of the superior's role, it is the superior who must ultimately define her or his role in psychological terms. Some superiors describe their office in broad terms and attempt to be available at all times to everyone for every kind of problem. This represents an unrealistic approach to leadership in contemporary religious communities. In the past, religious superiors usually did not have to travel great distances to meet with community members. The typical community lived under one roof, engaged in one apostolate, and avoided most of the pressures of secular life. They prayed together, ate together, worked together, and recreated together, with the resident superior participating. Spiritual needs were emphasized; temporal needs were minimized and considered uniform; and emotional needs were viewed as unimportant. The individual was perhaps not as prized as was the way of life. Most religious communities now stretch beyond the narrow geographical, temporal, and psychological boundaries of the past. Where common prayer is not abandoned as a practice, many do not attend because of schedule conflicts. Community members often do not make spiritual retreats together. Even in small communities, members rarely live in the same house. They frequently do not work together and sometimes have little knowledge about the kind of work others in the group perform. Because of different apostolates, different schedules, different living arrangements, and different individual burdens, spiritual needs, temporal needs, and psychological needs may vary greatly among individuals in the same community. Superiors no longer share with many of the community members a common background of religious formation, community experience, or previous assignments. These many changes have limited the parental function of religious superiors. They cannot be available at all times, because they cannot be perpetually present for a nonresident community. They cannot be available to everyone, because community members may be scattered thousands of miles apart. They cannot be available for every kind of problem, because they cannot appreciate or respond to many of the problems that arise in the diverse apostolates and complicated experiences of community members.

Religious superiors who either cherish the parental role or have it forced upon them by community expectations find difficult, and sometimes disastrous, those periods when all the community members return home—at Christmas time, for chapter meetings, during community week, or for special celebrations. Maternalistic and paternalistic superiors are overwhelmed on these occasions. Everyone comes with the burdens of the past year and a wish list for the next year. Some have fresh concerns, but others repeat the same problems year after year. Some seek advice, some want absolution, some need decisions, some only look for a listener, some ask for special favors. Whatever they want, no matter how important or how crucial, no matter how insignificant or how inane, they all want time, attention, and understanding from the superior. Some recite a modern version of a confession of faults. Others obsessively detail events since the last meeting, anticipating a benediction. A few bring gossip from which to unburden themselves. The more needy ones approach the superior early in the morning before first prayers, during mealtime, in the hallway immediately after community prayer, sometimes in chapel, or in the privacy that late hours provide. They do not respect office hours if the superior has the wisdom to establish them. Schedules and appointments are difficult for the superior to maintain, because one interview may last ten minutes or three hours. One provincial superior in administrative consultation with a psychiatrist discussed her dread of community gatherings. She felt emotionally drained and physically exhausted after such gatherings and normally took several weeks to regain her usual level of functioning. Consultation helped her revise her own definition of her position as superior, and by maintaining some firm limits she forced her community to modify their definition of the superior's role.

It is important for religious superiors to decide how they will carry out their positions of authority. In those decisions limitations of time, of energy, and of health, both physical and emotional, must be considered. Religious who have recently completed terms as superiors occasionally seek psychiatric care—often with a diagnosis of depression, but it might more appropriately be called delayed stress reaction. Characteristically, these patients have pushed themselves too hard, not keeping regular, healthy schedules in their lives, not setting aside time for proper rest or adequate recreation. Their unlimited availability for others exhausts their limited internal resources. Religious superiors are not exempt from the inexorable laws of physical and psychological existence. Poor eating habits, poor sleeping patterns, lengthy periods of excessive fatigue, prolonged high levels of tension, all take a physical as well as a psychological toll. If the superior fails to counterbalance the pressures of office through relaxation, recreation, private time, and vacation periods, the rate of emotional and physical deterioration accelerates. Spiritual decline may then occur, because superiors, like other religious, often decrease their prayer time when they find they are extremely busy. As time becomes more valuable, prayer seems to become less valued. Mother Teresa of India relates how her community discussed the increased demands placed on their work schedule, which already seemed stretched beyond their endurance and beyond the limits of time. They decided that they could only serve greater numbers and increased needs by setting aside two more hours each day for prayer.

Sometimes religious superiors make a conscious compromise regarding the demands of their position, gambling their physical health, their emotional stability, and their spiritual solvency against the number of years their term requires. They reason, "My term in office is only for so many more years. I can survive that long with less sleep, inadequate recreation, inattention to health needs, and a certain amount of physical and emotional deterioration. I can revitalize my spiritual life later when I am not so busy. I can renew abandoned friendships when I no longer have all these people pulling at me. I can get lots of rest when I'm old. I really don't need to take time off because I enjoy what I'm doing. My community needs me now, and I will make these sacrifices for them. God will take care of all those things I normally should take care of, because I will spend myself taking care of this community for God." Superiors who think this way neglect for the sake of community those personal responsibilities that cannot normally be avoided. Life does go on after a person leaves the position of superior, and the virtue of that continuing life depends not on the kind of star one followed or created as superior but on the kind of stability and integrity one preserved during the time in office. One religious superior required three years to recover from the deterioration that had occurred during her six years as provincial superior. Her recovery was financially costly, not only because it necessitated a lengthy period of hospitalization and intensive psychiatric intervention, but also because it prevented her from being a productive member of her community for several years.

Religious superiors labor under a severe psychological disadvantage in not being able to discuss with others many of their feelings, some of their decisions, and most of their conversations with community members. The position of superior frequently requires the exercise of control over personal feelings and spontaneous responses. Although it is important for the superior to control the outward expression of these internal reactions, it is also important to acknowledge their presence, and on occasion it would be helpful to discuss them with another person. Superiors sometimes make decisions that cannot be discussed openly because they cannot be disclosed publicly or because those who are involved would be offended. Superiors cannot discuss many personnel problems with anyone for reasons of confidentiality. Sometimes community members discuss matters of moral conscience with superiors, who then must be careful not to refer to this knowledge directly or indirectly. Religious authorities are separated from those inside the community by a wall of confidentiality that separates much of their decision making from the purview of others. The obligation of confidentiality is unilateral: it binds the superior but not the community member. As a result, an individual religious can represent to other community members any version of an exchange with the superior, and the latter is unable to respond. The account of the exchange may be accurate or inaccurate. The degree of inaccuracy may be slight or gross, unintentional and innocent or carefully contrived to undermine the role of the superior or to make the individual religious appear commendable in the eyes of others. Whatever the degree of distortion and whatever the reasons for it, the religious superior is usually not in a position to contradict the report, to defend the position taken, or to explain the reasons for the decision. Although these constraints infuriate many religious superiors, they would behave imprudently and in some instances immorally if they were to violate them.

In a private conversation many years ago, an archbishop discussed how he had acted toward a young priest who was having a problem with alcohol. At the annual priests' retreat the archbishop had approached the young man and in a kind and gentle manner had brought up the subject of the young priest's alcohol abuse. The archbishop had not rebuked him, but in a caring manner and in positive terms had encouraged him to correct his problem. Later the archbishop heard that the young priest was extremely angry over the meeting and was telling others that the archbishop had "shouted angry threats" and had treated him harshly and impatiently. Chagrined by the priest's interpretation of the encounter, the archbishop called him in for an appointment. When the priest arrived, the archbishop greeted him cordially and led him into a discussion of their earlier meeting. The archbishop finally mentioned that he had heard the young priest was offended by the meeting and asked why he was angry. The priest replied, "You spoke gently enough, but you never offered to shake hands with me." This exhausted the archbishop's patience. He ended his story, saying, "I got up from my chair, crossed the room, shook his hand, and threw him out."

Religious superiors have difficulty finding someone they can talk with candidly and confidently. Although they may trust friends within the community, they obviously cannot discuss confidential matters or personal feelings with them. Most superiors consider it inappropriate and irresponsible to discuss community affairs with outsiders, whether they are friends, relatives, or members of other communities. Laypersons rarely understand the complexities of religious life, and outsiders are unfamiliar with the special problems of a particular community. The idea of frank discussion with them sometimes raises concerns about scandal or at least impropriety. Spiritual directors may serve as resource persons for superiors in these matters; however, spiritual directors may not be able to set aside adequate time for this continuing task, which goes beyond the role of spiritual direction and sometimes beyond the competence of the spiritual director. In addition, it is inappropriate for a spiritual director to serve both as a resource person for a superior and as a spiritual director for members of that community. The professional counselor who is familiar with the issues and conflicts of religious life is one of the best sources of confidential support for the religious superior. Psychiatrists who are well acquainted with religious life sometimes serve as administrative consultants to religious superiors. In a setting of confidentiality and impartiality, the superior can benefit from the critical attentiveness, the analytic expertise, and the disciplined insights of the psychiatrist. Psychiatric consultation can help religious superiors expand their understanding of people and situations and establish a broader base for their decision making. In this relationship the psychiatrist can also help the religious superior evaluate his or her own affective reactions and maintain a healthy emotional balance.

Some sort of administrative consultation is one of several things that can enable a religious superior to cope with his or her leadership position. Religious communities are beginning to acknowledge that the leadership role is particularly difficult in this period of dramatic transition in religious life.

Accordingly, communities should be encouraged to improve their election process by joining new techniques of leadership discovery with old customs of prayerful reflection. They must learn to evaluate the leadership potential of candidates for positions of authority and place those abilities on a par with spiritual balance, emotional reliability, and physical stamina. In their selection process communities must avoid choosing superiors who lack leadership ability in an attempt to avoid problems the community is not ready to confront.

Superiors who exercise their authority in a parental fashion expose themselves to many administrative dilemmas that are not faced by superiors who approach their job in a more businesslike manner. Religious superiors need to define for their communities the day-by-day exercise of their office as well as the general nature of their administration. This definition should admit to the emotional strengths, the personal characteristics, the physical energies, and the psychological and spiritual needs of the superior, and not be primarily responsive to the excessive demands or unsubstantiated needs of community members. When a religious takes over the task of being a superior, he or she may experience an increased need for periods of recreation, relaxation, prayer, and spiritual enrichment.

Religious superiors, no matter how capable they are—no matter how fair, no matter how benevolent—experience the same kinds of harsh and unjust criticism that most persons in authority encounter in contemporary society. It is important for superiors to recognize that these responses of community members often originate in conflicts with authority figures somewhere in the past. The superior is a lonely figure behind an invisible wall that keeps former friends at a distance but offers no protection from the barbs of those whose insensitivity allows them to perceive the superior as insensitive. All the members of the community have the psychological freedom, although not the moral prerogative, to judge the behavior of the superior, to attribute motives to the superior, and to explain the superior to others who will listen. The superior, by contrast, is constrained from responding, sometimes because of greater emotional composure, often because of a better sense of propriety, and always because of a recognition of the bonds of confidentiality and the right to privacy.

13. Issues Regarding Confidentiality and Privacy

Persons who make religious vows are sometimes caught in conflict by the presence of opposing values. Religious superiors expect frankness and sincerity at the time individuals apply for admission and throughout their lives as religious. On the other hand, every religious has a need for privacy and confidentiality. The religious authority invites candid and open discussion on the part of the individual religious; the latter, however, may be cautious about the superior's expectations and maintain some personal reservations about self-revelation. Religious exhibited considerable naïveté about this in the past. They went to physicians who freely discussed their findings with the superior. Without their knowledge or permission their relatives and friends often supplied information to their superiors, and superiors sometimes talked too freely to their own families or friends about some of their community members, especially those who seemed to have problems. In those days and under those circumstances, individual religious appeared to have little right to privacy.

Several years ago a number of psychiatrists trained in a few psychiatric hospitals that were owned and administered and partly staffed by members of religious communities. Psychiatrically ill priests, brothers, and sisters from dioceses and religious communities throughout the United States were hospitalized in these institutions. It was often standard procedure for the staff to send reports regarding the religious patients to their bishops, provincials, and other major superiors. No one took the trouble to ask the individual patients to authorize such communications. In some cases, an ongoing dialogue between the staff psychiatrist and the religious superior decided the future of the community member, with little or no involvement of the latter. The psychiatrist rather than the superior often informed the patient about the conclusions that the psychiatrist and major superior had reached in their discussions. Religious superiors often sent their community members to these hospitals under the vow of obedience, and they remained there until the superior was willing to accept them back. On occasion, a religious superior virtually committed a religious to the hospital, and although the commitment had no legal basis, it was as binding on the individual as a court order would have been. Needless to say, the justification for admission as a psychiatric patient did not always depend on valid legal grounds or sound medical opinion. Although the majority of religious who entered these hospitals had bona fide psychiatric problems, some were ordered to go not because they had a psychiatric illness but because they had offended the superior in a grave manner or because their behavior represented a scandal to others.

Although religious superiors exercise their spiritual authority based on the individual's vow of obedience, they sometimes resort to the temporal power of their position and force submission from community members. In these instances the superior cannot claim virtue as a basis for the decision any more than the community member can claim his or her vow as the basis for compliance. Religious superiors on occasion may have good reasons to resort to power tactics in dealing with a difficult subordinate, but they should not expect to enlist others in their temporal stratagems under the guise of spiritual benevolence. Physicians and other persons who work with religious are not under a vow of obedience to religious superiors, and they should no longer permit religious superiors to encroach on the confidentiality of their relationship with the religious.

Father Luke, a priest in a northeastern diocese, had been

involved in sexual activity with a number of prepubertal boys. One of the boys told his parents, who reported the matter directly to Luke's provincial. Although the provincial had confronted other priests with sexual problems of one kind or another, he was completely startled when he received this information about Luke. The provincial recalled that he had recently told all the priests in his province that if any of them had any kind of behavior that could be scandalous, particularly sexual behavior, that individual should come to the provincial and discuss the problem openly and freely. The provincial made the unwarranted assumption that a person with clandestine behavior will come forward with a little encouragement and voluntarily reveal what is secret and unmentionable. Law enforcement officials do not expect wrongdoers to announce their identity, and they question the truthfulness of those who attempt to confess. Sex offenders are usually ashamed of their behavior and fear retribution from society. They must develop great trust in another person before they volunteer information about their aberrant behavior. The provincial was extremely angry at Luke because he was the first priest known to be involved in illicit and scandalous behavior since the provincial had made his pronouncement. He apparently believed that Luke had deliberately defied his prior invitation, which the provincial inwardly considered a magnanimous gesture. In addition, the provincial had entrusted several special tasks to Luke in the past, and he had valued Luke's unique abilities and his gifted service to the community. Finally, the provincial had on many occasions expressed a strong personal affection for Luke. As the provincial reviewed all the reasons why Luke should not be in this predicament, his wrath grew to immense proportions. He summoned Luke to a meeting and told him how completely disappointed he was in him. Then he told Luke that he must leave the province that day, that he must not discuss the problem with anyone, that he was stripped of priestly faculties, and that he was to admit himself to a particular treatment facility. After that meeting the provincial never had any direct contact with Luke again but only communicated through the assistant provincial.

Luke had gone through various phases in his adult sexual struggle, which began following his ordination. At first he was horrified that he could engage in pedophilic behavior, and he was too ashamed to mention it even to his confessor. Then he went through a period of extreme guilt and worked with his confessor to overcome the problem, but unsuccessfully. Then he experienced a period of laxity in which he separated his improper behavior from the rest of his priestly life and simply ignored the behavior and his feelings associated with it. Luke renewed his desire to control the problem during a retreat he made about one year before the report to the provincial. At that time, Luke's spiritual director had prudently recommended psychiatric help, and Luke had been undergoing psychotherapy for several weeks when the young boy reported the sexual encounter to his parents. The incident had occurred prior to the time Luke began psychotherapy.

Luke left the province as ordered by his provincial the day of their meeting. He went to the treatment facility, an institution specializing in the care of religious. He spent three days there for an evaluation. He took a battery of psychological tests and had three hours of interviews, each hour with a different staff member. The psychological tests were administered and evaluated by a graduate psychology student, and the interviews were conducted by a nurse, a social worker, and a person with a degree in ministry. As a result of this evaluation the provincial received a six-page letter discussing Luke's "very defensive manner," "his anxieties regarding his ministry," "his sexual immaturity reflecting family pathology," "his creative abilities that are limited by deep resentment of his father," "his acting out in hostility toward God," "his paranoid projections of his own inadequacies," "his sociopathic nature," "his distrust of all authority figures and fear of their power," "the conflict and disharmony between his emotions and his intelligence," "his need to provoke authority figures whom he distrusts and by whom he feels victimized," "his spiritual life which serves as a refuge from his emotional turmoil."

If one grants the possibility that the evaluation process did produce all this elaborate information, one must still question how appropriate and how ethical it was to pass this information on to Luke's superiors. These comments would surely intensify their anger toward him. A therapist could find value in some of the information provided in the report, but most of it was of no benefit to superiors making administrative decisions. The psychodynamic antecedents of behavior are the domain of therapists; the behavior and its consequences are the concern of superiors. The ethical violation of confidentiality was not relieved simply by obtaining Luke's permission to send a report to his superiors. The psychological duress exercised by his provincial permitted Luke no alternative. However, the patient's rights must be preserved, especially when he or she is not in a position to protect them. Nor was the violation of confidentiality removed by the usual disclaimer clauses, "Please respect the privileged nature of this communication. This report should be read only by the proper authority and should not be made a part of a permanent file." It seems seriously negligent to give another person confidential information and later on ask that person to keep it in confidence. An individual who does not initially safeguard privacy cannot pass the obligation on to others with whom that person has communicated indiscreetly.

The lengthy report regarding Luke concluded by recommending that he enter that facility for a twelve- to eighteen-month period to receive intensive psychotherapy and group counseling. It also recommended that his priestly faculties not be restored until the therapist there could advise it. The treatment facility did not have an opening for Luke at that time and placed him on a waiting list. The staff informed his provincial that he would be accepted when a place became available if "you indicate in writing your willingness to assume full financial responsibility for his care."

Luke could not return to his province, so he sought refuge with distant relatives in another city, and because of his anxiety and suicidal depression, sought psychiatric care there. He progressed rapidly in treatment and developed some sound insights. He became quite despondent when he learned from a priest in his province that the provincial had discussed Luke's situation with three or four priests in the community. Luke had previously been assured by the provincial and his assistant that they would respect his privacy. After about thirty hours of psychotherapy the psychiatrist wrote a letter addressed to the provincial and reviewed by Luke prior to being sent. The letter recommended with supporting justification that Luke be allowed to continue in outpatient treatment rather than to be institutionalized. The reply from the assistant provincial came within a few days, stating, "The provincial has reviewed the matter and his decision remains unchanged. We believe that the previous evaluation is a correct view of Luke's personality and his needs. He is to go for treatment as recommended. If he chooses not to accept inpatient treatment, the province will no longer assume any responsibility for him. This decision is in no way meant to punish him or to keep him from returning to the province." Sometimes it is important not to listen to what people say but to look at what they do; if what is said and what is done are not in agreement, the reality of the action cannot be erased by corrective words. The assistant provincial said that Luke was not being punished and was not being banished from his province. In reality the provincial insisted on institutionalizing Luke because the provincial was angry at him and not because Luke's treatment necessitated such an action. In reality Luke was never permitted to return to his own province. Luke accepted his confinement because he had to do so, and he cooperated with the program because he chose to do so. When he had successfully completed fourteen months of treatment, his provincial refused to accept him back in the province and only allowed him to exercise priestly faculties under severe restrictions. Luke found work in a remote diocese and eventually became incardinated there after the death of his provincial.

If a religious, whether in formation or in vows or in candidacy status, is sent to a psychiatrist for an evaluation, the psychiatrist should make it clear before beginning the evaluation that a report will be sent to the religious authority. An evaluation of this sort, requested by the religious superior, should be treated like any other evaluation resulting in a written report to the requesting individual. The authorization covers that evaluation only and allows communication only with the person or persons specified in the signed authorization. An excerpt from a consultative report addressed to the provincial of a religious community clarifies this point: "Sister Louise was seen for a total of five interviews, each lasting approximately one hour. In the first interview, I carefully explained to Sister Louise that I was seeing her in consultation for you, and that I could not give her the same assurance of confidentiality that I could give her if she were seeing me as a therapist. I explained to her that this was not intended to be a therapeutic encounter but that it was an evaluative process which would result in a written report to you with specific recommendations regarding her." In addition, Louise signed a statement authorizing the release of information to her provincial, who was named in the authorization. The written consultative report provided some specific recommendations with which Louise did not agree. Louise wrote an angry letter to the evaluator complaining that she had been betrayed. However, it was obvious from the letter that Louise was primarily angry at her superior, who had decided to reassign Louise. The superior based her decision principally on the psychiatrist's report, which indicated that Louise's present work placed her in a position of severe emotional conflict that she had been unable to resolve. Louise's complaint to the psychiatrist would have been justified if she had not been informed about the purpose of the interview or if she had not given her written consent for communication with her superior.

However, even after establishing legal safeguards, evaluators must be careful not to disclose to religious superiors information that they have no need to know or that would be of no value to them in reaching administrative decisions. In seeking the consultation, Louise's provincial indicated that Louise had been involved in sexual indiscretions with several men over the previous ten years. This behavior frequently caused considerable scandal and was a matter of great concern to her community. The provincial council was considering a recommendation of dismissal from community. The evaluative report referred to Louise's "confusion regarding directions in her life," "her lack of regular contact with her community," and "the impropriety of some of her actions." The report did not mention any of the sexual behavior that Louise discussed quite openly during the interview, nor did the report examine the background of Louise's behavior or conflicts. The report stated that "maintaining Louise in her present assignment contributes to her alienation from her religious community and indirectly encourages relationships and behaviors which are in conflict with her commitment as a religious and which are not likely to be emotionally fulfilling for her. An assignment in a more conventional setting might enable Louise to strengthen her commitment to the essential elements of religious life, to develop a more appropriate attitude regarding certain behaviors, and to avoid the more drastic step of exclaustration." Psychotherapy was also recommended for Louise but only if "she believes there is some value in treatment and accepts a treatment relationship willingly."

A treatment relationship is quite different from a meeting for an evaluation. The individual religious in therapy has every right to expect the same confidentiality that any other adult has in a treatment relationship. Sometimes a religious in treatment experiences pressure from the religious superior to permit the superior to have access to the therapist. If the patient cannot resist this pressure, the therapist nevertheless should resist it. If the superior and the therapist communicate with each other without the express permission of the patient, it may not violate the professional ethics of the superior, but it definitely violates the professional ethics of the therapist. Most religious superiors respect the strict confidence of the therapeutic relationship, but a few do not. There are also some therapists who continue not to respect the confidentiality of the therapeutic relationship with religious patients. These same therapists may be extremely careful not to violate the confidential relationship of any other patient: Perhaps they stand in awe of religious superiors. Perhaps they wish to maintain a good relationship with those superiors who have referred a number of patients to them. Perhaps they have always practiced that way and never realized how incorrect their behavior is. Perhaps they assume that the religious patient automatically authorizes such contacts.

Larry, a young man in religious formation, went to a therapist for four or five visits because he doubted his motivations for entering religious life. Later his novice master asked the therapist for a report, which the therapist sent without the consent or knowledge of the patient. The report contained statements such as "His presentation disclosed that he has a severe problem with masculine identification"; "For several years, he has had the recurring concern that his penis was of inferior size"; "He is without heterosexual experience, but he has been involved in sexual experiences with men"; "He speaks in delicate tones, exhibits a lisping quality in his speech, and he moves his body in womanly fashion"; and "He believes that he would be unable to satisfy a woman." After Larry had taken vows, his superior showed him the report. Needless to say, it was disconcerting to Larry. Three years later he sought psychiatric care. As a result of the report, he was experiencing doubts about his masculinity, and he had developed a number of obsessive thought patterns coupled with acute anxiety symptoms. After a brief period of therapy, Larry was able to recognize not only the unethical nature of the report but also its lack of validity as an appraisal of his psychological makeup. Since the report had created some genuine anxiety for Larry, it was assumed that it must have caused some suspicion and apprehension on the part of his superiors. With Larry's consent, the psychiatrist wrote a letter to his superior stating in part, "Larry has experienced some doubts in relation to his sexuality, but these concerns revolved around normal development rather than around psychologically deviant behavior. He has sexually matured in a normal manner." The letter was discussed with Larry before it was mailed to his superior, and Larry received a copy of it. The earlier report constituted a grave injustice. Superiors were given facts they had no need to know, opinions based on totally unreliable criteria such as "moves his body in womanly fashion," and conclusions that raised doubts regarding Larry's motivation for entering religious life. All this was done without Larry's permission by a pompous therapist who allowed his own responsiveness to a religious superior to supersede his responsibility to a patient. In regard to this case, two questions remain: If Larry's superiors had any confidence in the report, why did they not insist that the issue of his sexual identification be clarified before Larry was permitted to take vows, and why did the superior show Larry the report after he had taken vows?

Some few therapists and some institutions still provide summary evaluations to religious superiors as a matter of course, and a few religious superiors act on the premise that they have the right of access to treatment information. A therapist has the obligation to protect the privacy of the patient, and in order to do so the therapist must sometimes try to anticipate encroachment by the religious authority. The psychiatric treatment of Sister Loretta was being threatened by her superior, who told Loretta that she was going to telephone the psychiatrist to inquire about Loretta's care. Loretta had been extremely cautious about entering into a treatment relationship, and not without reason. On three previous occasions she had tried to establish a confidential relationship with priests whom she approached for guidance and spiritual direction. Each one had betrayed her trust either by divulging to others the content of her visits or by attempting an unsuitable level of intimacy with her based on her emotional disclosures. As a result, she was initially wary and secretive in her psychotherapeutic sessions. Her trust level was low, and she was not about to let her superior talk to her therapist. At this point she did not trust either of them. The superior became increasingly insistent that Loretta give her permission to contact the therapist, and when Loretta continued to object to this invasion of her privacy, the superior threatened to make the contact without her consent. At this point the psychiatrist suggested to Loretta that he write a letter to her superior subject to her review and consent.

In her conversations with Loretta the superior had posed four questions that she wanted to ask the therapist: Is this care necessary? Will the care create dependency on the psychiatrist? How long will the care take? What will the cost be? In his letter the psychiatrist addressed each question. "In my opinion Sister Loretta's psychiatric care during these past weeks has been absolutely necessary, and termination of that care at this time might seriously damage her emotional well-being." It was not necessary to say that Loretta had been suicidal during most of that time. "Psychiatric care normally orients patients toward healthy emotional independence, which includes emotional independence from the treating psychiatrist. Although this is not always successful because of the type and degree of pathology in the patient, resolution of this issue is part of the treatment relationship and must be entrusted to the professional competence of the treating psychiatrist." There was no need to explain to superiors that Loretta's overdependent relationships of the past had, in fact, contributed to her present desolation. "The duration of treatment is based on the relief of symptoms and the attainment of emotional stability. Treatment cannot be completed in time limits set by those who are not party to the treatment relationship. If others supply conditions of treatment, they are influencing the treatment process and must, in conscience, bear some responsibility for treatment outcome. The psychiatrist can only accept responsibility for treatment when he has charge of it." On occasion superiors recommend therapists who assure them that a fixed number of visits will produce beneficial results for the religious who come to them for treatment. The financial condition of a community may limit the amount of psychiatric care an individual religious may be able to afford; that is sometimes an unpleasant reality for the superior, the patient, and the psychiatrist. However, religious who regularly meet the intangibles of life and the complexities of the human heart should know better than to put a time limit or a price tag on the correction of emotional disorders or to have confidence in those who offer bargains in psychotherapy. "The cost of treatment depends on the duration of treatment and on the intensity of the treatment program. In my opinion Sister Loretta is seen on a frequency commensurate with her need. She is keenly aware of the cost involved and considers it seriously in her decisions about treatment." Her superior never bothered her again about the issue of treatment, which ended successfully. Loretta's superior asked legitimate questions, considering that she assumed responsibility for Loretta's bill. If she had written to the psychiatrist and asked these same questions, it would not have interfered with the therapeutic alliance or the progress of treatment. It was unfortunate that the superior tried to force Loretta to allow her to talk to the psychiatrist and then to intensify this threat by proposing to contact the psychiatrist without Loretta's consent.

Other superiors challenge the therapeutic alliance more forcefully. A particular psychiatrist had as a patient a member of a religious congregation of men. One day the psychiatrist's office received a telephone call, and the caller requested an appointment for a priest named Father Lane. Two weeks later when Lane arrived for his first appointment, the psychiatrist gradually became aware during the interview that Lane was the superior of his other priest-patient and that Lane had come to discuss that patient with the psychiatrist. To make the situation even more difficult, the priest-patient had markedly paranoid ideation. There were no good alternatives. After some preliminary comments about the ethical boundaries of confidentiality, the psychiatrist spent an uncomfortable hour avoiding comments about his patient while the superior talked freely about his own strong feelings and random thoughts about the patient. The superior's visit created an uncomfortable and insurmountable dilemma for the psychiatrist. On the one hand, he was not certain that he had the right at this point to disclose to the patient the fact that the superior had been there. The patient had some hostility toward the superior and some paranoid thoughts about the superior. These would certainly be increased if the patient became aware of the superior's visit. In addition, if the psychiatrist told the patient that the superior had been there, he might lose the tenuous trust of his paranoid patient. The psychiatrist believed that he had not violated the confidence of his patient because his contact with the superior had been unintentional from his point of view, and he had revealed nothing about the patient to the superior. On the other hand, if he did not tell his patient about the superior's visit, there was always the danger that the patient might discover it and then lose his trust in the psychiatrist for not mentioning it.

Therapists who treat religious patients should establish a straightforward policy regarding communication with their superiors. It is ethically sound if communication with religious superiors occurs only following explicit permission by the patient and with the patient having full and prior knowledge of what is being communicated. This can be arranged in one of two ways. First, the therapist may send a letter to the superior after it has been reviewed and approved by the patient with a carbon copy for the patient. Second, the therapist with the approval of the patient may invite the superior to come to the office for a three-way discussion. In this case, the therapist should discuss with the patient in a prior session the position of the therapist in relation to issues that the superior may mention. The conjoint interview with the superior present is less easily controlled by the therapist, but if the therapist and patient have reviewed topics openly and thoroughly in advance, this type of meeting can be productive and therapeutic.

Another problem regarding confidentiality confronts religious in this era of self-revelation. Many communities accept the popular notion that self-disclosure through "sharing sessions" brings a resolution of inner conflicts and provides a means of avoiding conflict with others. The privacy of one's mind, the sacred domain of individual thinking, is assaulted by this demand for "sharing." Religious authorities demand information from aspirants and novices in order to make judgments about their suitability for religious life. However, religious superiors may be facing some of the same legal limitations that employers face in regard to what questions may be asked. Perhaps to offset these restrictions, businesses as well as religious communities sometimes apply considerable pressure on individuals to expose themselves psychologically to those with whom they work or with whom they live. The preliminary task in this crusade for self-disclosure revolves around an intense insistence that those involved "own" their own thoughts, their own feelings, their own words and behaviors. On the surface this seems very appropriate. However, there sometimes seems to be a proscription against "owning" one's thoughts or feelings privately. They must be "shared," revealed to others, talked about in group settings, discussed without restraint and without shame. The "ownership" of one's external behavior, in the sense that one must be willing to be held responsible for one's words and one's actions, is a realistic expectation. External behavior impinges on the world of others and, in a sense, becomes something those others also own, since they are in receipt of it. People cannot avoid sharing something of themselves through their words and actions that become common ground between them and others. That common ground may be rough and discourage the approach of others, or it may be smooth and encourage their closeness.

The thoughts and feelings that a person has are "owned" in a much more private way. No one has a right to intrude into that private world or to insist that the individual share it with others. Entrance without permission is an invasion; entrance on demand is a violation. In one respect, an individual loses ownership of his or her thoughts and feelings in sharing them with others. Those thoughts and feelings enter into a new region of external, observable behavior, and the individual no longer has exclusive ownership of them. Religious superiors, and especially formation directors, sometimes insist that those under their jurisdiction disclose to them their private thoughts and personal feelings. The psychological advantage held by superiors and formation directors limits the voluntary aspect of such disclosures and weakens the truthfulness of individual religious.

Now it is common for small living groups to demand, sometimes subtly, sometimes patently, that members share their thoughts and feelings with the group. If a particular person refuses to participate in the rite of self-revelation, the inference is made that that individual is either hiding something horrible, having some serious emotional struggle, or opposing community goals. However, those who demand this self-disclosure are rarely in a position to give absolute assurance that confidentiality will be preserved. Even when others can promise privacy, that does not obligate a person to a full disclosure of self. If the chapter of faults continues to be practiced in some religious communities these days, the practice should be examined in terms of the psychological need for privacy and confidentiality.

Young children take a major step forward in emotional development when they learn to say no to authority figures. If young children never become able to do that, a psychological fixation occurs, and the realization of individuality and separate self is thwarted. Adolescents accomplish another milestone in development when they learn that adults cannot read their minds and so do not know what thoughts they think or what feelings they experience. It is important for adolescents to discover their separateness, their individuality, and that discovery process in part revolves around the privacy of their inner psychological life. They find their individuality by hiding their inner selves from others. They refrain from telling adults things because they want to "own" them internally, exclusively. In order to possess their thoughts and feelings as separate individuals, they must have the right and the ability to decide what they will reveal and what they will conceal. As adolescents become increasingly aware that they often cannot control what they think or what they feel, they need to learn that at least they can contain these thoughts and feelings undetected within themselves. Adolescents experience a wide variety of strange feelings and unusual thoughts as they become aware of the complex world that surrounds them. Thoughts and feelings that are at times aggressive, sexual, perverse, or bizarre move in and out of their minds, and they experience a common reaction, "If others knew what I'm thinking, they would hate me; if others knew what I'm feeling, they would think I'm crazy." Adolescents need to know that there are lines of demarcation separating their internal processes from their external behaviors. These ego boundaries must be under their control so that others may not trample through the territory of their minds and so that the secret movements of their thoughts and their emotions can be hidden from those whom they do not trust and from those in whom they simply do not wish to confide.

Adults also need to preserve healthy ego boundaries, and they do so partially by the same process of maintaining an intact barrier between their inner psychological functions and their external behaviors, recognizing that verbalization of thoughts and feelings moves those experiences from the secret side of that barrier to the exposed side. It is frightening to see adults whose ego boundaries are disintegrating. As they lose the line that makes their minds private places, they begin to believe that others are inserting ideas in their heads and that others are able to observe their thoughts. Their minds are no longer surrounded by a protective barrier that they control, deciding what can enter and what can leave. Instead, their minds seem to be enclosed by a sieve that allows an indiscriminate flow of material in both directions. These unfortunate persons have lost the ability to keep the internal reality of their thoughts and feelings separate from the external realities of the world, and the result is psychotic confusion. Psychiatrists sometimes treat religious who have experienced a partial disintegration of ego boundaries brought on by some assault on those boundaries. Occasionally religious superiors, formation directors, or spiritual directors, perhaps out of excessive zeal for their work and not because of inordinate curiosity, will force religious to disclose private matters that they are not willing to reveal or ready to discuss. A sister in therapy talked about her lasting mistrust of superiors, which began when her novice mistress coerced her into disclosing a family problem that the novice mistress was, of course, in no position to help her resolve. Community sharing sessions often place psychological pressure on some religious to divulge material that they later regret mentioning. As a result they may feel violated and thus alienated.

Religious may become participants in workshops of one sort or another that compel self-disclosure in the group setting. They may seek this kind of experience, but they may also be persuaded to participate because they were misinformed about the purpose of the group. When these workshops are designed specifically for religious, they seem to possess a kind of imprimatur that assures unwary religious that the meeting contains nothing hazardous to faith or morals. Danger to psychological integrity is usually not considered. These workshops are frequently conducted by persons who have some training in group process but no understanding of individual psychodynamics. Their goal is to bring the group to interact successfully without concern for the needs of any one individual.

During psychotherapy it became clear that Father Lyle had undergone a serious disruption of ego boundaries during a marathon session presented in his community by an itinerant group worker who claimed a special expertise in enabling religious communities to interrelate in new ways. Under the emotional duress of the lengthy session, the persuasive leader, and the pressure of peers, Lyle mentioned some homosexual feelings he had experienced several years earlier as a young priest. After the workshop ended, Lyle began to worry that his prior thought might now become a reality. He began to sleep poorly and dreamed of people chasing him through dark, lonely streets. He felt that members of his community doubted his good reputation and questioned his motivation in becoming a priest. He thought that several of the students in the college where he taught were suspicious about his sexual orientation and were talking about him in small groups. Lyle was able to re-establish his ego boundaries after a brief period of psychotherapy. His psychiatrist advised him to avoid group situations that might lure him into personal disclosures. As part of their personality structures some people have weak ego boundaries, which become more fragile under stress. If these individuals are then exposed to dynamic religious speakers or powerful religious events that evoke intense emotional reactions, their ego boundaries may dissolve. In these situations it is difficult to determine what part of their experience originated within their own thoughts and feelings and impulses and what part came from another source.

Poorly trained counselors rarely acquire the important skills of not asking ill-timed questions and of not asking any questions at certain times. Psychological integrity depends on psychic privacy. If a therapist moves too quickly into delicate areas, the patient becomes defensive, in a maneuver to protect restricted mental and emotional domain. Well-trained therapists respect this territorial integrity and wait until the patient is ready to disclose more of self. The wanton publicizing of private lives and the crass exposure of personal matters in exposé style destroy respect for individual privacy. Religious superiors, formation directors, spiritual directors, religious counselors, and members of religious communities would do well to imitate the style of well-trained therapists rather than the style of the sensationalists.

Information given with the understanding, expressed or implicit, that it be kept in confidence should obviously be considered confidential. Therapists, confessors, and spiritual directors regularly receive information that may not be disclosed to others, whether that assurance was explicitly expressed in a particular instance or only implicitly present by virtue of their professional role. Does a member of a religious community have a right to expect a confidential relationship when talking to the superior in the superior's official capacity? Does a member of a small living community have a right to expect confidentiality in discussing a personal matter with another member of the group? Everyone might wish that the answer to these questions were positive. The individual religious who expects confidential communication in both instances may be bitterly disappointed. Some religious superiors assume that such conversations are confidential, but others do not. Some peers in religious life accept the privacy of personal communications, but others do not. Rather than assuming that a matter will be held in confidence by a religious superior or a companion religious, it is wiser and more realistic to request before a matter is revealed that it be protected by confidentiality. In small living groups, unless there is some unusual bond that supports the value of privacy and that is expressly agreed on by all, there can be no assurance of confidentiality in personal matters.

Most people consider information to be public if they know it has been told to several persons. If an individual believes that only she or he knows a certain secret, the responsibility to guard that secret seems serious. However, if the individual discovers that several others are also aware of the secret, the responsibility to maintain secrecy seems to decrease in direct proportion to the number of others who know. Although the fact that others know a secret does not ethically release a person from a promise to keep the matter confidential, psychologically the obligation of secrecy is diminished. For many people, knowing a secret is a strain, but telling a secret is a relief. The person who knows a secret often avoids telling it primarily because the one who confided it may discover the breach of confidence. However, if several persons know the secret, an individual can assume that someone will divulge it sooner or later, and it will be impossible to discover who did so. It is a fact of life that extends inside religious communities that private matters disclosed in group settings are not likely to remain confidential. To wish that it were not so is idealistic. To believe that it is not so is naive.

Religious superiors, especially formation directors, wishing to understand individual religious as thoroughly as possible may approach relatives and friends as sources of information. They usually obtain information readily from these people; most laypersons regard religious as men and women of high integrity to whom they can entrust all kinds of private and confidential data, and consequently, relatives and friends are not likely to be discriminating in what they tell. However, the privacy of the individual religious should not be violated by the willingness of family and friends to provide information or by the skill of the superior in extracting information from others.

Community concerns about issues of confidentiality should include consideration of personal files and various community documents, such as the minutes of administrative meetings. Legal aspects should be reviewed by an attorney. There are also ethical and psychological considerations. What material should be kept in an individual's record? May disparaging material be placed in the record? How long should personal documents be preserved? Who should be allowed to have access to the records? If community documents contain unfavorable information about an individual in the community, what special safeguards must be provided? What responsibility does a superior have when derogatory documents come from another source? What rights do religious have to review their personal files and add comments to them or request that information be removed? One facility that treats only religious patients sends detailed discharge reports to the patients' religious superiors. These reports consist of six to eight pages of personal information that may have been meaningful to the therapists and relevant to the therapeutic work but that cannot possibly be meaningful to the superiors or relevant to administrative decisions. Although these are sent with the permission of the patients, signed authorizations do not license indiscretion on the part of therapists. This facility recommends that superiors receiving the reports "destroy these reports after a reasonable period. . . . these reports should not be seen as part of a community member's permanent record." Such a recommendation is appropriate, but it is not an adequate safeguard. The best protection for the patient is a carefully worded report that avoids discussing the emotional pathology that necessitated care, that summarizes the treatment process in general terms, and that makes relevant recommendations. If a religious undergoes surgery, the surgeon does not give the superior a detailed report of the surgical techniques or a description of the diseased tissues that were removed. The surgeon might recommend to the superior that the patient return to duty with certain restrictions. The more carefully reports are worded the less concern there needs to be about keeping them in an individual's file.

Prior to Vatican II and the ensuing changes in religious life, one could not have argued in favor of the kind of confidentiality that is discussed here. However, momentous changes in religious life have brought about a different psychological climate. The legal rights and personal liberties of the individual are not abolished by religious vows. At a time when the political and social environment intrudes upon and curtails the private world of individuals, religious communities should consider the value they place on privacy and confidentiality. Some religious make unfair judgments about those who desire psychological privacy and consider them negligent in contributing to community cohesiveness. A personal penchant for privacy does not inhibit community involvement. Some religious, enamored with openness, distrust confidential relationships as contrary to a shared life. If the purpose of confiding in another is to obtain advice or assistance or to unburden oneself, the interaction does not detract from community relationships. Of course, if the reason for confiding is to establish an intimate, exclusive relationship with the confidant, then the good of the community may be jeopardized. A confidential relationship binds two people together in a sacred trust that should not be accepted lightly or abandoned easily. To deliver a personal secret to another makes that other person an extension of one's inner self. Such trust should be given cautiously and received carefully. Religious do not take a vow of trustworthiness, because vows are superfluous where virtue should already exist. Unfortunately, a focus on special vows sometimes allows one to lose sight of common virtue. If the virtue of charity brings religious to hold human life in high esteem, they will extend that reverence to information about an individual's life, because that information remains part of the fabric of the person's life, no matter how recent or how remote the information is in time, no matter how public or how private it appears to be.

The access of religious superiors and formation directors to personal information about individual religious should be limited by two principal factors. The first of these is the individual's right to privacy. This basic right is not abrogated by religious vows, and religious superiors must never assume that an individual religious has voluntarily renounced it. Secondly, confidentiality may be an essential part of the relationship a religious has with a therapist, a spiritual director, a family member, or a personal friend. This bond of confidentiality should not be transgressed by the religious superior or broken by the confidant.

Therapists, particularly, must maintain high ethical standards in their treatment of religious and withstand the intrusive maneuvers of those superiors who assume they have a right to know what the therapist learns in treatment. Confidentiality is not adequately protected by the impotent clause in a report recommending that it be destroyed. Nor is confidentiality truly protected by the signed authorization that is not freely given. If payment for treatment depends on providing unnecessary information to superiors, the price is obviously exorbitant. The manner in which therapists give information to superiors should follow precise ethical guidelines, and the kind of material that is provided should aim at helping superiors make administrative decisions about the patient and not attempt to acquaint them with the etiology of psychological symptoms or the psychodynamics of pathological behaviors. Family members and friends must also respect the individual's privacy and not disclose information indiscreetly to religious superiors simply because they represent ecclesiastical authority.

As the right to privacy has gained recognition culturally and in religious communities, a more subtle route to personal information has been established. Self-disclosure in "sharing groups" sometimes reveals a greater amount of private material than lengthy questioning could ever uncover. Religious often are under considerable psychological pressure from superiors and from peers in routine community meetings or in special group settings to disclose personal material that they normally would only trust to others in whom they have the utmost confidence. Such groups can rarely produce the confidentiality they promise. Superiors sometimes encourage community members to reveal personal problems and secret conflicts to them with the implicit promise that the superior can then assist them in resolving these matters. This disclosure of private information by the community member moves the superior toward the role of counselor, which may be incompatible with the superior's other roles, as discussed in the following chapter.

14. The Religious Superior as Counselor

Today many religious superiors have had some training in general psychological principles as well as in specific counseling techniques. Some have completed regular college courses in these areas, and others have attended special short-term training sessions that purport to teach counseling skills to those who enroll. Some religious formation directors have advanced degrees in psychology or counseling. Education and experience in these areas can assist religious superiors and formation directors in understanding the emotional struggles of those with whom they work. However, it is important that those in authority who have this training recognize its benefits and its limitations and establish some clear standards for its use. They not only need to accept limitations in counseling skills imposed by their education and experience, but they also need to appreciate the obstacles to counseling techniques imposed by their position of authority.

A little bit of knowledge of psychology is as dangerous as a little bit of knowledge in other fields—perhaps more dangerous. If one miscalculates because of a limited knowledge of mathematics, others are likely to notice the errors and make the necessary corrections. If one has an inadequate knowledge of cooking and misguidedly volunteers one's incompetence, others will soon complain. Counselees rarely detect the shortcomings of counselors, because the counselees have no valid external criteria and no reliable internal criteria by which to evaluate a counselor's proficiency. It is self-evident when figures do not add up correctly or ledgers do not balance. There is incontrovertible evidence when the cook has ruined the roast. But when the counseling relationship enters a sour phase or when the realities of the counselee's experiences are not summed up accurately, who is to say that the counselor is inept? It is much easier to say that the counselee is resistive. This explanation is readily presented when the counselor is a religious superior and the counselee is a community member. It is difficult enough for a good counselor to have someone question his or her authority. It is even more difficult for a person in authority to have someone question his or her counseling skills.

Counseling involves more than the simple application of a few superficial techniques to a relationship that exists with another person. Counseling embodies a special kind of relationship, a unique kind of interaction. The counselor must accurately perceive the qualities of that relationship and must continually clarify them for the counselee. It is the counselor who defines the counseling relationship. The counselor's craft provides an openness to the counselee, an absence of bias, an avoidance of criticism, and a refusal to exercise authority in the decisions of the counselee. The counseling role also requires an empathetic stance on the part of the counselor. When religious superiors attempt formal counseling of their community members, they accept a dual task that may contain internal inconsistencies. On the one hand, the role of the superior carries a special obligation to support the rule, the vows, the requirements of community life, and the authority of ecclesiastical superiors. On the other hand, the role of counselor demands faithful concern for the particular problems of those individuals who seek understanding, a supportive hand through emotional turmoil, an unbiased listener who accepts their imperfections and does not judge them accordingly. The religious counselee may exhibit behaviors that violate reasonable requirements in community living, that openly or surreptitiously challenge the authority of religious superiors, that defy the rules of the community and of the church, or that are incompatible with their religious vows. If religious superiors have assumed formal counseling relationships with individual religious caught in such emotional conflicts and troubled behaviors, how should those superiors now proceed? Obviously, there are two directions superiors may take in such situations: one is to set forth the responsibilities of the individual; the other is to remain noncommittal about the present weakness of the individual. Some superiors deny the incompatibility of these two positions and attempt to hide the steel of their authority under the cloak of the kindly counselor. They overlook the glaring fact that the counselee finds conflict between the demands of life and the inadequacy of his or her responses and that this conflict brings the individual to seek assistance. In facing this dilemma, if superiors lean toward their authority role and use information gained in the confidential counseling relationship to correct, to control, or to censure troubled community members, they violate the counselor–counselee relationship. On the other hand, if superiors persist in their counseling role, their authority is gravely compromised, and they become powerless to confront the problem behaviors of those under their jurisdiction. The leadership position of the superior often supplies an important relationship for the distressed religious who experiences that authority as positive motivation to obtain help and strong incentive to make improvements.

Sister Martha entered psychiatric care because she had experienced a traumatic event in her life. Her lover of several years was killed in an airplane crash, and she could not recover from the loss. She became increasingly depressed as the months passed following his death, and she withdrew more and more from social contacts, particularly with community members. No one had known about her relationship, so no one perceived her loss or comforted her in it. However, there was one person who should have been aware of her loss because she should have been aware of the relationship. When Martha first met the man who later became her lover, she experienced some concern about her own romantic feelings toward him. Martha had a great deal of confidence in and affection for her major superior and went to her to discuss this beginning relationship. The superior apparently fancied herself to be a counselor and took Martha under her guidance. In her counseling role the superior took the position that a religious benefits from an intimate relationship because such a relationship encourages personal growth. The superior did not define what she meant by "intimate," and Martha chose not to ask. If the superior had been more attentive to her role as superior, she might have recognized the potential seriousness of Martha's relationship and advised Martha to avoid any further involvement. If the superior had been more competent in her role as counselor, she might have elicited the details of Martha's involvement and pointed out the emotional conflict she was creating. Martha did not disclose the depth of her relationship, because the counseling superior did not ask and because Martha did not wish to reveal that information to her authoritative superior.

Martha interpreted the superior's statements about intimacy as official sanction for her sexual involvement with her friend. One can argue that Martha could not have been that naive or innocent and that she heard what she wanted to hear. In fact, Martha heard accurately what the superior said, but she used those comments to support the course she already wanted to travel. However, if Martha's superior had assumed an authoritative role and directly advised Martha not to continue the relationship, Martha would have heard that admonition and acted upon it.

Martha went to her superior for advice, not counseling. She received poor counseling, which only confused her and encouraged her to enter into an illicit relationship. If she had received good advice from her superior, she would not later have needed psychiatric care to resolve the emotional conflicts she had experienced for many years, to cure the major depressive illness that had almost brought her to suicide, and to renew her commitment to religious life. The only growth she had experienced in the relationship was growth away from her personal values, her religious vows, and her community involvement. Everyone at some time needs the strength of a friend who says, "Please don't do that. It is not good for you. It is not right for you." If instead the friend says, "Let's talk about it over the weeks to come but in the meantime I won't give you an opinion and you do what seems right for you," perhaps that friend gives the cold stone of counseling to one who needs the warm bread of concern.

Some might claim that religious superiors no longer have much authority so they are free to enter into a counselor role with their community members. In spite of many modifications in the role of religious superiors, those changes do not support the idea that religious superiors have lost their power. They may acknowledge it less openly; they may refer to it less directly; they may exercise it less dramatically. However, religious authority still exists in the person of the religious superior, and euphemistic titles like "coordinator" or "facilitator" have not altered that reality. The fact that religious superiors remain people of authority seems indisputable. They still make decisions that affect the lives of their community members and the status of their corporate communities. If indeed religious superiors are not making decisions, then the members of their communities, both corporately and individually, are affected by their pusillanimity.

Superiors who attempt to avoid the authority of their position make poor religious superiors. Community members who attempt to avoid the authority of their superiors by assuming they have no authority behave imprudently. Formation directors also have authority, and rightly so. Religious communities these days sometimes select formation directors because of their warm and friendly personalities, characteristics often considered unimportant in the past. Communities may also choose as formation directors persons who have counseling skills. However, the congeniality of formation directors should not influence those in formation to overlook their authority, nor should their counseling skills persuade those in formation to forget their power. Whatever their level of affability, whatever their expertise in counseling, the fact remains that formation directors have authority, and their authority directly affects the lives, the futures, of those under their jurisdiction.

Some may disagree with any limitation on the counseling function of the religious superior. They may argue that the role of religious superiors and formation directors has always included the prerogative, in fact the obligation, to counsel individual religious. Some religious will attest to the great virtue and fine leadership of former superiors and directors whose excellence was based on the fact that they were friendly, available to everyone, easy to talk to, helpful in their advice, wise in their counsel. Obviously one treads on tradition in suggesting a curtailment of the superior's counseling role. Some communities require members to make a "manifestation of conscience" to the superior. Others strongly encourage complete openness with religious superiors. Attitudes of this kind imply that religious superiors by virtue of their position have special gifts and extraordinary graces that enable them to understand all those who come to them with problems. These attitudes also imply that religious superiors have some exceptional abilities to advise individual religious on what course to follow. These suppositions are unjustified in the case of many religious superiors and formation directors, even though some of them are remarkably wise and insightful people whose advice always deserves careful attention.

At one time most religious accepted the counsel of superiors as representing the will of God. Although that idea is no longer stated as openly and as often, it continues to exert a major influence in the lives of many religious. One cannot reasonably dispute the notion that religious superiors do receive special graces to carry out their particular duties, just as married couples and parents receive special graces for their needs. However, individuals may or may not cooperate with grace, so freedom remains part of the formula, and, barring some continuous miracle, grace builds on nature. By reason of their natural characteristics, some superiors are poorly endowed for the position they have acquired, and the grace of office does not miraculously equip them to listen gently, to reflect wisely, and to respond prudently. Some superiors do not spend enough time in personal prayer and private reflection to preserve that inner disposition that would allow grace to influence their exercise of office.

Individual religious who accept superiors and formation directors as steadfast sources of good counsel by reason of their position oversimplify the matter and in so doing expose themselves to influences that may be unreliable and inept and even damaging. Superiors and directors who assume that they acquire counseling aptitudes and perennial wisdom by reason of their position overestimate the matter and in so doing may expose community members to pretentious airs and poor advice. In one religious community of women, the superior, Sister Maria, was psychologically poorly equipped to function either in an administrative role or in a counseling capacity. She exhibited signs of chronic depression superimposed on personality traits that were immature and self-centered. For six stress-filled years the members of Maria's community regularly and dutifully approached her in an attempt to discuss their problems and to elicit her advice. Her responses rarely provided any indication that she even listened to their comments. Maria remained preoccupied with the welfare of the children in a school where she had taught for fifteen years. In interviews with individual sisters she often digressed into tiresome stories about the children, stories that she considered humorous anecdotes.

How should individual religious deal with superiors who are psychologically or experientially poorly equipped to listen, to evaluate, and to respond to the current problems and personal concerns of those who are under their authority? How should individual religious interact with superiors who have demonstrated an inability to maintain the confidentiality required by their office? Religious sometimes face serious conflicts in this area, caught between the expectations of authority or the requirements of the rule and their own legitimate concerns about the revelation of personal and confidential material to a superior whom they consider inadequate and unreliable. They must try to make a mature and judicious decision about the alternatives, recognizing that an individual cannot be forced to trust another person. To be compelled to expose oneself psychologically to another who does not inspire confidence violates one's sense of integrity and one's sense of fairness.

Sister Matilda began psychotherapy because she had experienced symptoms of depression and conflict with authority figures for many years. In treatment she related that as a young girl it was extremely difficult for her to discuss anything important or even to have a casual conversation with her mother. Matilda's verbal reticence developed in her youth because of her mother's constant faultfinding. Her mother criticized everything she did, how she walked, how she ate, how she dressed, how she laughed, how she talked. Matilda recalled the embarrassment and anger she felt when her mother corrected her grammar or her pronunciation in front of others. Matilda felt defenseless against her mother, whose sharp tongue, carping attitude, and domineering manner subdued everyone around her. Matilda tried to protect herself by withdrawing so that her mother could not humiliate her, by inactivity so that her mother could not criticize her, and by silence so that her mother could not correct her. When Matilda applied to enter a religious community, those in authority regarded her as an excellent candidate, for they interpreted her isolation as contentment, her inactivity as reverence, and her silence as serenity. However, her novice mistress construed her social withdrawal and uncommunicativeness as surliness. On one occasion Matilda hesitantly questioned a decision made by the novice mistress. She timidly and perhaps awkwardly asked the novice mistress to change her mind about forbidding the group of novices to go on a particular outing. Instead of encouraging this reserved young woman to express herself in this manner, the novice mistress was provoked by her "defiance," especially since it had occurred with the other novices present. After evening prayers the novice mistress called Matilda to the office and spent three hours demanding an explanation of her behavior. Under the gruelling questioning of the mistress, Matilda revealed the hidden alcoholism of her father, the rejecting and punitive attitude of her mother, the rivalry she felt toward two of her five siblings, and her own doubts about the existence of God and the value of her own life.

The next day in the novitiate appeared routine for Matilda and the mistress of novices. Each one carried on her usual schedule. Matilda hid her emotional reactions in the same manner that she had always hidden them. She had not cried during or following the interview, although she had not slept all night. The following morning her companions had no way of knowing that she had been emotionally violated and then abandoned the previous night. When Matilda came for therapy eighteen years later, she had still not forgiven her novice mistress. The incident between them remained a raw psychological wound, which was constantly irritated by superiors who tried to interact with her and by peers who tried to get close to her, and which now made her a reluctant participant in treatment. For the therapist, treatment was a cautious venture—not to ask too much, not to seem to pry, not to violate her trust in even the smallest way. It was extremely important to let her know that the therapist's "caring" did not necessitate his "knowing." As therapy progressed, she came to understand that even the therapist's "knowing" was not so that he could know but so that she could know and understand and finally be at peace because of understanding. She found that understanding, and it brought her peace and enabled her to forgive her mother for not understanding her, her novice mistress for profaning her privacy, and her psychiatrist for intruding into her inner turmoil.

It is obvious that some religious superiors and some formation directors have little or no ability for confidential listening or judicious counseling. However, no matter how inept they may be, they are unlikely to limit themselves in this particular role, first, because they have no definite criteria to use to evaluate their own competence and, second, because the ability to counsel others has become a remarkably popular and prestigious skill. Watered-down psychology has flooded the nation with an interest in self-disclosure, listening skills, and supportive liaisons. Emotional and social adequacy in today's society seems to require an ability to understand "where another person is coming from," and to be "present for" others. These simple phrases frequently conceal a counseling stance or a counseling need on the part of those who use them. Religious superiors who profess a desire to be "present for" every member of the community or to understand "where every member of the community is coming from" are in reality setting goals that demand of them endless discussion, constant availability, infinite tact, and boundless wisdom. Many religious who in the past tended to view the superior's role as that of a loving parental figure are ready to replace that model with a person who reads the latest pulp books in psychology, who exhibits at least some superficial techniques of counseling, and who uses current clichés in discussing personal distress. Because of the expectations of community members and because of the importance attached to the counseling role, religious superiors are tempted to assume a counseling mission and disregard their personal limitations or the constraints of their position of authority. It is important that individual religious avoid psychological exposure to unqualified persons who may wittingly or unwittingly violate their trust, even when those unqualified persons are their religious superiors.

The predilection to counsel people was depicted in a recent television play in a scene that should have been serious but that became vacuous and inane. The typical triangle of lovers had come to a melodramatic moment, with one of them brandishing a gun and threatening to kill the other two. In the play, a young priest was witness to this scene; he rushed toward the gunman saying, with profound inadequacy, "Let me counsel you! Let me counsel you!" Religious superiors, adequate or not, sometimes rush in with equal fervor, saying to the individual religious, "Let me counsel you." That may be the very moment when it would be better to say, "Let me be your superior, interested, attentive, concerned, but a person of authority in your life." The distraught individual in the television script might have been more reassured and calmed if the young cleric had said, "I am a Catholic priest, a person of faith, one who believes in the sacredness of life. Let me bring the force of my belief, the authority of my position, to calm the anger and to lessen the chaos that is present here."

Professional counseling and psychotherapy include specific, organized interventions in a person's life in an attempt to help that individual voluntarily make some positive and desired changes in self. Counseling and psychotherapy do not cure all ills, relieve all suffering, correct all evils, remove all faults, or solve all problems. These methods of assisting others are not the panacea that those who recommend them might wish them to be. A glib recommendation to undergo counseling sometimes permits those in authority to avoid their primary responsibility and to shift the complex burden of a refractory person to the fragile bond of a counselor-counselee relationship. Teachers refer difficult students to counselors. Courts refer delinquent adolescents and convicted criminals to counselors. Businesses refer overworked executives and alcoholic employees to counselors. Attorneys refer divorcing couples to counselors. There are special programs to counsel gamblers, people in mid-life crisis, incest victims, people with strokes, people with colostomies, pyromaniacs, rape victims, abusive spouses, abused spouses, and numerous other groups whose only homogeneity sometimes depends on two common labels, one descriptive of a life event and the other the label of counselee. These statements are not intended to minimize the value of therapeutic intervention and support in the lives of some individuals. However, some people do not benefit from counseling; some are unwilling or unable to participate; and some have problems that are not amenable to therapy. Society recognizes the reality that welfare programs do not alleviate the need for charitable contributions or release the financial obligation that some members of society have toward others for whom they are responsible. In a similar manner, counseling programs do not remove the need for loving relationships or release the professional obligation some members of society have toward others to whom they have some responsibility. The superior's obligation to be a person of authority in the life of an individual religious is not relieved either by referring that individual for counseling or by assuming the counselor role.

Father Mark came for psychiatric care on the recommendation of his bishop. Mark was fifty-five years old and had been a priest for twenty-two years. In a parish where he served as pastor ten years after his ordination, some of the parishioners disagreed with his policies and wrote a letter of complaint to the bishop. The latter had a reputation of being an austere but saintly person who genuinely loved the people of his diocese. The bishop never allowed Mark to respond to the charges that were made against him but indicated that he accepted them as valid, and he transferred Mark to a different parish. Mark came from a wealthy family, and he enjoyed the expensive gifts his relatives gave him. Possibly Mark's affluent background infected the thinking of the poverty-minded bishop. The bishop's negative attitude about Mark persisted, and he readily believed any disparaging comments he heard about Mark. At one time the bishop ordered Mark to attend a marathon session given in the area by a traveling therapist. Mark was the only religious in the group, and he found the experience emotionally degrading and humiliating. A few years later the bishop hired a mental health consultant to attend parish meetings in Mark's parish and to point out to Mark what he was doing wrong. On another occasion the bishop insisted that Mark admit himself to a residential program for religious. Mark agreed to go for an evaluation. The director of that facility wrote an ambiguous report to the bishop stating that if

Mark cooperated with their program, it could probably be of benefit to him but also indicating that Mark was not disposed to cooperate with the program.

In psychiatric care Mark was seen for a few visits to determine clearly whether or not there was a reason for him to be in treatment. Although the biased attitude of the bishop angered Mark, he adjusted reasonably well to the tribulations of his ministry under a superior whom others revered for his piety and gentleness, but whom Mark experienced as unjust, unforgiving, and unrelenting. With Mark's permission the psychiatrist wrote a letter to the bishop stating, "After several interviews with Father Mark I find no evidence of psychopathology and no reason to engage him in psychiatric treatment. Father Mark appears willing to cooperate with any assignment which you choose to give him, and he has expressed a desire to develop a more direct relationship with you and work on the resolution of any conflicts that may exist between the two of you." Although the bishop's repeated recommendations that Mark receive some kind of counseling did not in fact release the bishop from his obligation to interact more openly and more fairly with Mark, these recommendations apparently gave the bishop an unwarranted sense of benevolence in his confidence that he was doing all that he could for Mark.

Some superiors and formation directors have, through natural ability or extensive education, the knowledge and the skills to counsel others. Nevertheless, those who possess these capabilities must exercise sound judgment in their use and carefully distinguish between the role of a superior who has the skills of a counselor and the role of a counselor who has the authority of a superior. To know how to listen attentively, to be able to encourage others to express themselves more clearly and more completely, to value discussion rather than decision in certain situations, to be able to extend one's own understanding to encompass another's position, to be respectful and caring in responses, and to be judicious and thoughtful in recommendations or comments, all of these counseling skills aid superiors and formation directors in meeting more competently the psychological aspects of their roles. Although the normal relationship of superior and community member benefits from the presence of these skills, the uncurtailed use of these techniques can sometimes move the relationship beyond that of superior–community member to one of counselor–counselee. The change in relationship can occur easily because the two roles of the superior are not sharply demarcated. The responsibility to establish the character of the relationship rests with the superior, not with the community member.

If a religious superior discovers, for example, that one of the members of the community has a problem with alcohol, the superior has a choice of ignoring the matter or mentioning it to the individual. Some superiors choose to ignore situations of this kind; they assume an attitude of noninterference when a community member behaves in a negligent or destructive manner. These superiors appear to base this attitude on the premise that mature adults must make their own decisions in life, and superiors are not accountable for the behavior of individual religious. However, persons in positions of authority, whether their title is manager or pastor, superintendent or superior, governor or bishop, chief or coordinator, president or provincial, accept in their assignment the duty to expect, and at times to require, that those under their jurisdiction meet certain standards that those in authority are obligated to uphold by virtue of their office. The legal doctrine of *respondeat superior* holds those in authority responsible for the actions of those who are under their direction. Under this doctrine contractors are judged responsible for the actions of their workers, physicians are considered accountable for the acts of their employees, and religious superiors can be answerable for the behavior of those under their authority. Religious superiors who ignore the problem behavior of community members not only perform in a weak and irresponsible manner but also in a manner that increases their legal liability and places the reputation and financial assets of the community at risk. When a superior becomes aware of seriously inappropriate behavior on the part of an individual religious, the prudent and conscientious course to take is to confront that individual. After some patient listening and some prayerful reflection, the superior should suggest some measures the person may take to correct the difficulty. Father Martin, although well respected as a college teacher, had some serious psychological problems, but he avoided seeking professional help for them. The first manifestation of his emotional disturbance came in his abuse of alcohol. His mood became irritable and his behavior became erratic during the "happy hour" that his community regularly enjoyed before dinner. When he was not drinking, the members of his community regarded him as a person of considerable personal charm, with a keen mind and a facile sense of humor. Because of their admiration of him, they patiently tolerated his acrimonious and stormy behavior when he was inebriated. Martin invariably cultivated a close relationship with successive superiors, who became personal friends and in whom he confided, at least superficially. The extent of his alcoholism fluctuated over the years, but not because any of his superiors confronted him regarding his intemperance. He developed some physical illnesses as a result of his alcoholism, and the repeated admonitions of his physicians served as intermittent deterrents.

Martin had another pattern of behavior that was even more destructive, if not to him then certainly to others. He established a series of sexually exploitative relationships with women, especially women religious. These evolved out of his position as their teacher, as their confidant, and at times as their spiritual director. Although his superior may not have been aware of the number of these relationships, he could not have been ignorant of their seriousness. Some of Martin's victims, in seeking psychiatric help for their own confusion and conflict, on occasion obtained treatment from the same psychiatrist. At one point three or four of these distressed women, independently of one another, reported their unsavory liaisons to Martin's superior. Although the superior expressed some concern about their charges, he was defensive regarding Martin's involvement and assured each of them that his relationship with Martin would enable him to evaluate their stories and to persuade Martin to correct any serious deficiencies in his behavior. The superior maintained a pseudocounseling role with Martin, as he did with many of the community members, but that role was so ambiguous that it did not give him a base from which to examine thoroughly Martin's behavior. If not deliberately at least unconsciously, Martin used his close relationship with superiors to avoid their scrutiny, and he assumed a counselee position with them to escape from confronting his conflicts rather than to resolve them. Regrettably, the superior ignored his own serious responsibility to require some change in Martin's behavior and to advise Martin to obtain whatever professional help might be necessary to effect that change. Such superiors will eventually face their administrative responsibility if they find themselves subject to legal action based on this kind of negligence.

If a formation director discovers that a novice is involved in an erotic relationship with someone outside the community, the director has an obligation to discuss the behavior with the novice and at some point to make some careful but definite recommendations. If the formation director assumes the role of counselor and sets up a series of appointments to analyze and resolve the problem, some awkward predicaments may arise. Once a counseling relationship has been established, what does the formation director do if the novice reveals a homosexual relationship with another novice or with a professed member of the community? What obligation does the formation director have toward the novice as well as the other community member? What obligation is there to the entire community? Can the formation director act on this knowledge without the permission, or even with the permission, of the client? Well-trained counselors and therapists deal with this kind of information in a nonjudgmental manner and focus their attention on the needs of the counselee without feeling obliged to evaluate or to influence the behavior of those who are outside the therapeutic relationship. In order to ensure this attitude of detachment and maintain therapeutic objectivity, most therapists will not treat two people who have a significant relationship with each other, such as two friends, two college roommates, two people who work closely together, two members of the same family unit, or two religious who live together in a small community. Neither will therapists usually accept as patients persons who are already well known to them or who have some other relationship with them. For example, a counselor who teaches in a college introduces a conflict of interest in accepting one of her or his students as a counselee. How can religious superiors and formation directors assume a counselor's nonjudgmental attitude toward persons about whom they have an obligation to make judgments? How can religious superiors and formation directors achieve therapeutic objectivity toward community members with whom they have another, more important relationship? How can a formation director be the director of several persons and the counselor of one of them? How can a religious superior relate consistently to all community members and deliberately arrange a special, exclusive counseling relationship with one of them?

If the superior, in the process of confronting an individual religious regarding his or her problem behavior, suggests that the two of them get together at regular intervals to discuss the behavior and to discover its causes and its significance with the goal of helping the individual gain control over it, then the superior has become counselor and must relinquish the role of superior. One cannot, in fairness, play opposing parts. When a superior arranges regular appointments for a community member who exhibits emotional difficulties or inappropriate behaviors, there is the implication that a formal counseling relationship is established, and, as a result, the responsibilities of the superior change. Characteristically, superiors govern and care for community members independent of whether or not they have problems, but counselors guide and care for others because they have problems. Superiors must recognize the difference between taking care of another in a relationship of administrative obligation and taking care of another in a relationship of therapy. Spouses and friends take care of one another, but they do not treat one another's problems. It is characteristic of adolescents to have difficulty caring about friends without trying to cure all their hurts, all their faults, all their difficulties. Idealistic adolescents struggling with their own inner confusion claim the ability to understand their friends as no one else has and the power to help their friends as no one else can. Sometimes religious superiors find it difficult to establish their identity in their new role, and in a regression to an adolescent pattern, they set out to help others meet the challenges of life rather than facing the challenge of their own leadership role.

When superiors fail to recommend reliable and accessible sources of help to community members who have a definite need for assistance, those superiors place themselves indirectly and inadvertently in a counseling role. If a religious has a severe pain in the abdomen and if the superior makes the judgment that there is no need to call a doctor, the superior implies that she or he is competent to make that determination and thereby assumes responsibility for the course and outcome of that physical suffering. If the pain leaves in a short time and does not return, the superior and the individual religious may assume it was only an intestinal spasm. If the pain is associated with an infected appendix that ruptures and causes intestinal gangrene, the individual religious endures a prolonged illness as a result of the superior's wrongful and inexpert judgment. Superiors who make decisions about the level of therapeutic intervention required by community members always assume a grave responsibility. This is particularly true when they not only determine the kind of treatment that is necessary but also decide that they have the expertise to provide that treatment.

When religious superiors promise or even imply that they

will assist others in resolving emotional conflicts or reforming problem behaviors, they offer a counseling relationship and in so doing withdraw the caring concern and the subtle influence of their authoritative role. The desire to counsel others attracts some religious superiors so strongly that they encourage the members of their communities to relate to them in this role. The attitude "Come and talk to me anytime about anything that may be troubling you" has the aura of "band-aid" counseling. It is an open-door policy that leads to an empty house. No one can be available all the time. Superiors who are able to limit their availability to the community by establishing office hours, by asking individuals to make appointments, by being absent from the community for personal reasons thereby indicate an unwillingness to serve as counselor-in-residence during their term of office. Father Michael, a formation director in an order of men, was always available, or tried to be, for those in his care. Besides his routine duties Michael spent many hours counseling those in formation. Although his counseling efforts exhausted him, there was never any indication that his work was psychologically productive for anyone. It was more like "emotional hand-holding." For some it proved detrimental; it was tranquilizing and mildly addictive and so kept them from confronting some painful issues. Periodically Michael became overwhelmed by the stress of his availability and sought refuge in a residential treatment facility. It would have been more just and more beneficial to allow the directees to obtain professional help, in which case Michael might not have needed it himself.

The superiors and formation directors who want to be counselors to their community members are like the parents who want to be friends to their teenagers. Adolescents need friends, but they also need parents, and when parents become "buddies," they lose their parental role. Adolescents recognize the difference and withdraw from those parents who trade the burden of parental authority for the comfort of camaraderie. Being a friend to a teenager is easier than being a parent to one. Being a counselor for individual religious is easier than being a superior for a group of religious.

Religious superiors and formation directors are in positions of authority that require them to make important decisions about the lives of others and to accept some legal, and perhaps moral, responsibility for the behavior of those under their jurisdiction. They may fail to meet this obligation of their office if they are incompetent or untrustworthy in guiding others, or if they are unwilling to exercise their authority by confronting others and by making explicit recommendations to them. Superiors and formation directors may also avoid their responsibilities as authorities by shifting into the role of counselor. Good counselors do not take an authoritative position in the lives of those whom they counsel, and they remain detached from additional interrelatedness with their counselees. Superiors abandon their authoritative role in order to counsel community members, and they establish a special place in the community for those whom they counsel. This incompatibility in being superior and counselor is present whether the superior is adequately trained or totally unskilled.

Superiors set up a counseling relationship when they arrange regular appointments with a community member for the purpose of helping that individual understand and thus change some emotional responses or problem behaviors. Superiors implicitly assume the responsibility, if not the role, of counselor when they decide whether or not an individual religious needs therapeutic assistance or when they determine the kind or extent of therapy that is needed. On the other hand, even appropriate referral to a psychiatrist or other therapist does not resolve difficulties for every individual, nor does it absolve the superior of the obligation to continue to be interested in the individual's welfare and to make equitable decisions regarding the individual's situation. Sometimes it takes the harmonious combination of the best of superiors exercising wise and patient administrative authority and the best of therapists exercising precise and penetrating therapeutic skills to motivate an individual religious to the resolution of deep emotional conflict.

15. Resolution of Celibate Conflict

For years religious communities have been acutely aware of emotional conflicts in many of their members, and religious superiors have watched those conflicts affect the quality of religious life. Some of those in conflict exhibit disturbed reactions and problem behaviors that reverberate throughout the entire community because of their magnitude. Other religious, less obviously unsettled, disrupt the harmony of every group with whom they live by forging a chain of unrewarding relationships and unpleasant experiences. Another group behave appropriately in their community setting but demonstrate emotional disturbance in relationships outside the jurisdiction of the community. There are others whose emotional disquiet has little effect on anyone else but destroys their own tranquility, saps their vitality, and limits their potential. Whatever level of psychological conflict religious evidence, their communities increasingly recognize the related costs in wasted lives, community contention, public scandal, and the economic burden of treatment programs. Although research data fail to establish a higher incidence of psychiatric illness among religious compared to laypersons, these studies do not include those emotional problems that may exist in religious for years causing personal distress and community disturbance but that are never confronted as individual treatment issues.

Married persons sometimes say to their spouse, "You must change, and if that requires psychiatric intervention, then obtain that help, because if you do not change, we cannot continue to be together." Employers make similar statements to employees, and friends do the same to friends. But religious superiors rarely take such a firm stand. Instead of insisting that individual religious with severe emotional conflicts obtain appropriate treatment, superiors frequently offer them substitute programs that do not provide the help they need. Superiors often recommend that emotionally troubled religious participate in human-potential workshops, growth experiences, psychology courses, consciousness-expanding retreats, marathon therapy sessions, renewal programs, and encounter groups. Involvement in these programs rarely produces any permanent relief or lasting improvement, but the superior obtains the temporary advantage of believing that something is being done and some change will occur. Some emotionally troubled religious proceed through a lengthy list of these experiences and as a result become among the most psychologically pampered people in contemporary society without gaining any benefit from these opportunities.

Married persons sometimes discover that they are unable to continue in a marriage unless the spouse makes some deep and drastic changes. Marriage tribunals recognize the importance of emotional stability and maturity in determining the validity of a marriage contract. Unresolved emotional conflict or psychiatric illness in one spouse can cause years of marital strife, destroy the emotional health of the partner, induce or intensify physical illnesses in both parties, and undermine the personal integrity and spiritual values of both. Just as emotional instability or immaturity can severely limit the ability of an individual to engage in a valid marriage contract, so similar limitations can make a person unable to meet the essential requirements of the religious life. It is unlikely that any workshop, class, or group experience could help unstable religious examine the obligations of religious life and their own ability or lack of ability to meet those obligations. Individual psychotherapy might compel an individual to contemplate the alternatives. However, religious are often reluctant to begin psychotherapy, and superiors, who sometimes are the only ones who can influence the individual religious to accept treatment, often fail to make the recommendation. In recent years religious lifestyles have changed, exposing religious to increased public scrutiny. Religious who are emotionally unstable are more visible to those outside the community and more embarrassing to those inside the community. Changing circumstances may oblige superiors more frequently to say to community members, "You must make some changes in your emotional reactions and attitudes if you wish to remain in religious life. Psychiatric care may assist you in making those changes, and you should consider obtaining that kind of help. But if you cannot make those changes that bring you to an emotional state that is compatible with religious life, then we must be separated."

One can distinguish five groups of emotionally conflicted persons in religious life: The first group tries to hide from emotional conflict and to deny the importance of their own emotional reactions. The second group exhibits psychiatric symptomatology that can develop from a variety of emotional difficulties. The third group experiences conflict because their emotional immaturity brings them into contention with others. The fourth group encounters a normal amount of emotional dissidence, but their inner struggles do not cause psychiatric symptoms, social disharmony, or personal disquietude. In the fifth group, emotional conflict develops as a result of their inner ambivalence in relation to vocational commitment. Each of these groups will be considered in the paragraphs that follow.

Persons in religious life who reject their own emotional reactions inevitably encounter emotional conflict, because they are unable to practice good mental hygiene. Good physical hygiene helps people ward off physical illness, and good mental hygiene helps people avoid psychological conflict and emotional illness. However, in order to practice good physical hygiene, individuals must have some awareness of the way their bodies function and the things they can do to keep their bodies healthy. Similarly, in order to practice good mental hygiene individuals must have some awareness of the way their minds and emotions work and the things they can do to keep themselves emotionally healthy. Religious characteristically regard their spiritual development as their primary goal. Their intellectual advancement, which was not always considered important, is now a greater priority, partly because of improved standards and higher requirements in the professional fields in which they work. More and more religious share society's concern for good physical health, centering around habits of exercise, diet, and demands for an unpolluted environment. But religious are sometimes solicitous about their spiritual progress, their intellectual improvement, and their physical health while ignoring the breadth and the depth of their emotional reactions. Daily living involves a variety of emotional responses, which may vary from a quick breath of annoyance or a sharp flash of attraction to an overwhelming cascade of rage or a bursting fire of passion. Some religious suppress their awareness of these internal events and thereby postpone the possible pain and the potential growth associated with emotional conflict.

Emotion adds a dimension to life that contributes to its richness. Emotion reminds people that they are created to span the two worlds of spirit and flesh, belonging completely to neither. On the one hand, ascetics cannot fully escape into the world of spirit, because feelings of loneliness, of tedium, of love, of lust renew their contact with physical reality. On the other hand, those who seek only material pleasures know a sense of guilt and sadness, however faint, that keeps saying, "There is something more. There is something more." Neither the pietist nor the materialist can successfully avoid the reality of his or her emotional responses, because those responses do not disappear simply because they are ignored. They may be repressed, but they live on like subversives under a military regime, sometimes attacking openly and suddenly and quickly disappearing, sometimes secretly sabotaging all productive efforts, sometimes gaining brief, chaotic control, but always continuing to struggle until either they are recognized as worthy participants or they bring destruction to all. Emotions are not alien forces in people's lives. They are lawful constituents of internal government, sometimes unruly, sometimes too boisterous, sometimes too quick to act; yet emotions are filled with a kind of mysterious wisdom that recognizes danger from far away and knows where great treasures are hidden. If all emotional reactions were eliminated, the world might be better, but it would not be as bright; the world might be simpler, but it would not be as beautiful; the world might be more peaceful, but it would not be as colorful. Those who repress their emotions pay a heavy price for the uncertain tranquility they obtain. When emotion is curtailed, so is enthusiasm; when emotion is constricted, so is joy; when emotion is suppressed, so is empathy. Those who repress emotion may appear secure and stable as they meet the everyday demands of life with apparent self-assurance and equanimity. Underneath this exterior calmness they are fragile, because they lack the strength that comes from emotional resilience. Their inflexibility makes them vulnerable to unexpected or unusual stress, which may cause psychological disintegration and psychiatric illness.

Emotional conflict in religious sometimes produces the same kinds of psychiatric symptoms that other people develop in response to certain life events. The unresolved conflicts of developmental years, immediate pressures that exceed personality strengths, or psychophysiologic factors that include hereditary predisposition—one or a combination of these may bring about psychiatric illness in the form of generalized anxiety, specific phobias, obsessive thought patterns, compulsive behavior patterns, depression, or the more serious symptoms of psychosis. In addition, religious are especially prone to develop psychosomatic illnesses, because they characteristically repress many of their emotional reactions, which nevertheless disrupt their physiological equilibrium sufficiently to cause physical illness. The education and training of psychiatrists equip them to treat this range of illnesses through psychotherapy and the judicious use of psychotropic medicines. Most laypersons who experience major symptoms of emotional distress are willing to accept psychiatric care. Religious, however, often discount the significance of emotional reactions and interpret psychiatric symptoms as spiritual signs. Consequently, they may seek spiritual direction as a source of guidance in their emotional turmoil, which they view as a spiritual affliction. Spiritual directors and those who do spiritual counseling are usually unable to determine whether or not a psychiatric illness exists in a person who exhibits uncertainty and instability.

Father Ned sought psychiatric care because of mental confusion. Several months previously he had made an eight-day retreat during which he tried to decide whether he should continue in his campus ministry work at a state college. The retreat director from whom he sought guidance told Ned that if he prayed and approached the altar, God would let him know what he should do. Ned prayed fervently and during his prayer heard the message inside his head, "Leave the college." He found comfort in the experience and shortly after the retreat resigned his post. He was assigned to parish work, but within a week he regretted his previous decision. He approached a different spiritual director, who advised him to return to campus ministry because his immediate unhappiness with his decision indicated that it was not God's will for him. When his superiors allowed him to return to his campus ministry work, Ned felt that it was a certain sign of God's approval. However, within a few weeks he again experienced the kind of anxiety and confusion that he had previously encountered on the college campus. He became increasingly agitated and found a new spiritual director to guide him. This director told Ned that the message he had received during retreat must have been from an evil spirit, since it had not brought him peace. Therefore, he should disregard that incident and remain in campus ministry. This advice did not calm his agitation or reduce his confusion. A friend recommended that he see a psychiatrist.

At the time of Ned's first interview it was obvious that he was seriously depressed. He had lost twenty pounds in the previous six months, and he slept fitfully about four hours each night. He could not concentrate on things he read and had stopped watching television because he could not follow the story. He thought about suicide frequently and at the same time feared that he had an incurable illness. He tried to pray but wondered if God were playing tricks on him. He expressed the hope that his new spiritual director would guide him to the truth. On his first visit to the psychiatrist he suspected that someone had followed him to the office in order to destroy his reputation at the college. All these symptoms had been present during that time when his spiritual guides were advising him of the need to discern God's will. Further interviews revealed that Ned's mother had died six months before he made the eight-day retreat. He was not certain how he felt about her loss, because it was difficult for him to forgive her for her demeaning attitude toward Ned's father, who had been dead for about fifteen years. Ned's father, a well-educated but unsuccessful man, had played a subservient role in the family. He went through a lengthy period of depression following military duty in World War II. Ned had two brothers and two sisters. Both brothers had been under psychiatric care, one for depressive illness, the other for a manic-depressive illness. Before the eight-day retreat Ned had had difficulty performing his campus duties because of poor concentration, indecisiveness, feelings of self-depreciation, insomnia, irritability, and a melancholy mood. His depressive illness had made it impossible for him to think things through in a coherent manner, and his job had become more than he could manage. He became desperate and sought spiritual direction in the hope that God would resolve his conflict. The degree of Ned's depression diminished his powers of reason and prevented his making good decisions. In addition, his depression created a sense of urgency that made him unable to evaluate the advice of spiritual guides or the meaning of certain events. After several weeks of psychotherapy and the use of antidepressant medicine, Ned regained his emotional stability and performed his campus duties at his usual level. He continued in treatment for a while and worked out a change in career plans.

Ned's spiritual guides did not recognize the gravity of his illness even though his symptoms were relatively incapacitating. One of the spiritual directors with whom he consulted had a reputation for his criticism of psychotherapists "because they ignore spiritual values." Psychiatric illness with symptoms less advanced than Ned's affects decision-making abilities, creates vulnerability to the suggestion of others, and produces susceptibility to autosuggestion. The latter probably accounts for the message Ned received during the retreat. Good psychotherapists do not ignore the spiritual realities of a patient's life, but neither do good spiritual directors ignore the emotional realities of a person's life. Before they decide that thoughts that come into a person's mind come from God or from the devil, they should determine whether or not those thoughts may originate in emotional conflicts within the individual. Since most spiritual directors do not have the training or experience to make that determination, they should be extremely cautious in giving prophetic answers that may further confuse a person who is already emotionally disturbed. Although many psychiatrists and other professional counselors consult with one another regularly, spiritual directors typically avoid such consultation. Perhaps they believe that their contact with God makes human consultation unnecessary. However, spiritual directors are not exempt from the pitfalls of pride and the detours of self-deception that people encounter on their pathway to God. Nor are they immune to the psychological distortions that readily occur when one person sets out to help another through a psychological crisis or a spiritual dilemma.

Another group of religious, who are without psychiatric symptoms, manifest a kind of emotional immaturity that creates conflict for them and for others. Their immaturity may make it difficult for others to live with them because they are excessively sensitive, overdemanding, or unwilling to carry their share of responsibility. They may demonstrate their immaturity in a flirtatious attitude that does not seek intimacy but only attention, in a rebellious stance that is not intended to produce change but only disturbance, or in a lighthearted manner that does not arise from inner peace but from childlike indiscretion. Emotional maturity does not develop automatically at a specific age. Some who enter religious life in their adolescent years continue the process of maturation and become healthy adults. They use their formation years as an opportunity for spiritual growth and as an environment for continued emotional maturation. Others who enter religious life long after their adolescence sometimes exhibit serious maturational deficiencies. Age is not the door to maturity, nor is experience the key. Ability in superficial social graces may hide emotional immaturity, and intellectual acumen may temporarily conceal the fact that emotional immaturity impairs judgment. Social disguise and intellectual veneer are lost when people live in the confines of community life or under the restrictions of enduring relationships. Age alone does not provide assurance that an individual entering religious life has achieved emotional maturity. In fact, formation programs for late or delayed vocations have high rejection rates because of the emotional immaturity of candidates.

In recent years religious communities have modified some of their criteria for the acceptance of candidates, and the shift in focus corresponds with social changes. A few decades ago scholarship, leadership skills, and social ability were not high priorities in either the selection or the formation of religious. Habits of industry, simple piety, and a certain docility were considered more important, and in some communities healthy ancestry and a strong body were assets for admission. Emotional maturity was not a major consideration in those days, and, as a result, religious communities admitted an inordinate number of persons with personality deficiencies. Research into the emotional difficulties of persons in religious life reveals a high incidence of dependent personalities, aggressive personalities, sociopathic personalities, depressive personalities, and paranoid personalities. In these individuals the process of personality development was arrested at an immature stage that religious formation years neither detected nor corrected.

As religious communities moved out of the cloister, the classroom, and the "cloth," different credentials became valuable. Increased interaction with the laity required sophistication and personal poise. As the authority of the church diffused downward, talents for leadership became important. Urbanization and rapid technical advances made higher education and graduate degrees vital to contemporary religious. Religious leaders became aware of the need for emotional stability, so that religious could deal with outsiders consistently and appropriately, participate in leadership judiciously and harmoniously, and achieve higher levels of educational and professional excellence. Religious communities turned to mental health professionals to assist them in evaluating the emotional maturity of candidates for religious life. Psychological testing and psychiatric evaluation searched for personality factors predictive of emotional maturity but independent of the candidate's value system, transcendent motivations, force of dedication, and spiritual commitment. Although emotional maturity is neither a substitute nor a prerequisite for the personal dedication, spiritual worthiness, or genuine desire necessary to enter religious life, emotional maturity is a requirement for healthy involvement in religious life.

Those who are emotionally immature do not achieve maturity through some brief experience of treatment. They do not attain psychological adulthood by journaling, by participating in a growth workshop, or by attending a renewal program. Emotional maturation is an unfolding process that begins in infancy and continues well into adulthood. If that process is warped or thwarted by unhealthy early experiences, it is not corrected or completed by some brief experience in adult years. A deficiency in emotional maturation is more difficult to correct than is a problem of psychiatric illness, with its accompanying symptomatology. The latter represents a deterioration in psychic stability, but emotional immaturity represents a defect in components essential to psychic stability. Those entering religious communities need not be fully mature before they are accepted, but it is important that their maturation process move in the right direction and within the parameters of an age-specific timetable. The narcissism of infancy, the doubts of early childhood, the inferiority of early school years, the rebellious needs of early adolescence, and the identity conflicts of late adolescence should be worked through at the appropriate time. If adults in their late twenties still engage in these struggles, they may be fixated in a phase of development that will keep them from achieving emotional maturity. This kind of emotional conflict requires patience but firmness on the part of religious superiors. Psychotherapy may bring some improvement in behavior but rarely alters the basic problem. The deficiency usually remains a source of trial for the individual and a source of turmoil for the community.

Sister Nancy at age fifty-two came to a psychiatrist because her superior insisted that she do so. Nancy had been a nurse for twenty-six years but had frequently been moved from one assignment to another and from one living group to another. She seemed to adapt rather easily to these changes and apparently had never questioned why she was transferred so often. In the psychiatrist's office Nancy conversed easily and trustfully, although she had difficulty keeping on one topic. Even with support from her therapist, she could not pursue a subject to any firm conclusion. On occasion she would playfully dismiss this failure by saying she was "simply a scatterbrain." She had no deep ties with any community members but enjoyed a number of superficial relationships with them in which she saw herself as someone who brought them cheer and laughter. She sometimes wondered why these friends rarely asked her to participate in their activities. Through the years Nancy had engaged in some flirtatious relationships with laymen that followed the normal behavior patterns of twelve-year-old girls. During treatment Nancy expressed a desire to make all kinds of changes in her life and during every visit brought in new ideas about what she should change, without ever acknowledging the specific steps necessary for her proposed changes. She searched for a "growth experience" in every possibility offered in the region, whether it was a workshop on dreams, an encounter group, a class on journaling, or a course on sensate focusing. Nancy's emotional immaturity made her unable to benefit from the experiences of adult life that normally produce growth, because those experiences could not span the distance between the mentality of a middle-aged woman and the emotionality of an early adolescent. Psychotherapy did not produce any of the changes that Nancy naively expected to find, but after several months in treatment she was better able to cope with the isolation she experienced in community.

Those in religious communities who are emotionally mature experience conflict also, but their conflict is neither debilitating nor incapacitating. Although emotional maturity provides stability, it necessarily includes flexibility and adaptability to meet the demands of diverse situations. Mature individuals possess a sense of personal worth independent of the successes or failures of daily living. Their inner strength allows them to be sensitive to the needs and to the reactions of others, but their integrity and their confidence are not disturbed by the shallow appraisal of casual observers. They integrate their experiences into a meaningful whole, and, although they recognize that opposing forces are at work within them, they establish a clear hierarchy of values. They distinguish between beneficial and detrimental influences in their lives, and they avoid confusion in deciding where new experiences fit. The mature religious is no more without conflict than is the mature layperson. However, the mature layperson and the mature religious use their emotional conflicts as motivation for change, not guilt, as a source of self-appraisal, not self-doubt, as a measure of the distance still to go, not a signal to avoid the journey.

In the past, religious life attracted some individuals because it provided a shelter from worldly concerns and temporal demands. Although religious life has never provided a refuge from emotional conflicts, recent changes in religious communities have intensified some past conflicts and have introduced some new ones. The majority of mature religious meet this increased conflict with prayerfulness and patience and, as a result, improve their coping skills. They desire greater intimacy than they find, but they come to accept the limitations of community living. They strive to be open to others, and in the process they learn more about the privacy of their own hearts. They try to evaluate their experiences from the solid core of self and refuse to trust themselves to the uncertainty of others' convictions. They walk their own path of faith within the borders of moral law, religious obedience, and personal commitment rather than crawling along a protected course provided by some inconstant guide. They take responsibility for their talents and their opportunities but still remember that these are the gifts of continuing creation. Because they enjoy broader experiences, greater freedom, and an awareness of their own inner strengths, they find obedience more difficult but more necessary. The pain of their losses accentuates the mystery of their lives but does not distort their vision. They seek to improve their relationships with others but recognize that all their communication skills cannot prepare them for their face-to-face meeting with God. They grow in their appreciation of community liturgies, but they do not lose their attachment to silent prayer, which foreshadows the loneliness, the quiet, the abandonment of death. They know that, no matter how much they discuss their problems or with whom, the resolution of emotional conflict comes as a private achievement, not a public victory.

Emotional conflict occurs when the incompatibility of emotional reactions remains unattended and unchecked. Since emotions represent forces that move a person in one direction or another, it is important that the individual manage emotions in such a way that he or she is not pulled in opposing directions simultaneously or toward one goal that is incompatible with another desired goal. When individuals seek two opposing goals, they strain their inner integrity and create emotional distress. People could achieve continuous inner harmony and eliminate the need for conflict resolution if they could successfully suppress their desires for incompatible goals. However, emotions do not take their cues from reason; instead, they respond primitively to the excitement of the sensory world. Although reason neither initiates emotional response nor controls its first momentum, reason can be used to separate the individual from situations that excite emotions and also to assume control of those behaviors that emotions incite. Emotional conflict can be reduced if people acknowledge that they have incompatible emotional drives and learn to recognize situations in which those contradictory drives are being aroused, fostered, and finally accepted. People can avoid some emotional conflicts if they honestly admit that certain circumstances, particular situations, or specific associates excite emotional reactions that oppose other important goals. The alcoholic who is determined to quit drinking can ease the problem by taking a longer route home to avoid the familiar tavern where drinking friends congregate. But if the reforming alcoholic walks past that favorite tavern and stops to gaze longingly through the window, an emotional conflict occurs that is likely to be soothed by a glass of cold beer or a shot of whiskey.

A great deal of emotional conflict can be avoided by meeting the conditions that are attached to decision making. Most people recognize a reckless lack of foresight in an individual who purchases a valuable article without any consideration of its cost or any provision to pay its price. However, every purchase has its price, every contract its obligations, every decision its conditions. When people enter a contract but are unable or unwilling to meet the conditions of the contract, they are caught in a situation that produces conflict. They have incurred an obligation that they now wish to vacate. Obviously they should not have agreed to the contract, or now they should find the means to fulfill it. If indeed they absolutely cannot meet the obligations of the contract, then it should be invalidated. Persons who buy valuable articles for which they cannot pay keep them uneasily, guard them suspiciously, and enjoy them incompletely. Predicaments like these leave individuals with anxiety because there is no acceptable solution, guilt because there is default, depression because there is inevitable loss.

Each decision that people make involves a price to pay and conditions to meet. The pleasure in a decision comes from first anticipating and later obtaining the goal the individual desires, but continued satisfaction depends upon meeting the obligations incurred in the decision. A married person remains happily married when he or she is willing to pay the price of a marital relationship. Marital happiness is not purchased by pronouncing the wedding vows, nor is marital fidelity simply a matter of avoiding adultery. The marriage relationship entails a dedication of time by each spouse to the other so that the necessary exchanges of words and thoughts, of feelings and love can occur. The marriage relationship requires of each spouse the modification of behavior patterns, not because those behaviors are immoral or illegal or unrefined, but because they are in this relationship indelicate, and therefore they strain the tenuous bond that holds two people in a union of love. The marriage relationship contains the obligation for both spouses to curtail personal interests, to alter personal schedules, and to change personal priorities so that their patterns of living can mesh together in harmony rather than clash in constant friction. A marriage commitment that accepts the sacrifices of self inherent in a marriage contract provides the lasting happiness that is the wish of every wedding day.

In a similar way, religious can only obtain continued satisfaction by paying the price of the choice they have made in entering religious life. Some religious consider their commitment in terms of moral boundaries that they view as barriers within which they must function. Religious life is not simply a matter of sexual continence, external compliance, and worldly detachment. A decision to enter religious life creates conditions that cannot be defined in legalistic terms any more than the obligations of a marriage can be defined in terms of a property agreement. Commitment in religious life requires some of the same sacrifices that a marriage relationship requires, although the rewards are considerably different. In the past religious were bound by schedules, customs, and rules that, although they did not accurately define the relationship of the religious to God or to the community, held the religious in a structure that encouraged those relationships. Greater freedom sometimes demands greater sacrifices. Religious now have more control over their time schedules, but this freedom leaves them with a personal obligation to give the time to prayer that is necessary to sustain their spiritual life and to give the time to one another that is necessary to sustain their community life. They too have an obligation at times to surrender their personal interests, to change their individual schedules, to modify their patterns of behavior, to shift their personal priorities because a complete commitment to religious life carries obligations such as these. Religious create an irresolvable conflict for themselves when they fail to respond to the conditions of the vocation decision they have made.

A married person should have a sense of ownership that does not convey possessiveness of the spouse but rather a total acceptance of the contract and its conditions. Married people own the relationship in which they have invested, and in another way they are owned by the sacred bond they have established with one another. Perhaps the popular idea about owning one's feelings should be extended to include the importance of owning one's decisions. Religious should develop a similar sense of ownership for the life they have chosen.

For the purchaser who will not pay, the contractor who will not meet his or her obligations, the decision-maker who will not live by the conditions of the decision, there is a conflict of personal integrity. Increasing numbers of religious experience a conflict of integrity these days, as they exhibit not just an indolence toward the responsibilities of their vowed state but a denial that such responsibilities arise from their contractual relationship. If religious sometimes neglect their responsibilities, if they stumble in their dedication, if they let emotion weaken their resolve, if they fall short of their own high purpose, they must exercise patience and perseverence with this evidence of their human frailty. But if they deny the obligations they have assumed, if they refuse to pay for what they have purchased, if they refuse to acknowledge the responsibilities in the decision they have made, they exhibit intellectual dishonesty and experience psychological demoralization. They relinquish their personal integrity when they disavow what they vow, reject what they accept, and disown what they take as their own. It is not an oversimplification to say that the only good way to be a wife or husband is to be a good wife or husband, and the only good way to be a religious is to be a good religious.

In the past two decades change has struck religious life like an earthquake strikes a forest. Nothing will ever be the same again. Some sacred trees have fallen; some saplings have been swept away; dislodged boulders have left fertile ground behind; crevices have formed that will no longer support life. Religious communities cannot recapture the same tranquil landscape they knew before Vatican II. They have been shaken by the sudden loss of magnificent traditions and the unexpected departure of respected friends from their ranks. They have abandoned fields of labor that now lay barren because the increased mean age of community members, the decrease in new vocations, and the loss of institutional affiliations have reduced their productivity. In characteristic fashion, religious look for providential design in these awesome events and search through the losses looking for hope and signs of new growth. The tremors of change in religious life have also brought less regimentation but more self-direction, less structure but more self-discipline, less demand but more dedication. The greatest concern of many religious in this period of turbulence is the viability of the celibate life. A former patient recently wrote to her psychiatrist, "I know my gift of celibacy is not to negate my desire for someone but to enable me somehow to use that desire in serving others. I offer the lack of that relationship to God and seek it in God. I ask God to fill that space he has created in me and which I return to him as my gift." The real question is not whether a celibate life is a viable option in the modern world. The real question is in what kind of community will those people gather together who continue to choose celibacy as a voluntary, vowed option. Religious life as it now exists demands the sacrifices that are part of celibacy, but religious life does not create the commitment of celibacy. Something in human nature that transcends immediate reward, material gratification, and temporary satisfaction raises a special few to seek another measure in their lives, and the phoenix of celibacy takes flight.